How to Ride Just About Everything (except a horse)

By Paul DuPre

GREATLAKES LIVING PRESS
Suite 2217—Tribune Tower
435 N. Michigan Ave.
Chicago, Ill.

Library of Congress Catalog Card No.: 75-9296

ISBN: 0-915498-03-0

Cover design by Joseph Mistak Jr.
Cover art by Jack Hasley

Contents

ACKNOWLEDGEMENTS

Many good friends and authorities on various subjects furnished photographs, drawings and technical and historical information. Among the many to whom I am indebted, my special appreciation is due to the following:
Hang gliding experts Wayne Christenson, Paul Makis, David Snook and Steve Naffziger. Hovercraft designer/builder Mike Pinder. Recreational vehicle authorities Bob Stewart, Sheldon Walle, Lloyd Bontrger, Herb Ebendorf and John Jenkins. Outboard motor expert Greg Kissela. Surfing historian Michael P. Moser. All-American Soap Box Derby general manager Ron Baker and Firestone's Bob Troyer. Experienced hitch hiker Phillip A. DuPre. ORV modification expert Tom Wallner. Skateboard champion Chris Yandall and industry authorities Frank Nasworthy and Nigel Jackson. League of American Wheelmen's Marilyn Johnson. Jet Ski (Kawasaki) information director Doug Freeman. Water skiing researcher Pat DuPre. Roller skate manufacturer Joseph Shevelson; *Skating* Magazine editor Barbara Boucher. Motorcycle Safety Foundation president Charles H. Hartman. American Automobile Association managing director J. Kay Aldous and research editor Melitta Hartung. Motor Vehicle Manufacturers Association of the U.S. Inc. statistician Earl Creer and public relations officer Bernice Huffman. National Ski Patrol regional director Randall M. Schultze; United Airlines public relations director Jim Kennedy. Sailing authorities Bob Link, Hank Evans, Duke Best, Paul Swenson and Charles Mann. Polaris race team manager Bob Eastman and information officer Burney Soderlind. Finally, my publishers for their patience and tolerant attitude toward deadlines, Pat Matsumoto for her careful editing of the manuscript, and my wife, who keeps me well insured.

INTRODUCTION

"A load of books does not equal one good instructor"
—Chinese Proverb

I have been fascinated most of my life with ways of overcoming natural forces of one kind or another—air resistance, water resistance, gravity, the wind, ground friction . . . and I have tried also to utilize those forces instead of working against them. The result for me has been a great deal of pure fun, coupled with strong admiration of those who conceived the various activities discussed in this book, plus a deep respect for the natural forces which govern our lives and often save us from self-destruction.

There are many fun activities which, because of space and other considerations, I have been unable to discuss in this book, although they have provided me with countless hours of thrills and enjoyment. Included among these is flying—omitted because you cannot legally learn to fly the way I did—with a book, an airplane and a buddy who had already tried it. A course of authorized instruction by a licensed instructor is required by law. And it is the only intelligent way to learn to fly these days.

As life and leisure equipment get more sophisticated and more complicated and as regulatory organizations continue to reach out with ever-growing tentacles to stifle various forms of outdoor recreation, it will become increasingly difficult to learn and to participate in many of the activities discussed herein.

My advice, therefore—whether you are fifteen or fifty—is to seize every opportunity for outdoor fun. And it is my hope that this book may help you find as much fun, thrills and relaxation as these various activities have given me over the years.

Paul DuPre
May, 1975
Chicago

Paul DuPre, a life-long outdoorsman who was swept over a 150-foot waterfall in a homemade raft at the age of six, has written extensively for magazines and newspapers, lectured and appeared on radio and television shows. As a teenager he joined Britain's famed Desert Rats in North Africa. Since then, between writing assignments, DuPre has raced various vehicles, explored remote areas of Mexico, piloted flying machines including hang gliders, operated a ranch in California, mined gold, dined on exotic and not-so-exotic outdoors foods, climbed mountains, and slept under the open sky as much as any man can.

You and Jean-Claude Killy

Remains of what must have been skis have been found in Scandinavian bogs and have been dated to 2,500 BC. A carving on a rock face in Norway dating back to 2,000 BC shows a man on skis. So skiing has been around a long time. A Californian who rejoiced in the name of "Snowshoe" Thompson brought skiing into the USA in 1856 from Norway, where it was used primarily as a means of getting about the mountains in snow. Olympic competition among skiers began in 1924.

Skiing is fun. It is excellent exercise, it improves the lung performance . . . and is a good way to meet healthy girls (or vice versa). (Photo courtesy United Airlines)

Skiing is fun. It is excellent exercise, it improves the lung performance, teaches body coordination and muscle control and is a good way to meet healthy girls—or for girls to meet strong, outdoor-type fellows.

If you decide to take up skiing and happen to be a close friend of Jean-Claude Killy, Stein Eriksen, Genia Fuller, Jimmy Heuga, Pat Karnik or any other champion skiers, many of whom have turned professional, you will probably learn quickly and easily. Lucky you. Otherwise, head for a ski slope on weekends or whenever you can get there and take lessons under the direction of some of the world's greatest ski instructors. The cost is far less than you may think. For instance, if you live in the Midwest, you can drive 30 minutes from Milwaukee to Oconomowoc and attend the Ray T. Stemper Ski School. For $65 you get five professional lessons, plus five lift tickets, plus rental of skis, boots and poles, plus a warm, friendly chalet to relax in and nurse your aching muscles at the end of the day. Add to this, say, two nights' lodging, your meals, tips and a few beers and your total cost for a five-lesson ski course and a weekend of fun comes to around $160. Group lessons cost $3 each, private lessons $15.

Rates are similar at Wisconsin's Wilmot Mountain where the ski school director is well-loved Helmut Teichner who—well into his sixties and in spite of one heart attack—skis and teaches seven days a week throughout the season. And when the Midwest snows disappear, Helmut heads for the Rockies to get in some serious skiing. Incidentally, Wilmot—in spite of its low rates—is among the top revenue producers for ski resorts in the country. Over 110,000 Americans have learned to ski at Wilmot. Teichner's school teaches the popular, fairly new, Graduated Length Method (GLM). It is a fast, economical way to become a proficient skier.

Here are a few tips from Helmut Teichner (spoken with just a trace of his delightful Austrian accent):

"Skis cannot be ridden like a sled. On skis you are not a passenger—you are in complete, sole control. And control must be learned. In spite of the cartoons, there is little, if any, danger of injury if you learn properly at the outset. Don't take lessons from a well-meaning friend. Learn with a seasoned, trained and fully qualified instructor.

At Wilmot we follow a sequence of well-programmed lessons, step by step. We use the American teaching method incorporating the GLM approach starting beginners on short skis, only three feet long and progressing on up to the right size for each person's weight, age and other factors. With practice between lessons, a new skier can ski most hills under control after as little as three lessons. I do not advise a beginning skier to go out and buy a lot of equipment. Rent it until you have graduated to full-length skis and have determined the extent of your interest in the sport."

Discussing the GLM teaching system, Crystal Mountain (Michigan) ski school head Bob Meyer says:

"The GLM system has revolutionized ski teaching and we now have far more people coming to learn to ski. The age spread is now greater. Parents are starting their children at younger ages, and older people, into their sixties and seventies—are discovering that skiing is for them, too. Learning to ski by the GLM is faster, easier, more natural and less expensive than the old methods."

Most US ski schools now teach the graduated length method, but at first there was a good deal of resistance by instructors to the new teaching system. Some purists felt that the way they had learned was the right and only effective method of teaching new skiers. Others saw it as a threat to their livelihoods since it shortcut the learning by several lessons. Offsetting these objections are the facts that:

- People, who gave up on the conventional learning methods after a lesson or two, found they could ski after all when learning with GLM.
- Although it is true that the average beginner takes fewer lessons and learns faster by the GLM system, more people are taking up the sport since it's easier to learn.

Actually, several different approaches to teaching the GLM technique are currently in use at different ski schools in the USA. Most popular seems to be Head-way system, pioneered by Karl Pfeiffer, ski school head at Killington, Vermont, with strong support from the Head Ski Company. But all short-ski methods do one thing—they get you into parallel skiing from the start without going through the cumbersome snowplow and stem stages.

Remember the Old Snowplow?

First, let's look at those old bugaboos, the snowplow and the stem (which is really a kind of half-snowplow)—which are still taught and sometimes used by even proficient skiers. The snowplow is primarily an effective method of slowing you down and stopping you. It and the stem enable you to turn once you are gliding uncertainly down the beginner's slope.

The straight snowplow which slows you down and brings you to a relieved stop is accomplished as follows:

You are gliding straight down a gentle slope with your skis more or less straight and side by side, the way you started, knees slightly bent. Now you want to slow down and stop so you force the heel ends of your skis farther apart, leaving the tips of your skis close together (but not touching). At the same time you bend your knees a little more and angle them in toward each other and apply weight evenly to the inside edges of your skis. Keep your poles clear of the snow—you don't need them while snowplowing. What happens, of course, is that your two skis, in a V-shape and with the inside edges digging into the snow, cause you to slow down and stop.

To perform a snowplow turn, you do the same thing. Separate the heels of your skis, keeping the tips close together. Now, to turn right, you shift all your weight onto the *left* ski (which is pointing to the right) and you begin to turn right. And vice versa if you want to turn left. If you are learning to ski by the snowplow method rather than by GLM, it is helpful at this point to make left and right turns all the way down the slope (the beginner's slope, of course). Just get your skis in the snowplow position and switch your weight from one ski to the other to make wide S-curves. If the slope is not steep enough to keep you moving or if your snowplows seem to slow you down too much, bring your skis back together in between turns to gain momentum. Once you have gained a little more speed, start making snowplow turns again. And again and again. As you begin to turn in the direction your turning ski is pointing, edge that ski a little more—in other words, bend your ankle in so that more weight is on the inside edge of that ski. Also, lean your shoulders over the ski that is turning but don't change the position of the hips.

Why Not Straight Down The Hill?

The fun of skiing is in making turns as you traverse down a hill. If you just follow the fall line (the most direct route to the bottom), you will not only gain too much momentum and travel too fast for safety, you will also fail to improve your skiing technique very much. And skiing, like most sports, is more enjoyable when you get better at it.

Another reason against skiing straight down the hill is that you will reach the bottom too soon (that is if the combination of speed and your own lack of skill have not already dumped you in the snow) and you will feel that such a short amount of time wasn't worth the price of the lift ticket. And it probably wasn't. Then you have to line up again for the lift and get back up there for another trip down.

As you descend the hill, you traverse from side to side, quite often traveling completely horizontal to the vertical line of descent. As you need more speed, you use your ski poles and the slope of the hill.

As you traverse the hill, obviously one ski is on higher ground than the other. The higher one is known as the uphill ski and the lower as the downhill ski. As you traverse, have your skis side by side, about six inches apart. What stops you from side-slipping down the hill? Edging. That means, most of your weight will be on the downhill ski, because of gravity. You bend both ankles so that the uphill edges of both skis bite into the snow more than the downhill edges. Also, as you traverse, keep the uphill ski slightly ahead of the downhill ski. Your knees and hips lean away from the downhill ski.

The Stem and Christie

Now let's consider the stem. This is an easy maneuver to learn, and it is a great help to the beginner. Let's say you are sliding down a gentle slope, skis side by side, and you want to make a turn to your right. You put the left ski farther out and turn it into a half-snowplow so that the tip is pointing right. You edge that ski slightly and apply more weight to its inside edge. As you begin to turn, you bring the other ski up alongside the turning ski and, voila, you are turning right.

Another method of turning is the christie. You start with a slight snowplow and as you turn, twist the upper part of your torso so that one shoulder is pointing in the direction of your turn. Now you push the heel ends of your skis in the downhill direction, bending your knees to transfer more weight on the forward part of your skis. Turn and gradually apply more weight to the outside ski and you will find the heel ends of your skis will slide downhill. Use your poles to maintain forward movement. When you use the christie in conjunction with a stem turn, you perform what is known (naturally enough) as the stem-christie.

With a little practice and some professional help you can easily master these turns in a few lessons. But if you learn the graduated length method you virtually skip this "kindergarten" stage and start on parallel skiing right away.

Practice and professional help will enable these youngsters to enjoy a lifetime of outdoor pleasure, beginning, rightfully, in the company of their parents. (Photo courtesy United Airlines)

When you observe proficient skiers traversing a hill with both skis close together, almost touching, and using body English to make graceful turns, you are watching parallel skiing—beautiful, fluid, natural. The reason why traditional ski instruction has always included the snowplow, the stem, the stem christie and other variations on these basic themes is to enable you at least to be able to turn and stop at will—under control—and to give you confidence and the "feel" of skiing. Once you have learned these movements, you progress on to parallel skiing, where you virtually unlearn what you have already learned and start in on an entirely different method of skiing.

Using normal skis, six or seven-feet long, it is extremely difficult for most people to learn parallel skiing without going through the preliminary snowplow and stem stages. For one thing, when you stand up on full-length skis that are close together as in parallel skiing, you feel very unbalanced, since, by comparison with length, this is a very narrow base on which to support your entire weight—especially once you start moving. And when you first get on full-length skis, since you have normally never moved around on anything longer than a pair of ice skates, you tend to get them crossed and all tangled up, and you keep falling over.

GLM—Doing It The Easy Way

·The graduated ski length method (GLM) solves this problem by starting you off on skis that are only three feet long. Not all that much longer than your shoes or a pair of ice skates. Now your base is theoretically wider in comparison to length. Prior to the GLM, approximately one-third of all Americans who tried to learn to ski gave up after their first lesson or two. They decided they just didn't have the amount of coordination necessary or that they just weren't built for it. And you know something? They were right. But if they had persisted, they would probably have eventually learned the necessary coordination and would have found out that they were built for it after all.

It is easy to turn on short skis. You are sliding downhill (on three-foot skis first day) and you want to turn so all you do is you jump slightly, with knees bent and move the heels to one side. If you are turning left, you jump the heels toward the right, and vice versa. You are now skiing in the new direction with no trouble at all. You are amazed, unbelieving, almost, at how easy it is to ski with short skis in the parallel position.

You now advance to continuous turning. Now you discover that you can make turns without actually jumping—you merely weight the tips of your skis more than the heels and, using a little muscle power, you turn one way, then the other, "christie slipping" into the turn. Your GLM instructor keeps a critical but friendly eye on you to make sure you're doing this thing right and he usually assists by calling out

"One-two-three-four. . ." This helps you develop smooth rhythm. As a beginner, you must be careful not to pick up too much speed—continuous turns slow you down and keep your descent well under control. Yes, you will have falls at first. But even these are fun and you will find yourself laughing gaily as you get back up. When you are on short skis, getting up is easy. Move your feet so your skis are facing across the hill, not down it. They should be together and your body half-lying on the uphill side of your skis. Place the uphill hand on the ground and push yourself back onto your skis. One thing about falling with short skis—you are not at all likely to twist an ankle since three or four-foot skis are too short to exert that much leverage.

What's Another Foot, More or Less?

Your instructor will usually graduate you to the next length ski for your second lesson, and you continue doing your jump-and-christie turns on four-foot skis. Sometimes, if you seem to be getting the hang of it pretty well at the end of your first lesson, your instructor may take you into the five-foot stage next and probably move you onto a steeper slope. Before you know it, he's got you parallel skiing on six or seven-foot skis on the intermediate hill. All you need now is more practice and continued expert instruction and you'll be up on the big hills with skiers who have been skiing lots longer than you have. And all because you learned the GLM instead of spending all that time messing around with the snowplow and stem and trying to learn how to keep your seven-foot skis uncrossed.

Getting Up The Hill

There are three basic ways of getting up the hill in preparation for your traverse back down: 1. side stepping 2. the herringbone walk and 3. the lift or tow. Of these, the last is fastest, less exhausting, more comfortable and less chilling. On the other hand the first two are free.

There are occasions when you need to get up a hill other than by lift or tow. For instance, at many ski resorts there is no tow or lift on the low-altitude beginner's slope. Also, when you are skiing down a slope perhaps you hit an unexpected mogul (bump) and find yourself separated from your skis and rolling in the snow. The thing to do here, in the words of an old song is to "Pick yourself up, dust yourself off. and start all over again." Well, not all over, but you will probably want to go back up at least a few yards above the mogul and try it again. You will have to do this by non-mechanical means—i.e., either by side-stepping or using the herring bone. Sometimes you want to try skiing a hill that does not seem to get much use—mostly because it has no lift. Later on you may become interested in ski touring, or cross country or Nordic skiing. Then you will have to be able to climb hills on your own, so you might as well learn now.

Before you start charging up a hill, however, you must be sure you can walk on skis. You start on a flat surface. Do not lift your skis off the ground as you normally lift your shoes up as you walk. Using your poles for balance and assistance, slide your skis forward, keeping them flat on the ground. Slide one at a time about the distance of a normal step and use the right pole in conjunction with the left ski and the left pole with the right ski. Gradually take longer "steps" and develop a smooth rhythm. After a while, try it without poles. Then when you have enough confidence in your ability to walk forward in a smooth series of sliding steps, you are ready to try sidestepping.

Pick a gentle slope for your first try at sidestepping up a hill. Stand at right angles to the hill and move the uphill ski a short "step" away from the downhill ski. At the same time, dig the uphill edge of the uphill ski firmly into the snow. Using the poles for balance and support, lift up the downhill foot and place it alongside the other, again digging the uphill edge of the ski into the snow. Then move the uphill ski again, dig the edge in and follow with the downhill ski. And so on up the hill. It is a slow way of climbing a hill, but it'll get you there.

The herringbone walk will probably get you there faster. You face uphill, separate the tips of your skis, keeping the heels close together and start up the hill. Use your poles behind you for extra support. Lift first one ski, then the other, turning your ankles inward so that the inside edges of your skis bite into the snow. Keep your knees bent and your weight forward. If you look back at your tracks you'll see why this method of climbing a hill is known as the herringbone.

Ski lifts vary from a slow-moving rope which you hold while it pulls you up the hill, to gondolas and huge, multi-passenger cable cars. In the last, skiers ride seated while their skis ride in an outside rack. The chair lift, when it is at the bottom of the hill, has a seat that is about the same height from the ground as a chair seat. Which makes it convenient to sit down. While waiting for your chair, you stand with skis side by side and the knees bent with your back to the approaching chair. The chair will catch you behind the knees, and you'll be sitting as it continues up the hill. Hold both poles together with one hand, baskets down, and hold onto the chair support with the other hand.

The action with a rope tow is to stand with skis parallel with the rope, both poles in one hand. Then with the hand nearest the rope, grasp it lightly and gradually tighten pressure until the rope is pulling you along. Don't grab the rope or you may lose your balance.

Equipment

It is virtually impossible to make recommendations regarding ski

Look, Ma! No hands! While waiting for your chair, you stand with skis side by side and the knees bent, with your back to the approaching chair, which catches you behind the knees and whisks you up the hill.
(Photo courtesy United Airlines)

equipment, clothing, boots, bindings, etc., because the type of ski best for each skier depends upon his height, weight, age, ability level and type of skiing he does or intends to do. Until you have graduated to full-length skis and become reasonably proficient, you should use rented equipment—the rental cost is often included in the cost of your lessons. When you reach this stage, your instructor will recommend equipment that is best for you. As far as clothing is concerned, today's modern fabrics have made possible the development of lightweight, warm, comfortable ski clothing that is in the height of ski resort fashion. If you are on a tight budget, you can usually get by wearing good warm sweaters, slacks and a serviceable windbreaker. It is better, when the pocket book is thin, to spend more money on good boots and bindings than on fashionable ski suits. Goggles are a must, of course, as are good ski gloves or mittens.

One sad note: the days when any youngster bitten by the ski bug could easily get a job at a ski resort in return for bed, board, lift tickets and a few dollars a day, alas, have gone. Ski resorts just don't have enough jobs available for the thousands of young "ski bums" who apply every season.

Safety On The Slopes

Just as there are idiots who insist on jeopardizing their own safety and that of other motorists on the roads, so there are jerks who deliberately cause safety hazards on the ski slopes. Othmar Schneider, head of the ski schools at Boyne Mountain and Boyne Highlands, Michigan, in a thirty-six page illustrated booklet titled "Skiing Tips", published by Sears, Roebuck & Company, lists nine basic safety rules that are worth repeating:
1. Check snow and slope conditions before skiing.
2. Never ski alone, especially on strange slopes.
3. Be in complete control at all times. Do not go on slopes that call for skills beyond your ability.
4. Check equipment carefully. Use the safety straps on your skis to prevent accidents.
5. Ask ski patrol for any information you need. Report any accident promptly.
6. Do not attempt to ski without preliminary instruction by a qualified instructor.
7. Watch out for frostbite on bitter cold days.
8. Avoid overtiring yourself. Stop skiing while you still feel like taking another run.
9. Practice courtesy—you're not the only person on the slope.

It would be neither proper nor intelligent to think about ski safety without considering the National Ski Patrol—a corps of unpaid, dedicated, highly trained men and women who are capable skiers. They are also expert toboggan handlers, good climbers, have excellent knowledge of navigation both by day with compass and map and by night using stars if necessary. They are as essential to the operation of a ski resort as are the lifts and snow grooming equipment.

An important activity of the National Ski Patrol is accident prevention, and this is a task which members handle in the most diplomatic way possible. They offer suggestions concerning safety to skiers rather than orders or rebukes. They give friendly warnings of trail dangers and unsafe practices. They do not act like ski slope policemen (which they are not).

Ski Patrol members wear rust-colored parkas with a gold-colored cross on the back bearing the words NATIONAL SKI PATROL. On the front of the parka the ski patrol member wears various merit badges.

These dedicated men and women patrol the ski slopes, constantly alert for hazardous conditions. They watch skiers and note any that appear to be having difficulty breathing, are in pain, having problems with their skis or bindings, or trouble skiing the slope they are on. They put in long days and do not quit until every last skier is accounted for. If a skier is believed missing, the Patrol goes out and finds him. The Patrol knows how to get an injured person quickly off the slope and into the First Aid Station for proper medical treatment. Sleds, toboggans, snowmobiles, stretchers are used as needed. The blue belt the Patrol member wears contains more than twenty items comprising part of the member's individual First Aid Kit.

They buy their own parkas and their own ski equipment, undertake rigorous, lengthy training and must pass strict tests. And for what? The chance to ski free is only part of the reward they receive. They enjoy the opportunity their skills give them to serve other skiers and the sport they all love so much.

They have saved countless lives since their origination in 1936, and have helped thousands of skiers who are hurt, lost, ill, have problems of one kind or another, or need information.

The National Ski Patrol issues ten safety tips:
1. Recognize your own abilities; take lessons to improve. Get in good physical condition before skiing.
2. Check ski area map for any slope problems. Note locations of converging trails, avalanche slopes. Report accidents by locations.
3. Obtain suitable equipment. Adjust safety bindings properly. Wear safety straps to avoid runaway skis.
4. Ride lifts and use tows carefully. Follow posted instructions. Keep your ski tips up. Carry ski poles by the shaft not by straps over the wrist.
5. Don't wear loose clothing or flying scarves on lifts or tows.
6. When skiing do NOT drink alcoholic beverages.
7. A skier who stops on slope should look up the hill before starting

down.
8. When overtaking another skier call out "On your left" or "On your right."
9. Don't block trail or path of other skiers when stopping on slope.
10. Fill in your "sitzmarks" (depressions in snow made when you fall). These are danger spots for other skiers who follow.

Publications For Ski Buffs

An excellent book on the GLM system is *Ski GLM* by Morten Lund, published by The Dial Press, New York. It is available in libraries and in most bookshops.

For those who want to learn the traditional snowplow method, *How To Ski Just A Little Bit* by Margaret Bennett, published by Simon & Schuster, New York, may be helpful. In among many pages of purely girlish chit-chat there is a little instruction (in keeping with the book's title), a few good tips, some cute illustrations and some high school-type verses.

Skiing Tips by Othmar Schneider, published by Sears, Roebuck and Company, contains sound, helpful information and instruction, plus a few "commercials" for S & R ski clothing and boots.

Skier's Directory is an annual listing of over 500 places to ski, stay, etc., with directions how to get there, trail maps, costs, and other information. Published by Ski Earth Publications, Inc., Boston, Massachusetts, the directory is available on newsstands and bookshops.

The Skier's Bible by Morten Lund, published by Doubleday, New York.
Skier's World by Morten Lund, published by Ridge Press, New York.
Expert Skiing by Morten Lund, published by Doubleday, New York.
Skier's Paradise by Morten Lund, published by Putnam & Sons, New York.
Finds of Skis From Prehistoric Time, in Swedish Bogs and Marshes, published by Stabslitografen, Stockholm, Sweden.

Crosscountry Skiing Is Cheap

One of the reasons why crosscountry skiing is now America's fastest-growing winter sport is that it is a lot less expensive than Alpine or downhill skiing. Your equipment costs far less, you don't have to buy lift tickets, and you are away from expensive ski lodge accommodations and costly meals. Like present-day Alpine skiing, crosscountry (also called Nordic) skiing originated in Scandinavia.

A crosscountry ski trip can consist of half a day, a day, or it can become a camping/skiing vacation. You can try out the trails in solitude (making sure someone knows which way you are going), you can make it a family activity, or you can join a touring club and go along with the gang.

Crosscountry skiing includes some of everything . . . herringbone

One of the joys of cross country (Nordic) skiing is the family activity it promotes. No family? Then join a touring club and go along with the gang. (Photo courtesy United Airlines)

hill climbing, downhill skiing, traversing, healthful exercise, skiing the virgin forests and hillsides or following marked trails (which is safer). You take a backpack with a few supplies including matches to light a fire to warm up when you feel chilled, perhaps a can of soup, some instant coffee or tea, maybe a pack of raisins to munch on, a compact first-aid kit, a map of the area and a compass, ski wax and wax remover, a lightweight folding shovel, a roll of toilet paper, camera and film, etc. If you are camping, of course you will need more gear—a sleeping bag, single-burner cooking stove, more food, change of socks and perhaps an extra garment or two . . .

Crosscountry skiing is really an extension of hiking. You do not keep the skis rigidly together as in downhill parallel skiing. Your skis are lightweight—usually laminated birch with hickory edges, hickory with laminations of polyethylene, fiberglass, etc. Your movements are free and easy. You use your poles, lean well forward, and take long, gliding steps. For turning and stopping you can use any standard ski technique—the snowplow is popular with crosscountry skiers. You can also use kick-turns, skating turns or the simple star turn consisting of merely stepping around to the new direction. You use your poles alternatively—left pole with right ski, right pole with left ski. Once you get going and the way ahead seems fairly smooth, you can make better time by double-poling—using both poles together to propel yourself along on your skis.

You can rent crosscountry skiing equipment just as you can Alpine skis, boots, bindings and poles at a ski resort. Rental costs for crosscountry equipment usually run around $5 to $8 a day for skis, boots, bindings, and poles. If you have definitely decided to make crosscountry skiing a family acitivity (and it's one of the finest family sports there is if you are located near an area where it can be done), then it would probably be more economical to buy the gear for each member of your family rather than rent. If there are five in your family group, rental would cost you at least $25 each time. For about $75 each, you can outfit your family of five with everything you need. Of course, the more you are able to spend, the better the equipment you can buy.

Variations On A Theme

Over the years ingenious ski buffs have found ways to make their skis do more than traverse a hill or make crosscountry tours. Ski sailing is more popular in Europe than in the USA. The skier holds aloft a large, kite-shaped sail with a rigid frame of bamboo, aluminum, or other light-weight material and holding the frame, ski-sails both downhill and on more level ground. This variation of the sport is growing popular in Japan and is being revived in this country to some extent. It flourished here for a few years, back about the turn of the century but faded away as skiing became more and more challenging and sophisticated. Of course, you do not have poles along for balance or propulsion. Ski sailing would not be practical on regular ski slopes because of the hazards it might present to other skiers.

Wheeled skis are slowly coming into their own—primarily as a means of off-season training for crosscountry competition. The wheels are prevented from rolling backward by rachet stops. Roller skate wheels or urethane wheels of the type used on skateboards are usually attached to special skis by means of "trucks"—an assembly which secures the axles to the underside of the skis. The trucks are bolted on, and there are thick rubber cushions which premit the wheels to cant from side to side so that ski "edging" can be simulated.

At one ski resort in Vermont, the skiing season ends with a riotous race down a small slope by the restaurant and cafeteria workers—bus boys, waiters and waitresses, cooks, etc. Instead of using skis, these fun-lovers use serving trays which they try to stand up on while sliding down the hill. It is a very funny event to watch.

Hang glider and kite enthusiasts have discovered that skis on a slope, plus a hang glider or a kite towed aloft by a winch, is a great way of flying down the hill. Wherever their wing descends, they land on their skis and continue down until they have enough speed to become airborne again. At some ski resorts, flying skiers may be seen soaring about several hundred feet above the ground when conditions are right.

Skis Work, Too

Aside from their contribution to sport and outdoor leisure, snow skis have through the years made contributions in other ways. In Norway, in some areas, skis are the only means many people have of getting about. Hunters use them as a means of tracking and following game. Many fishermen who depend on fish for their livelihood or to feed their families during the winter, find skis their best means of reaching lakes and rivers where they can make ice holes and catch fish.

In the years 1861-1862, the Reverend John L. Dyer carried some thirty pounds of mail daily over an Indian trail that was always about three-feet deep in snow. He used skis that were almost ten feet long and a single pole.

"Snowshoe" Thompson, credited with bringing skiing from Norway to the USA, carried mail for twenty years using oak skis. His trips totaled ninety miles each. Light aircraft used in Canada and Alaska have skis fitted for winter landings and takeoffs. During World War II, the Finnish troops, clad in white and using skis, did terrible things to the Russian troops who were trying to conquer the country. They virtually skied rings around the Reds, picking them off like ducks on a

lake. The American Tenth Mountain Division in World War II found skis
extremely helpful in northern Italy. The English trained a Commando
detachment on skis which got behind enemy lines and caused the
Germans quite a few problems. The Norwegians, too, continually
harassed the occupying troops by coming upon them swiftly and
silently on their skis and vanishing into the mountains. The Germans
also had well-trained ski troops which were very effective in northern
Europe and in Russia and Poland.

Apart from the wonderful National Ski Patrol, other search and rescue teams use skis to find lost travelers in isolated snow-covered
mountain areas.

Skis and the art of skiing have certainly contributed a great deal to
mankind in many ways, not the least of which is the economic impact
that some six million American skiers have.

Read These Crosscountry Ski Publications:
Crosscountry Skiing Guide, published by SKI Magazine, N.Y.
The Pleasures of Crosscountry Skiing by Morten Lund, published by
    Outerbridge & Lazard, Inc., New York, is an instructive and quite
    definitive work on this recent winter sport.
The Crosscountry Skiing Handbook by Edward R. Baldwin, published
    by Charles Scribner's Sons, New York, is also an excellent instruc-
    tion book on the subject.
Complete Crosscountry Skiing and Ski Touring by William Lederer
    and Joe Pete Wilson, published by W. W. Norton & Co., New York.
Ski Touring: An Introductory Guide by William E. Osgood and Leslie
    J. Hurley, published by Charles E. Tuttle, Co., Rutland, Vermont.
Ski Touring Guide, prepared by the Ski Touring Council, Inc., New
    York.

For Information About Crosscountry Skiing, try:
Ski Touring Council, Inc., 342 Madison Ave., New York, NY. 10017.
Nordic Division, US Ski Association, 1726 Champa St., Denver,
    Colorado.
Far West Ski Association, 812 Howard St., San Francisco, California
    94103.
Central Division, Ski Touring Council, 4437 First Ave. South, Minnea-
    polis, Minnesota 55409.
Rocky Mountain Division, Ski Touring Council, Steamboat Springs,
    Colorado 80477.
World Wide Ski Corporation, 2305 Canyon Blvd., Boulder, Colorado
    80302.

Follow That Boat!

The French think they invented water skiing around 1920, but we know different. The *Guinness Book of World Records* rightly credits an Englishman, Mr. S. Storry, with riding on a single plank behind an early motor launch years before that. He was more accurately an aquaplanist rather than a water skier. Back in 1914 a "plank-riding" contest was held and Mr. Storry won it, stiff upper lip and all.

Naturally, Americans improved on this sport, making it a multi-million-dollar business as well as one of the world's fastest-growing water sports. The Yanks got into the act in 1922 when a folla by the name of Ralph W. Samuelson was towed standing upright on two curved planks in Lake Pepin, Minnesota. Shortly afterwards, Fred Waller rode on two planks behind a powered boat on Long Island Sound. Soon Fred improved on his double aquaplanes and in 1925 was granted a patent for what he called "Dolphin Aqua-Skees".

Aquaplaning became the "mother" of water skiing, which immediately fell under the influence of a much older sport—snow skiing. An aquaplane is different from a ski in that it is curved upward at the front and has a pair of "reins" fastened to each side of the front curved portion of the board. The rider holds onto his rein, as the board is pulled behind a boat by a towline fastened directly to the front of the board (aquaplane).

From these earlier attempts to ride the water evolved today's highly engineered and well-made water skis and the sport as we now know it.

Water skiing is safe and fun to do and to watch. It is especially fun to watch when performed by those attractive, healthy-looking young women at Cypress Gardens in Winter Haven, Florida, where water shows are held every day. Cypress Gardens was started by two of America's early water skiers, Dick and Malcolm Pope, back in the twenties.

Water Skiing Equipment

Water skis are not expensive. You can get a good pair for under $100. If you're willing to pay $150 to $200, you've got some of the best water skiing equipment made, although competition and specialized skis can cost considerably more.

The best water skis today are made of fiberglass and one of the top manufacturers of laminated fiberglass skis is Taperflex of America, Inc., a company that has pioneered water ski designs. No one water ski design is suitable for every water skier. The type of ski you purchase should depend on such factors as your skill and experience (and lack of same), improvement objectives, speed ranges at which you will be skiing and your weight. Some manufacturers make one type of ski and sell it to novices, intermediate skiers, advanced skiers and even competition skiers. This is like giving small children, teenagers, adults and elderly people all exactly the same style, size and capability of bicycle.

First of all consider what size ski you should buy. Weight, boat speed and skier's skill are the most important factors to be considered. Height doesn't enter into it. The faster the boat speed the smaller skis you need, generally speaking. Smaller skis maneuver better and are known as slalom skis. Few skiers will be content to merely follow the tow boat. In a very short time you will find yourself crisscrossing the boat's wake—slaloming. And soon you will be skiing on a single slalom ski. Then turning, skiing backward, riding rough water, jumping and so on. What are you trying to do—become a champion water skier? It could happen . . . water skiing is not all that difficult.

Before you finalize your purchase, check all hardware for any sharp or protruding edges. Make sure that runners or binders are not loose— even a tiny bit. Look for chips, scratches, dents, cracks and other damage that may have been inflicted during handling. Beginners and novices are advised to choose a good combination pair of skis—that is, one straight recreational ski and one rigged for slaloming. Intermediate to good skiers would need a concave ski with performance characteristics related to making fast, smooth turns, wake jumps with "soft" landings, and fast, smooth, lengthy skiing without over-tiring. A wide-tunnel, concave, slalom-type ski is probably best for the really good to excellent skier. Wider tunneling increases the ski's concavity, giving it better holding characteristics in higher speed turns.

Let's consider water ski construction. Fiberglass has three basic advantages:

1. Materials used in fiberglass manufacture are available within very precise specifications so that density, weight, flex, tensile and sheer strength and other characteristics can be engineered into the skis under rigid controls.
2. As these materials are utilized in precision molds the possibilities of variation are appreciably reduced. In advanced ski designs even small variations can make a difference in performance.

3. Fiberglass skis have longer appearance-life—the materials are more resistant to ski surface abrasions and deterioration than most other materials used in laminated water ski manufacture.
The following chart, by courtesy of Taperflex, will help you select the size ski best for you.

SLALOM SKI SIZE GUIDE

SKIER's WEIGHT	BOAT SPEED					
	26	28	30	32	34	36
− 100	64″	64″	64″	64″	64″	64″
100-115	66″	66″	66″	64″	64″	64″
115-130	67″/68″	66″	66″	66″	66″	66″
130-145	67″/68″	67″/68″	66″	66″	66″	66″
145-160	67″/68″	67″/68″	66″	66″	66″	66″
160-175	67″/68″	67″/68″	67″/68″	66″	66″	66″
175-190	69″/70″	69″/70″	67″/68″	67″/68″	66″	66″
190-205	69″/70″	69″/70″	69″/70″	67″/68″	67″/68″	67″/68″
205-220	69″/70″	69″/70″	69″/70″	69″/70″	67″/68″	67″/68″
220 +	69″/70″	69″/70″	69″/70″	69″/70″	69″/70″	69″/70″

CHART NOTE: Obviously these weights, speeds and dividing lines between sizes must be regarded as approximate. The chart is designed to be a guide to the average good skier. If you consider yourself average or less choose the bigger ski at the dividing line. If better than average, or plan to become better, choose the smaller size.

Consider concave-bottomed skis. The concave shape tends to hold in turns so that the ski doesn't slip away from the skier's line of travel. However, the degree of concavity should be in harmony with the complete ski design. Added to concavity, quality skis have beveled bottom edges which help make the ski turn easier and adds stability when a skier is cutting through the wake of a towing boat. It sends the water out and away from the ski so that the spray does not hit the skier's rear leg as he slaloms and does not tend to "wrap around" the ski and swamp it when it is driven deep into the water on a pressure turn. Shape and size of bevel affect the turnability of the ski. When tournament skiers talk about "tuning" the edges of their skis, they are referring to the beveling on their ski bottom edges.

Let's Do It

Engineers and other fun-loving guys at Mercury Marine (which has a big stake in the growing popularity of water skiing) make available an instruction sheet on skiing and towing which points out what several books on water skiing and every qualified instructor tell us—that the best place to learn to water ski is on dry land. This is where you get the "feel" of your skis and towline.

First, put your skis on, making sure the harness is snug and comfortable to your feet. Now "feel" the towline by having someone pull you up from a sitting position. Keep your elbows straight and your knees slightly bent. This approximates the actual pull of the boat once you are underway. No matter how fast your towing boat is travelling, you should never have the feeling that your arms are being pulled out of their sockets.

The next step is to get into shallow water—about three feet deep is ideal. Sit down on your skis just back of your feet with your head—and hands holding the towline handle—just above the water. Tilt back a little to raise the tips of your skis just above the water level. Now yell to your boat driver "Hit it!" or some similar signal, and he will throttle forward evenly, giving you a rapid, steady pull. As water pressure forces your skis up, hold them straight and hold the same position you practiced on land. Knees bent, arms straight, head up. Resist the tendency of the skis to wobble as you come up to the surface of the water. Once you're up and planing, keep your knees bent to help maintain balance. Keep your feet flat on the skis. If you lean forward with more weight on your toes your heels will probably come out of the bindings and you'll likely take a spill.

Now let's try turning. To turn right, press down on your left ski and lean your body over to the right. Do the reverse for a left turn. To make a start from a boat dock, which you may have to do sometimes, it is easiest to sit on the edge of the dock with ski tips pointing upward out of the water with about ten feet of towline coiled beside you on the dock. When the rope tightens, transfer your weight from your seat to your feet and hold your arms straight ready for the pull. This usually results in a nice, smooth tow.

Ski towlines are usually one-quarter to one-half inch in diameter and made of synthetic material such as nylon, polyethylene, or of linen or manilla hemp. Twenty-five feet is an average length for a towline, but for a beginner up to seventy-five feet may be needed to keep you in the smoothest water in relation to the wake of the boat. Anything longer tends to drag.

What To Wear

You can water ski in a pair of shorts or lightweight slacks and a T-shirt if you wish. Or, more commonly, a bathing suit—any style. If you ski in cool weather you will find a wet suit more comfortable. Whether you are a good swimmer or not, and whether you are skiing in deep water or shallow water, it makes safety sense to wear a life jacket. Besides, it helps keep the cool breeze off your chest! An alternative is a lightweight supporting waist belt. Water skiing gloves are available or you may wear any light-weight gloves for better grip on the towing handle and to protect your hands from possible rope burns. Some skiers wear goggles but they are really not very practical for although they cut down the glare of the sun's rays and their reflection on the water, they soon collect water splashes and cut visibility.

Lady water skier, top of a three-skier pyramid, drops off during a performance at Lake Pleasant, Arizona. (Photo courtesy Jim Tallon)

Your Towing Boat

Any boat of sufficient horsepower can be used to tow water skiers. A careless, reckless or "show-off" driver can jeopardize your safety and start you off with bad practices which may inhibit your ability to learn to water ski. In addition to your driver, the towing boat should carry an observer who watches you the whole time until you are reasonably proficient. If you feel yourself taking a spill, don't fight it, let yourself fall backward . . . it doesn't hurt unless your towing boat driver is a hydroplane champion and has the machine under him to back him up. In that case you've no business skiing with him.

Get Out And Practice

We have covered the bare basics here—enough instruction to get you on your skis and enjoying recreational water skiing. Expertise and trick skiing come later, with lots of practice and some expert instruction, if you can get it. It is important to take it a step at a time. Be sure you are completely at home on your skis and can handle yourself behind a boat driving at speeds up to forty miles per hour before going on to jumping and hot-dogging. Most of your skiing will be done at under thirty miles per hour, however. Remember to keep your arms straight and knees slightly bent but your back straight and head up.

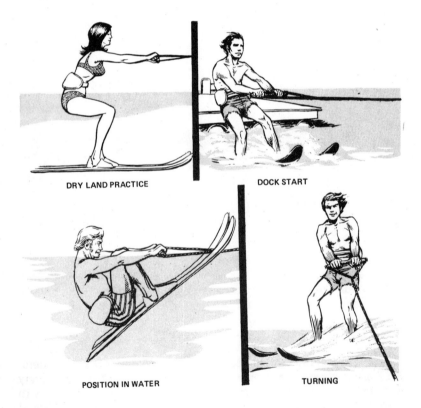

DRY LAND PRACTICE   DOCK START

POSITION IN WATER   TURNING

For Records Buffs

In July 1972, Wayne Grimditch made a water ski jump of 169 feet.

That's length, of course, not height. Wayne was seventeen years old. Barbara Clack at twenty-seven did her best for the distaff side. She jumped 111 feet in July 1971. The *Guinness Book of World Records* gives the world's longest non-stop water skiing run as 818.2 miles. It took young Marvin Shackleford thirty-four hours and fifteen minutes to cover this distance. That was back in 1960, and it is still a very impressive accomplishment.

The world-speed record was for a long time held by Danny Churchill who hit 125.69 mph at the Marine Stadium, Oakland, California in 1971. Sally Younger, a pretty, expert seventeen-year-old water skier, had previously recorded 105.14 mph at Perris, California.

If you can't afford to buy skis, try it barefoot. Just kidding, of course—you have to be an expert water skier before you can try kicking off the ski and going it without one. The record for barefoot skiing is sixty-seven minutes—thirty-six miles—by Stephen Northrup. John Taylor hit over 87 mph in 1972 on Lake Ming, California, riding on the soles of his feet. A gal with tough feet is Haidee Jones, an Australian, who did sixty-one mph. Aside from Miss Jones, all the champions named above are Americans.

Walking On Water

Water skis are not your only means of traveling over water on your feet. What about the "Water Walkers" marketed by Hammacher Schlemmer Inc., N.Y.? These are made of molded polystyrene plastic and will support close to 250 pounds (per pair). Junior sizes are available for smaller water walkers. You can not only stand and walk on the water but you can also water ski, after a fashion, behind a slow boat such as a rowboat.

"Ski Buoys" are another product enabling you to ski behind a rowboat, sail boat, or other slow-moving boat. "Ski Buoys" can also be used successfully behind a motor boat as they are better made and engineered than the Water Walkers, which are nevertheless fun things to play with on calm water. Ski Buoys are made by Recreational Products Division, Lockley Manufacturing Co. Inc., New Castle, Pennsylvania. They are fifty-seven inches long and have a "skeg", fin or keel at the rear for stability. They are buoyant foam floats with slalom-shaped bottoms. You slip your feet into them like a pair of snowshoes or moccassins. They offer an easy way to learn to water ski since they eliminate the usual beginner's bugaboo of getting up on a plane. With Ski Buoys you simple stand on the water, hold onto the towline and wait until the boat pulls you forward. You can also hold aloft a large kite or sail and be wind-propelled. These unusual skis support about 200 pounds per pair yet they weigh only four pounds each. They make you look like an experienced skier first time out!

Polystyrene "Water Walkers", marketed by Hamacher Schlemmer, N.Y., enable you to walk on calm water, once you have learned to balance. (Photo courtesy Hamacher Schlemmer)

Ski Power

Kawasaki, the motorcycle people, have come up with a new water skiing development—a high-powered, self-propelled motorized ski. It is called the Kawasaki Jet Ski, and it will hit thirty-five mph in fairly calm water. This strange-looking cross between a motorcycle, a snowmobile, a surfboard and a water ski has a two-cycle, two-cylinder, 400cc, water-cooled engine, with an impeller-pump-type adjustable jet diaphragm carburetor, an electric starter with Bendix-type drive, water proof solid-state ignition system, and a watertight engine cover. The Jet Ski develops twenty-six horsepower at 6,000 rpm and twenty-four pounds of torque at 5,000 rpm.

Here's how it works: a jet pump at the front of the unit takes in water, pressurizes it and expells it at great force in a jet through a rear directional steering nozzle. There is no propeller and no rudder.

Riding the Jet Ski

Place the unit in shallow water—as little as eighteen inches will suffice. Make sure there is no debris in the water nearby and be sure there are no swimmers close by. Standing behind the craft grasp the handlebars and drop down on one knee into the riding area. Pull the choke out (unless the engine is already warm) and apply a small amount of throttle. Press the start switch and as the engine bursts into life push the choke in. Warm the engine for about a minute—you must make sure that vapor or water spray is coming out of the rear nozzle before trying to move off. Now apply full throttle and pull your other leg up into the riding area so that you are in a kneeling position. After you get the hand of it you can stand, although the kneeling position gives you better control. As your Jet Ski moves forward, move your own weight as far forward in the riding area as possible. Use "body English" to achieve balance until the unit reaches planing speed. The bow will drop and the craft will level out in the water. Now you can decrease throttle and start learning how to maneuver on your strange, new mount. It steers just like a bicycle and almost as easily. When turning, avoid decreasing throttle pressure since this decreases the

Kawasaki's Jet Ski is safe and easy to operate, as this young 8-year old demonstrates. (Photo courtesy Kawasaki)

thrust of the jet pump and the boat may not turn or will turn slowly. Increasing throttle pressure, therefore, enables you to make sharp, tight, smooth turns.

Once you are familiar with your new toy and have mastered the basic maneuvers, you can stand by raising the handlebars slightly and placing one foot near the front section of the foot pad area.

Stabilize yourself for a moment and slowly rise to a full standing position bringing the handlebars up with you.

If you lose your balance and fall off, no problem. The craft is virtually unsinkable. As you let go of the throttle control on the handlebars, the boat instantly slows down and circles until you climb back aboard.

These are expensive toys, but they are tremendous fun. Here are the statistics: length six feet 10 inches, width, two feet, height twenty-six inches, dry weight 220 pounds, fuel tank capacity three point five gallons, gasoline consumption one and one-half gallons per hour at twenty mph—less at higher speeds. Cruising range is over two hours, giving you a distance of fifty to seventy miles. Maximum speed is well over thirty mph in calm water. Turning radius is nine feet.

To purchase one of these funtastic units, or get more information, see your nearest Kawasaki dealer or write to Kawasaki Motors Corporation, USA, 1062 McGaw Ave., P.O. Box 11447, Santa Ana, CA 92711.

Water Ski Books

Water Skiing For All, by Walter N. Prince, published by Greenberg, New York. Written in 1956, this is still a standard instructional work.
Better Water Skiing For Boys, by James Joseph. Published by Dodd, Mead & Co., New York.
Let's Go Water Skiing, by Thomas C. Hardman & William D. Clifford, published by Hawthorn Books Inc., New York.

Riding on Blades and Wheels

(1) On the Ice

You can just imagine the guffaws that came from deep chests and hoarse throats when the Scandinavian that invented ice skating fixed a narrow "blade" of wood to his shoes with the idea that these gadgets would enable him to slide across the icy surface of a lake or river! That was about as outrageous in those days as was the Wright Brothers' contention in later years that a wing-type gadget and a gasoline engine, would allow men to fly!

When Hans (or whatever his name was) finally learned how to balance on his wooden blades, the skeptics laughed on the other sides of their faces when they watched him glide swiftly across the ice while they had to walk—carefully and slowly.

"You know, he may have something there", a few of his erstwhile critics probably remarked. And then they asked him to show them how to do it. Maybe Hans' first skates were not made of wood—perhaps he used bone. It was the resourceful Hollanders, though, who realized that metal was the answer.

Later on, one Dutchman named Hans Brinker (notice how all those northern European men are named Hans?) revolutionized speed skating by developing a skate that would grip the ice as well as slide on it.

An American choreographer named Jackson Haines developed free-style skating which liberated skaters from the rigid, mechanical movements that had been associated with ice skating in the past.

And then tiny, beautiful Sonja Henie showed the world in a series of extavagant Hollywood movies just how graceful and effortless ice skating can be. An Olympic gold medal winner, Sonja Henie won no less than ten world figure skating championships. For the male side, Ulrich Salchow of Sweden won ten world figure skating championships in the early 1900s. Recent U.S. Olympic figure skating champions have included lovely Peggy Fleming and Janet Lynn; both beautiful young women possessed of unusual grace on the ice as well as superb athletic ability.

What is the best age to learn to ice skate? Any age, from the time a child is old enough to walk to the time when a person is getting too old to walk. A great many retired people, bored when cold weather keeps them off the golf courses and beaches, take skating lessons and become really good at it.

Among non-skaters a myth seems to be perpetuated that ice skating is a sure way to break a few bones. After all, they reason, ice is a very hard, solid thing to fall on—you are bound to get hurt. Fortunately, simple physics prove that falling on the ice is far less dangerous than people may think. There are two kinds of falls—one is when you are standing still or barely moving, and the second occurs when you are moving quite fast on the ice probably trying a trick beyond your capabilities. In the first case you may wind up with a slight bruise on your rear end, although, since this is a slow fall, you have plenty of time to use your hands to break your fall. However, a bruised rear end is no big deal, unless you happen to be an avid streaker—in that case it is amazing what you can accomplish with a little makeup or talcum powder.

If you fall while moving quite fast on the ice you actually hit the ice while still moving forward, which considerably lessens the impact. Again, a bruise now and then will probably be the total extent of your injuries. It is possible, though rare, to break bones while skating, twist an ankle, sprain a wrist. These injuries occur much more frequently in one's own home or back yard.

Let's Shop For Skates

There are basically three types of skates you can buy today—hockey skates, figure skates and speed skates. Hockey skates have short, high-rocked blades for fast, easy maneuverability and instant stops. Figure skates feature a hollow-ground blade and a saw-tooth toe-tip for easier control. Speed skates have long, almost level blades to allow you to obtain maximum speed with minimum effort.

As a beginner, you should make your first pair figure skates, you're not ready for hockey right away, and you are certainly not yet ready for the speed trials. Usually skates are purchased attached to skating boots although you still occasionally see the old type which can be temporarily attached to almost any boot and removed after use.

The figure skates with boots attached are best for two reasons: first, you will find it easiest to learn on figure skates and second: figure skate boots are higher and give more ankle support.

When buying first skates either for yourself or for a child, do not make the mistake of buying the cheapest, thinking they are good enough for a beginner. Nothing could be farther from the truth. Since youngsters grow rapidly, you may be inclined to buy cheaper skates; however, many skate rink shops will take the skates your child has grown out of in trade on a larger size, for there is always a market for good used skates. Or, you may prefer to place a small classified ad in your local newspaper which will usually bring a buyer to your door.

Incidentally, you may decide to buy a good pair of used skates yourself in this manner instead of starting with new ones. Nevertheless, do
buy good skates, new or used.
Generally, I don't recommend learning on rented skates. You often
do not get a perfect fit, and rented skates usually get a lot of use and
are not properly cared for—blades are often dull, rusty; boots sometimes distorted and do not provide proper support, etc.
When purchasing a pair of figure skates make sure they fit properly—tightly around the ankles, and when laced all the way up there
should not be much movement of the foot within the boot. Obviously,
you do not want the boot too tight, either. Let's say, snug. Good skating boots have built-in arch supports, and it is wise to make sure boots
have these supports before making a purchase. A pair of socks should
be worn when fitting your skates. Some skate boots have blades
riveted on, some have them attached by screws. Generally, screws are
best since blades that are riveted on are often not riveted along the correct line of the boot; many factories merely position the blade exactly
along the boot's center line whereas most experts agree the blade
should be fastened to the boot slightly to the inside of the center line
to help offset the tendency to turn the ankle in.
The skates should be laced all the way up, quite firm over the ankle
area but a little looser at the top and bottom so as not to restrict circulation.

Dress For The Part

Beginning skaters often make the mistake of dressing too lightly.
Perhaps they are guided too much by deceiving visions at ice shows of
skating stars wearing skates, boots, a short, flimsy-looking dress and
apparently little else. The truth is that the beautiful legs that look bare
actually are clad in tights that, though not as warm as woollen slacks,
are a lot warmer than bare skin. Under the flimsy dress there is often
warm, thermal underwear—especially during practice. In fact, professional skaters turn out for practice frequently bundled up like Eskimos
almost—sweaters, tights, slacks and plenty of warm undergarments.
In spite of some charming old engravings that one sees in antique
shops or art galleries from time to time, it is never advisable to wear
one of those flowing, long scarves when skating—they are a definite
safety hazard both to the wearer and to other skaters. Most serious
skaters buy skate boot covers. Usually made of wool or other warm
material, the covers are fastened over the skate boot for extra warmth.
Custom dictates that girl skaters wear white boots and male skaters
wear black boots. Other differences in clothing include the fact that
instead of tights and a short upper garment, male skaters wear warm
slacks (often over thermal "longies"), undershirt, sweater and—when
skating under freezing conditions—a jacket. Apart from the cold

outside air it is well to remember that air rising up from ice is usually rather on the chilly side.

Come On—The Water's Frozen

Now that you are dressed and equipped for it, the time has come to get on the ice. Before you start your robot-like walk to the rink or edge of the pond, lake or river, you must remember to put your blade guards on your skates. You bare blades won't stay sharp very long, especially if you walk on concrete or hardtop.

You're never too young. This lass tried again—and made it! (Photo courtesy UPI).

Like most things, learning to ice skate is best done with a professional instructor who is not only an expert skater, but also an experienced teacher. If you are learning this way, the proper way, your instructor will be with you as you step onto the ice and will hold you firm and steady until you are on balance and ready to put his or her previous instructions into practice.

If you decide to try it on your own, make sure you have something or someone to hold on to. When you are sure of your balance, walk around on the ice, gaining confidence and getting the feel of the skates. Finally, when you think you are ready to try gliding or skating, stand still with both feet side by side. Don't look at your feet. Stand erect with your back straight and look ahead. Now bend your knees slightly and turn the right foot outward at about a 45-degree angle. Keeping that right skate blade firmly on the ice, transfer most of your weight to your left foot and push against the ice with the right skate, using the entire blade, not the tip. This will cause you to glide forward on the left skate. Make sure your weight is centered on the blade of the left skate as you glide foward.

Now lift the right skate clear of the ice as you glide forward on the left skate and place it alongside the other, finishing your glide on both skates.

Now repeat with the left pushing and gliding forward on the right skate, bringing the left alongside the right. See? You're skating! Do this simple exercise a number of times to give yourself confidence and to learn how to center your weight exactly over each blade.

You are now ready to progress to the next skating plateau—skating on one foot. Using the instructions given above, glide forward with both feet parallel. Now ease your entire weight onto one foot, keeping the other blade in contact with the ice. Center your head, and consequently the center line of your body, immediately over the skate blade which is bearing your weight and lift the free skate clear of the ice and slightly to the rear of the other. Now you are virtually skating on one skate.

If you do not carry out each movement exactly right and center your weight correctly over the blade you are likely to find yourself sitting down on the ice rather rapidly. In other words, you fall down on your rear end. Well, this is your first attempt at skating, isn't it? You expect to fall down a few times. Even top skating professionals sometimes fall—you think you're better than a pro? So fall! Now that you are sitting on the ice, perhaps still sliding foward, you find yourself wondering where are the broken bones and excruciating pains you may have expected? Well, now you know that falling on the ice is no big deal and except for an occasional bruise, you are not very likely to get hurt at all.

The best way to get back up on your skates after your brief sit-down is to roll over onto one knee. Supporting yourself on the knee and your hands, bring the other foot up until the skate blade is flat on the ice, close to the knee that is supporting you. Now carefully rise, placing the other skate alongside the first and stand upright, ready to try again. And again, and again . . . Do not stay sitting on the ice—as soon as you land, start getting up right away. If there are other skaters on the ice you present a hazard sitting there. Also, you will get a very cold rear end! Another problem you may create is that other skaters and instructors may think you need help and rush to your aid—you don't you don't need any, so why bother them?

Stay towards the center of the rink or pond during your first few lessons so that you hinder the other skaters as little as possible, since the more experienced skaters will be using the perimeter. In any case, most other skaters will keep well out of your way—they've all been through what you are now going through and they understand . . . so don't pay any attention to other skaters—concentrate on what you are doing.

Where's The Brake?

Now that we've got you going on the ice, we should explain how to stop other than by merely slowing down and losing momentum until you come to a halt. The beginner's "brakes" are the snowplow, which means bringing the toes closer together than the heels, making the two skates roughly into the shape of a big snowplow. Here's how you do it: get yourself gliding forward with both feet parallel, between a foot and a foot-and-a-half apart. Bend the knees, lean slightly back and turn your toes in toward each other while pushing the heels apart. Hold this position and the increased friction on the ice surface will cause you to come to a stop.

Wrong ways of stopping include running into the rail at the edge of the rink or into other skaters, falling down, etc. As a beginner, stick with the snowplow. You can use the one-skate plow for stopping, if you prefer—glide forward with the feet parallel, then turn slightly to one side letting one skate go forward as you turn the toe in. As you become accomplished you will learn other, faster and more spectacular ways to stop, but the snowplow will do for now.

Getting Fancy

So far we have learned how to skate forward in a straight line, more or less, and how to stop. Now let's try some curves and turns. Get up a little speed and then bring both feet parallel to each other as you glide forward. Now lean the entire body, from the feet up toward the side in the direction you wish to turn. Then try turning in the opposite direction by leaning that way. It is important that the entire body from skate blade to head leans in the direction of the turn. Do not bend the legs and most important of all, do not bend the ankles.

Quite early in your skating lessons you should learn to skate backward, which isn't as tricky as it looks. Start with both feet side by side about a foot or so apart and stationary, toes slightly pointed inward. By means of a slight shuffling, begin moving backward very slowly and as you do, apply more weight to the insides of the skate blades. As you begin to glide backward the heels will separate and your feet become farther apart. Force the heels back together until your skates are again parallel. Then once again separate the heels and apply weight to the inside of the blades. This is an easy way to learn to skate backward. A slightly less-easy method is by twisting the body weight from side to side. Begin with feet side-by-side about a foot apart and stationary, then twist your body from the waist to move both heels to one side, then twist the other way to move your heels in the opposite direction. And so on . . .

The foregoing are the basics of ice skating—once you have mastered these steps you can progress in a number of directions. Speed skating may be your thing—the objective, of course, is to see how fast you can skate. Style and technique are of lesser importance—it's how fast you can get around the course that counts.

A Norwegian named Oscar Methison won no less than five world speed championships in the years prior to World War I. A Finnish skater, Claus Thunberg, also won five during the late 20s and 30s. Russia's Rimma Zhukova established a women's world speed record in 1953 by skating 5,000 meters in 9 minutes, 1.60 seconds. A year before a Dutchman, Ard Schrenk, had covered the same distance in just under eight mintues and did the 10,000 meters in a fraction of a second under fifteen minutes (See Guinness Book of World Records).

Fame and fortune may be won at the graceful ice sport of figure skating. Sonja Henie, ten times world champion (including three Olympic gold medals) and star of many Hollywood ice skating extravaganzas, earned an enormous fortune judged to be close to fifty million dollars. For many years her name was virtually a household word. Today a great many figure skaters become professionals each year and turn to teaching, modeling, performing in ice shows, endorsing products, owning, managing or working in "pro shops" or sporting goods stores, etc.

A natural progression of figure skating is ice dancing—either solo or with a partner. Waltzes, fox trots, tangos, rhumbas, ballet, blues, jazz, swing . . . they can all be performed by the serious ice skater. Records and tapes may be purchased of well-known waltzes and other dance music, recorded especially for ice performances by some of the world's top orchestras and recording companies.

Then there's hockey, which also offers fame, fortune (and a liberal share of injuries) to those who become good enough to turn professional and play for big-name teams. It is believed ice hockey games originated in Holland in the seventeenth century but became popular in the last century when games began to be played in Canada. Incidentally, our northern neighbor has won nineteen world championships including six Olympic titles. In 1971 Hungary beat Belgium in a world championship game by the incredible score of thirty-one to one.

Professional hockey star Bobby Hull has been clocked at very close to thirty m.p.h. on the ice. Bobby has also been credited with the fastest puck speed of over 118 m.p.h. Hockey is a very fast game and not without its hazards. Gordon (Gordie) Howe who played twenty-five seasons with the Detroit Red Wings, had his face repaired at various times with a total of more than 500 stitches. Statiticians have lost count of the number of split skulls, broken bones, smashed teeth, etc., that have resulted from playing hockey.

Publications and Help

An outstanding instruction book on ice skating is *Basic Ice Skating Skills* by Robert S. Ogilvie, published by J. B. Lippincott Company, New York and Philadephia.

An older, but excellent book is *Skating* by Putnam and Parkinson, published by the Ice Skating Institute of America, Fort Myers, Florida. The ISIA published and distributes a good deal of literature designed to further the cause of ice skating. The Institute is a trade association for boot and blade manufacturers, rink operators, municipalities that maintain skating facilities, and others with a commercial interest in ice skating.

The United States Figure Skating Association issues national rules governing figure skating competition and publishes a directory of USFSA committees, competition officials, clubs, etc. The USFSA also publishes a magazine called *Skating*, and makes available a series of tests to enable figure skaters from beginners to experts to measure their progress and ability. Address of the group is 178 Tremont Street, Boston, Massachusetts 02111 Phone (617) 542-4550.

A course of individual instruction programs covering various aspects of ice skating which consists of casettes, a book of photographs, etc., is available from the author of *Basic Ice Skating Skills*, Robert S. Ogilvie, 421 Wingate Rd., Baltimore, Md. 21210.

Hockey Digest, published by Century Publishing Co., 1020 Church St., Evanston, Ill. 60201, is directed primarily at ice hockey fans.

The International Skating Union, Postfach 7270, Davos, Platz, Switzerland, issues official International Competition Recordings by the world-famous orchestra of Max Greger ($4.80 airmail) and the Union governs both figure and speed skating competition internationally.

The Sportswoman magazine features women in all sports and often publishes comprehensive articles on female ice skaters. Address is P.O. Box 2611-S, Culver City, Ca. 90230.

Manufacturers

Most skate blades used in the U.S.A. for figure skating are manufactured in Britain. U.S. skate boot manufacturers import the blades and attach them to their boots or sell them separately. Most hockey blades are made in Canada.

Largest skate boot manufacturer in the United States in Reidell

Shoes, Redwing, Minnesota. They use British blades for their recreational and figure skates and Canadian blades for their hockey boots. The company also makes most of the professional skates boots used in the country. Other manufacturers are Hyde Shoe Company, Cambridge, Massachusetts, and Oberhamer Company, St. Paul, Minnesota. Although most blades used in the U.S.A. are imported, there is one major American blade manufacturer—Nestor-Johnson, Chicago, Illinois.

Figure Skate Manufacturers

Companies that sell skate boots with blades attached as well as boots and blades sold separately:

Gerry Cosby & Co., Inc.
Madison Square Garden
3 Pennsylvania Plaza
New York, NY 10001

SP-Teri Co.
2490 San Bruno Ave.
San Francisco, Ca. 94134

Hyde Athletic Industries
432 Columbia St.
Cambridge, Ma. 02141

Strauss Skates, Inc.
1751 East Cope Ave.
St. Paul, Min. 55109

Riedell Shoes, Inc.
Red Wing, Min. 55066

Skate blade manufacturers:

Nestor Johnson Mfg. Co.
1900 N. Springfield
Chicago, ILL 60647

Olympiad Skates
797 Dodd Rd.
St. Paul, MINN 55107

Skate boot manufacturers:

Daust Lalonde, Inc.
4343 Hochelaga St.
Montreal, Que. HIV 1C3

Oberhamer Shoe Co.
683 N. Dale St.
St. Paul, MINN 55103

The Garcia Corp.
329 Alfred Ave.
Teaneck, N.J. 07666

G. Stanzione
50 W. 56th St.
New York, NY 10019

Harlick & Co.
893 American St.
San Carlos, CAL 94070

(2) On Hardtop, Concrete and Rink

The Dutch, who featured prominently in the early days of ice skating, discovered certain difficulties pursuing their sport on a year-round basis—especially when there was no ice. So they developed roller skates, which were sometimes called wheel skates and sometimes parlor skates. Actually, the basic idea for roller skating was the brainchild of a Belgian performer who mounted wooden spools to wood strips which he nailed to wooden shoes. He then gave performances of rolling across the stage while playing the violin. Some people saw the dawning of a new sport which, unfortunately, received a severe setback when the Belgian, during a performance in England in the 1760s, concentrated more on his violin playing and too little on his rolling with the consequence that he skated through a large mirror. This did neither himself nor the new type of locomotion any good at all. Didn't help the mirror all that much, either!

The next episode in the saga of roller skating unfolded at a beer house in Berlin, where the enterprising proprietor had guests served beer by young ladies on early-type skates. The skates had only two iron wheels each and guests were treated to many views of petticoats and other unmentionables as the waitresses struggled to keep their balance. This beer stube, was extremely popular with the young men about town.

The French got into the act with a three-wheeled skate—two fore and one aft—then produced the "Volito", a skate with five small wheels in a straight line. This skate could not make a turn without tremendous frictional drag. Today it is to be seen in the London museum.

Then about 1850 a German composer, Meyerbeer, put a roller skating scene into his opera "Prophete", and by the 1860s the new sport had reached England where it became tremendously popular and led to the building of roller rinks in almost every town in the country. The sport soon reached America where skates underwent much-needed improvement. A chicago man, A. F. Smith, introduced the pin bearing which allowed the wheels to turn more easily, and he himself gave demonstrations in Chicago before an audience of more than 3,000 in 1882. It is said that Smith performed more than 200 fancy figures on his skates at the Chicago Casino Rink, and skating on rollers, or wheels, became quite popular.

Although she looked fast on the screen, Raquel Welch was no big deal on roller skates. Back in 1884 in a Roller Race at Madison Square Garden in New York, a man named Donovan skated 1,091 miles to win the six-day event.

Motorcycling and automobiles displaced the sport for awhile about 1910, and it is interesting to note that Harley Davidson, a great pioneer in the motorcycle industry, was one of the best roller skaters of his day.

The Exhibition Rink in Milwaukee, Wisconsin, was opened in 1883 by Levant M. Richardson who developed the ball-bearing roller skate with a rubber cushion found in most skates today. Skaters could now turn within a fourteen inch circle.

Pigtails and skirts flash as a roller skater performs a pirouette on a concrete rink. (Photo courtesy UPI).

Dance skating was introduced in 1934 which further increased the popularity of the sport, and today there are nearly 20,000,000 roller skaters in the USA.

The largest manufacturer of roller skates, the Chicago Roller Skate Company (which goes back to about the turn of the century) makes dozens of types of skates to serve all needs—from as little as $13 a pair to as much as $100 per pair.

The Roller Skating Rink Operators Association of America, formed in 1937 "to encourage the highest standard of rink management and to

stimulate the development of roller skating as a recreation and sport", ·
is affiliated with the Amateur Athletic Union of the United States and
with the world governing body over competition roller skating, the
Federation International de Roller Skating (FIRS), headquartered in
Barcelona, Spain.

The RSROA publishes a booklet titled "This Is Roller Skating"
which the beginner will find useful. Among the tips in the booklet is
the No. 1 rule—make sure your skating boots or shoes are properly
laced and tied securely. A loose lace can result in an accident. One at a
time, shake each skate, listening for rattles that indicate something is
loose. A loose wheel or truck assembly can also cause a spill on the
rink.

Clothing and Equipment

Clothing worn while roller skating should be comfortable—loose
enough to allow complete freedom of movement, but neat and attractive, too.   You can buy a pair of roller skates for a few dollars or you
may prefer to rent them at the rink skate shop. Special skating boots
are available, with skates attached; occasionally you will find skates
you can fasten to your own shoes or boots, provided they are sturdy
enough. For this type skate, boots are best because of the additional
ankle support they provide.

One reason for the popularity of this family fun sport is that it is easy
to learn and become quite good at it. Many handicapped persons become excellent roller skaters. You can take up roller skating at any
age—some roller rinks have special programs for the elderly and quite
small children learn fast.

How To Start Skating Right Away

Posture is of the greatest importance. Your body weight should be
supported directly over the ball of your foot rather than the heel. Erect
body carriage is a great help—the back should be firm but not rigid,
head up, eyes straight ahead. Do not look down at your skates.

Professional instruction is offered at every roller skating rink, and it
is inexpensive. It is also the fastest and easiest way to learn. But if you
can already ice skate you may decide that you can become a proficient
roller skater without lessons. Or, even if you cannot ice skate, you just
may, for whatever reason, decide to teach yourself. It can be done if
you go about it the right way.

Do not attempt to use your normal walking motion on skates. This is
not walking and requires different movements and different balance.
When walking, your leading foot extends out in front of you and your
body weight is pitched forward. On roller skates this type of movement results in your supporting skate sliding out behind you, and you
end up in an ungraceful heap on the rink. Try to visualize one skate as

the carrier of your body which is propelled forward by a slight push with your other leg. The pushing skate is held on the rink surface with enough body weight to ensure the longest possible push and to allow for sufficient adherence to the skating surface.

Once you start moving foward, try to maintain an even, natural flow of movement rather than moving in spurts, using fast steps and then coasting and slowing down. A smooth flow of skate movement uses a good follow-through during the pushing stroke. Don't be in a hurry to transfer your weight to the next carrying skate. Use a long, smooth push. The follow-through is important, and the entire leg is used in the push. Put your body weight over the pushing skate and push out to the side and back using pressure on the inside of the pushing skate. This will propel the carrying skate forward, and your body weight is then gradually transferred to this skate as the pushing skate falls behind. Your pushing foot should be held onto the surface of the rink until your knee straightens and flows off the floor in a "carried" position. Once your pushing leg and skate are free of the surface it is referred to as the *free* leg or *balance* leg. Do not lift it off the rink in a kicking movement as this deprives you of a full push.

As your free leg assumes the task of carrier, your knee will rebend and glide forward alongside the other skate. Presto, you are roller skating!

How to Stop

An easy way to learn how to stop on roller skates is this: Stand still with the right skate behind the heel of the left in a "T" position. Keeping the body upright, bend both knees and push off on the left skate. Now return the right skate to the "T" position as you are coasting along on the left skate. Press the middle of the right skate against the heel of the left as you gradually lower it to the rink surface. As it touches, transfer your body weight to the right (rear) skate and friction of the skate moving sideways on the rink will act as a brake and you will stop. How fast you do this determines how quickly you will stop. Try to resist a tendency to lunge forward while stopping by supporting your body with a firm back and by leaning very slightly against the direction of travel until you have stopped. There are several stopping methods, but this is easiest.

How to Steer

When you reach the end of the rink you will have to make a turn or land up on the rail. Turning is accomplished by leaning the body weight in the direction you wish to turn.

What happens when you lean is that leverage is applied to the rubber cushion-mounted skate wheels which changes their pitch and results in the skates following a curved path in the direction of the lean. A turning lean is always to the side of the skate you are using and correct leverage is applied from a firm, straight upper body. Hips and shoulders should be in line, and your body square to the line of travel. Do not try to use "body English" by leaning from the waist and pulling your skate in the direction you wish to turn. This looks terrible and results in poor balance and loss of control. When your entire body leans, transmitting pressure to the skate you are using, you need very little angle of lean to turn in a deep arc, so don't over-lean or you may fall.

In addition to making curving turns you will want to completely change directions sometimes. One way to do this is by using what skaters call the "three" turn, so-called because of the path traced by the skate during this turn.

Use a good push onto the carrying skate to begin the turn. The skate in use must be made to "roll" through the movement. Your weight is carried firmly over the skate and your body turns into the new direction. You then transfer your weight carefully to the front wheels and using the elasticity of your "wound-up" body the skating foot is snapped around to rematch the normal body position. Your free leg is carried behind during this turn, and the front wheels of the skate are used as a pivot. Your rear wheels slide around in contact with the floor but do not carry much of the body weight.

Avoid kicking the turn around by swinging your free leg into the direction of the turn. This tends to pull you off the carrying skate and ruins the turn.

How To Skate Backward

Once you are able to skate forward, following the simple directions above, you will have no trouble learning to skate backward. Best way to learn is with an instructor or a friend. Have your partner stand in front of you and skate forward supporting you during your first backward movements by placing his or her hands under your elbows with your forearm resting on top of your partner's. Stand erect and don't look down. Balance your weight over the center of both skates, toes pointing inward slightly. As you are pushed backward by your helper the skates, because of their angle, are driven apart to about shoulder width. You then reverse the angles, turning heels inward, toes outward. Pressure is maintained to the inside of both skates. What you are doing is the scissors, and you can use this movement to skate backward by yourself.

Forward Scissors

The scissors movement, which we have just used as a means of learning to skate backward, has many users. It provides a means of skating forward while keeping both skates in continuous contact with the surface of the rink. Start with your weight evenly balanced on both skates. Maintain a firm, upright stance. Now bend both knees slightly by dropping them forward. With heels together and toes about forty-five degrees apart, exert side pressure on the inside of each skate and force the feet apart to about shoulder width. With continued pressure to the inside of the skates the toes will now turn inward and the skates are pulled together. The movement is then repeated, retaining a continuous, smooth movement. Scissors helps train you to support your body in motion, and develop muscles used in "edging" the skates.

The Fun of Roller Skating

A major part of roller skating's attractiveness is its social nature. The neighborhood skating rink is an excellent place for an evening of fun in the company of people whom you know, like and with whom you share a common interest. It is also a great place to meet new people. Countless successful romances and a great many marriages have resulted from roller rink meetings. Music is a traditional part of roller rinks and dances can be enjoyed on wheels with a partner—waltzes, fox-trots, tangos, rhumbas, even the twist. Skating is a healthful form of exercise, yet it is a sport in which you can indulge fully without physical strain. This activity is one of the few recreations outside of the home in which entire families can participate. Skating parties are a popular group activity with church memberships, fraternal organizations, schools and colleges. No cancellations due to poor weather, so advance planning can be completed for a more successful event.

But there's a serious side of roller skating. The Girl Scouts have a skating program in their merit badge assignments, and more than one million Girl Scouts have earned merit badges in roller rinks. North American championships are held annually in roller hockey, figure, dance and speed skating. Over the past quarter century, the use of roller skating programs in municipal recreation areas and youth service organizations has increased tremendously. One reason is that rinks can be concrete areas, asphalt (hard top), tile, wood, composition, terrazzo, and other surface materials. Floors that are intended for considerable roller skating use, however, should be properly finished. There are a number of firms specializing in roller skating floor finishing.

Roller skating is certainly one of the least expensive sports in the world. A few dollars' worth of skates and you are a participant. Charges at roller rinks vary—YMCA's that have rinks usually charge about 75 cents for non-members and 25 cents to 50 cents for members. Many rinks charge only 25 cents admission, and at additional cost offer skate rentals, professional instruction, periodical amateur competitions, snack bars, skate shops, etc.

More Information

Address of the Roller Skating Rink Operators Association of America is 7700 A St., Lincoln, Neb. 68510. The RSROA has a considerable amount of information that can be of value both to the beginning skater and to those who are interested in the sport from a professional standpoint.

Another group, the United States of America Confederation (USAC) works toward uniting and strengthening competitive aspects of the sport and anticipates acceptance of roller skating as an Olympic Games competition in the near future.

The Roller Skating Foundation of America promotes roller skating on behalf of all commercial enterprises with an interest in the sport and for skaters themselves. Its address is 515 Madison Ave., New York, NY 10022.

Some skate manufacturers are: Chicago Roller Skate Company, Chicago, Illinois; Sure Grip Skate Company, Lynwood, California; Union Hardware, Division of McGregor-Brunswick, Torrington, Connecticut; Douglass-Snyder Skate Company, Dayton, Ohio; Globe Union Skate Company, Milwaukee, Wisconsin; Stevens Manufacturing Company.

For The Record

Roller Skating was "big" in Britain before it caught on in the USA. From 1925 to 1939 Britain was undefeated in all international championships. Portugal won eleven titles from 1947 to 1972 (see Guinness *Book of World Records*). The fastest official world's record is 25.78 mph by an Italian who clocked an unofficial record in 1963 of almost 35 mph. David Letters, a twenty-seven-year-old sociologist from Gloucester, Massachusetts, roller skated across the country recently—a total of 3,750 miles in four and one-half months. An English girl in 1962 skated twenty miles and 1,355 yards on a rink in one hour and the record for a mile on a rink is 2 minutes 25.1 seconds by an Italian man. A Canadian, Clinton Shaw, roller skated from Victoria, BC to St. John's, Newfoundland (Canada) on the Trans-Canadian Highway in 1967—a total distance of 4,900 miles. And that was before the gasoline shortage!

Recent roller skating champions include pretty Natalie Dunn of Bakersfield, California, who won the 1974 Senior Ladies US Amateur Roller Skating Championship; Sue McDonald of Steubenville, Ohio, and Ronald Sabo, of Painesville, Ohio, who won the 1974 World's Pair Roller Skating Championships in La Coruna, Spain and Laura Gernannt of Fort Lauderdale, Florida, who won the title of 1974 American Roller Skate Queen.

Skateboarding: Surfing For Inlanders

Riding skateboards used to be essentially a children's game; however, some interesting things have been happening to this former child's pasttime over the last couple of years, and today skateboarding probably appeals as much to older youths and young adults as it does to the small fry. In fact, skateboarding is a whole new sport which is in its infancy, just as surfboarding was a quarter century ago.

Moreover, surfers have discovered that a skateboard on a paved parking lot, sidewalk, or asphalt or concrete slope is a good substitute for a surfboard on the rolling waves. Surfers and even skiers are using skateboards today as training devices, and many sophisticated skateboards now being built are designed with that purpose in mind. In *The Complete Book of Surfing* author Peter L. Dixon describes the skateboard as the "Link trainer for surfers."

Many skateboard enthusiasts, however, prefer to consider skateboarding a separate, younger and rapidly growing sport only distantly related to surfing.

Modern skateboards are designed, engineered and built with technology acquired through the development and manufacture of roller skates, skis, and surfboards.

Skateboard Styles

A skateboard is basically a flexible hardwood, laminated or fiberglass board of any length up to about forty inches. They are commercially available although some enthusiasts make their own which are often as long as forty-eight inches. Widths and shapes vary, depending upon the skateboard's use. One of the leading manufacturers, Bahne Skateboards, Inc., makes three basic styles—a thirty inch skateboard for general downhill use, a twenty-seven inch "slalom" board, and a twenty-four inch "hot-dog" board for special tricks and for training by hot-dogger surfers. Infinity Skateboards offers their "Gun"—thirty-one inches long, six wide and a "hot-dog" version twenty-three inches long by six and five-eighths inches wide.

Surf is always "up" for this ardent young surfboard rider who practices on his skateboard in his backyard. (Photo courtesy Don Kremers, *SURFER* Magazine).

A gently sloping, traffic-free street sets the stage for action on a skate-board. (Photo courtesy Frank Nasworthy)

Many people view the skateboard as basically an elongated skate or a mere board secured to four skate-type wheels and consider their price—sometimes as high as $45 each, to be inordinately high. However, the modern skateboard, made for today's serious aficionado of the sport, is highly engineered and precision-balanced. It has to be, considering the fact that when skateboarding you have only one pivot point instead of two—rather like riding downhill on one ski. Skateboarding requires a good deal of coordination and balance, and developing these necessary abilities pays off in the great freedom and excitement that skateboarders enjoy.

Most popular and probably best skateboard wheels are made by Cadillac Wheels Company in Encinitas, California. This company was started by young Frank Nasworthy on a total capital of $500. Within a year and a half the young entrepreneur had grossed close to a quarter million dollars, demonstrating the rapid growth of this new sport. Cadillac furnishes wheels in three configurations: No. 1. "Originals", the most popular general-purpose wheels measuring 1-7/8 inches in diameter and 1-1/8 inches wide; No. 2. "Da Kine", wheels 1-1/2 inches wide and more expensive, and No. 3 "Big Wheels", 2-1/4 inches in diameter, 1-1/8 inches wide. Each style has its devotees— some swear by one type; some by another. Greater width is the key to increased tractions, whereas larger diameter wheels produce higher rotation speeds.

Modern skateboards have come a long way from the original "skooters" and early skateboards kids used to put together using any old wheels and a flat board. Specifically engineered "soft" urethane wheels, laminated boards with a precise degree of flexibility, carefully calculated balance and weight—these are the reasons for the high cost of what may seem to the uninitiated to be a simple kid's toy.

Riding The Sidewalk "Surf"

Anyone who can roller skate can learn to ride a skateboard fairly easily, as can many youngsters who have never tried roller skating.

There are various ways of getting moving on a skateboard. Some push the skate board by hand and then run after it and jump aboard. Others start with one foot on the board and one on the ground using the ground foot to push until momentum takes over. Another method is to start from a standstill with one foot firmly on the skateboard. Then push with the other until the board gets rolling at a fair rate of speed, gathering momentum with the decline of a sloping, traffic-free street.

To change direction, you merely move your weight and point of balance, as in surfing. By shifting the weight in various ways, all kinds of hot-dogging tricks can be performed on a skateboard, as on a surfboard. As with most sports, practice breeds proficiency.

Be a Safe Skateboarder

The really good skateboarder scouts the slope before starting to get the feel of the degree of incline, what hazards may be encountered and how and where to stop. Skateboarders who know what they are doing do not compete with pedestrians for the sidewalk or with cars in parking lots and on the road. They make sure they do not overshoot a turn and roll or fall into the path of traffic. Some skateboarders insist on ankle supports, and hot doggers and trick riders often wear helmets as protection against head injuries in the event of a bad spill. Helmets are mandatory in skateboard competitions.

The responsible skateboarder checks for the following hazards prior to using his equipment: bumps, loose gravel, gratings, manhole covers, drains, bad concrete seams, broken glass and other debris, soft tar, fresh cement, patches of oil or grease, trees, lamp posts, curbs at sidestreets, etc. It is also wise to check out your skateboard carefully everytime you use it. Look for cracks, breaks, loose trucks, loose wheels, bad bearings, and all other signs of damage or wear.

Hints From The Champion

Chris Yandall, National Skateboard Champion, kindly passed along the following thoughts concerning his sport:

"Skateboarding in our perspective is a beautiful, flowing, stimulating, outrageous, fun sport, into which we put a great deal of thought and effort. Skateboard enthusiasts like to ride down asphalt, hardtop or cement slopes—preferably with inclines between twenty and thirty degrees.

"There are two ways of skateboarding down such a hill—first, with full control, able to make controlled stops at will, and second, without proper control which often results in cuts, bruises, concussions, fractures and other unpleasantness. Skateboarding is similar in some ways to downhill skiing where the skier picks a line of traverse down a hill and sets out a pattern of control using his ski edges and his own body to effect maneuvers. In skateboarding, the wheels act as the medium between the ground and the body. The skateboard "trucks" must be kept tight. Some enthusiasts like to ride with loose trucks which makes it easier for "hot doggers" to make radical turns. However, as you pick up speed, loose trucks cause wobbling which often leads to loss of full control. With practice you can ride the two inside wheels in your fast turns—this beats skateboarding with loose trucks every time.

"The arms play a definite part in the mechanics of skateboarding, and the head is another balance element. The torso, legs and feet must develop new muscles to take on the stress of performing controlled turns on hills or self-propulsion on flat surfaces.

"A simple S-curve at any radius allowed by the angle of descent requires different applications of pressures by the legs at an allowable angle of lean. The rest is practice, lots of it. Scratches, bruises, cuts, yes. But a great feeling of accomplishment as you gradually master the relatively new art of skateboarding. And a great deal of fun, too."

Who Makes Them?

Three leading manufacturers of sophisticated skateboards, who ship their products throughout the USA are:

Bahne Skateboards
P.O. Box 326A
Encinitas, CA 92024

Cadillac Wheels Company
P.O. Box 563
Encinitas, CA 92024.

California Surfing Products
P.O. Box 216
Encinitas, CA 92024

Infinity Surfboards
414 Pacific Coast Hwy.
Huntington Beach, CA 92648

Riding The Surf

No thrill quite equals the tremendous exhilaration that you experience when you ride the surf shorewards, either with or without a surfboard.

The actual origin of surfing seems lost in antiquity. We are fairly certain that it originated in the Tahitian and other South Pacific islands, although there are many different views as to when surfing for fun first began. One theory is that recreational surfing developed out of Pacific man's earlier needs to observe and spear fish. Forerunners of today's scientifically engineered, lightweight surfboards were probably mats woven from coconut and other fibers.

Surfer "Owl" Chapman racing the soup at sunset and demonstrating his fine form. (Photo courtesy Moe Lerner, *SURFER* Magazine.)

Islanders would likely lie flat on their bellies on these mats and allow the incoming waves to bring them to shore, while watching the water beneath them for fish which could fall victim to their strong arms and swift spears. Natives of the various South Pacific groups of islands migrated by catamaran, canoe and raft to the Hawaiian Islands where they found fruit, game and fish in abundance as well as surf just begging to be ridden.

When the English explorer Captain Cook landed there in 1778 recreational surfing was well established. For many years only kings and their sons and brothers rode the long, carved wooden surfboard called the *olo*, made from lightweight wood similar to balsa. Later, surfing privileges were extended to other young men. Commoners were permitted to ride the waves on much shorter boards called *koas*, carved from harder and heavier woods. Both of these early types of surfboards may be seen in the Bishop Museum in Honolulu, Hawaii.

The father of modern surfing is generally considered to be an Hawaiian known as Duke Kahanamoku, who revived it after early Christian missionaries had decided that since Hawaiians enjoyed it so much it must be sinful.

Kahanamoku, the Good Guy of Surfing, in the early years of this century won three gold medals for swimming at the Olympics, and in his subsequent travels he introduced surfing to California, Australia, New Zealand and other places wherever he could find good surf. He began surfing seriously at eight years of age and is still considered the greatest surfer who ever lived.

The development of lightweight polyurethane foam and fiberglass cloth and coatings, may be thanked for today's lightweight, balanced, scientifically shaped and beautifully finished surfboards.

Surfing is a sport that can be enjoyed by both sexes and by people of all ages, although agility and physical fitness are important. Nevertheless, one sees many gray-haired surfers expertly riding the waves as well as youngsters.

You shouldn't take up surfing unless you are an experienced, strong swimmer who does not tire easily.

Since most good, strong swimmers who swim regularly enjoy robust health, people taking up surfing usually have the degree of fitness necessary for this strenuous sport. I emphasize fitness—not strength. Many skinny little twelve-year-old girls as well as boys are competent surfers. Fast reactions, endurance, complete control, agility and a fine sense of balance are absolute essentials.

Try Body Surfing First

Before purchasing your first surfboard and taking lessons it is usually a good idea to start with body surfing—that is, riding the surf flat on your belly, without a board. This is a lot of fun, and it accustoms you to the "feel" of riding the waves.

Body surfing is usually done in fairly shallow water—a long, gradually declining sandy beach going far out into the water, is really

good to start with. However, if the water is too shallow and the incoming waves fairly fast, you stand the risk of being scraped along the
bottom, which can not only take the skin off your belly and chest but
can also take all the fun out of the thing. When you start body surfing it
is best to walk out to where the waves are breaking. The water should
be at least as high as your thighs, but no higher than your chest. Face
the shore and turn your head so that you can watch the incoming
waves behind you. Try to judge it so that you push off the bottom and
start swimming as fast as you can just before the wave breaks. As it
breaks, if you have timed it right, it will catch you up in the foam
(called "soup" by the surfing fraternity) and carry you shorewards
leaving you thrilled and probably breathless on the sand when the
wave is spent.

After a little practice you can start farther out and graduate to the
next step in body surfing—riding the "break." This is the technique of
catching the wave diagonally, or even at right angles, just before it
breaks into "soup" and then *sliding* along and down the "wall" of water
that rises up from the main water level and crests at the top. This area,
inside the wave, so to speak, is often hollowed out and is therefore
known in surfese as the "tube" or "trough." The crest of the wave is
over your head, and you are lying on your stomach. Keep your arms to
your sides and hollow your back a little by forcing your head and
shoulders back. You are now being carried ashore by the wave. To
catch the break and slide along the tube or trough takes lots of practice
and above all, timing. You must be swimming as fast as you can with
the water at the moment you are overtaken by the break just below the
crest of the incoming wave. Swim fins are a great help in achieving this
speed.

You must take a good, deep breath as the wave reaches you for you
are lying face down and it is going to be difficult to breathe regularly in
this position while being swept along by the wave. With practice you
can make turns, cut up and down the trough and do many of the tricks
done on a surfboard. Many enthusiasts surf this way and never go on
to using a surfboard.

Surfing With An Inflatable "Board"

Inflatable air mattresses, mats, or even inflated rubber toys can be
used by small children on the soup of small waves near the shore. At
many beaches, rubber surfboards may be rented and may be
purchased at surfboard stores (called surf shops), department and
discount stores, etc. These "mat-boards" are designed and made
exclusively for surfing. They are very buoyant and can be used by older
children or even adults to develop an interest in surfing and a degree of
surfing skill before going on to the big boards.

Many flat-bottomed items can be used for surfing—the author's interest in the sport started at the age of six on a beach on the Cornwall coast, in the South of England, long before this area became the popular surfing Mecca that it is today. We little tykes used to "borrow" trash can lids, take them out to where the waves broke, drop them onto the water, and quickly jump aboard. At low tide the waves would carry us ashore beautifully. Many a large baking tray vanished from a puzzled mother's kitchen in those days, as we discovered these made perfect "skimmers" to ride along the sand in very shallow water.

As in body surfing, swim fins are helpful in achieving the speed needed to catch the waves if you use a small board or inflatable object. After some practice you will find you can surf this way in a kneeling position and if you use a rigid board or stiff rubber mat, you may even be able to graduate to a standing position. But don't expect to make too much progress with an air-filled surfboard or a flat "belly board"— these items are not designed and engineered for surfing as are the more sophisticated surfboards.

Whichever type of surfing you do, in cold water it is well to consider wearing a wet suit which helps retain body heat. Surfing of any kind consists of short periods of rapid movement with the surf and long periods of paddling back out and waiting for the right wave. Unless the sun is warm and the water not too cold, you will soon find yourself covered in goose pimples and feeling uncomfortably chilled without a wet suit. This is bad surfing for several reasons:

Your circulation slows down and your muscles do not respond as quickly.

You lose some of the agility necessary for this sport.

Your concentration tends to waver and you lose interest, which makes you an inefficient surfer.

You soon feel just plain miserable.

Some body and small-board or inflatable board surfers oil or grease their bodies to retain body heat. This is not done by the experienced surfers on the big boards because the slightest touch of oil or grease on the smooth surface of a well-finished surfboard will send the surfer off the boards and into the water immediately.

Boat Surfing

The Polynesians and Hawaiians, in addition to inventing surfboard riding, also originated the idea of riding the surf in canoes, dugouts, catamarans, dories and kayak-type boats. Again, this sport probably originated as an outcome of fishing. The young men would return from their fishing trips, and when they got close enough, would save some energy by allowing their boats to ride the surf in to shore . . . sometimes for quite long distances. I have personally tried it in several parts of the world and it is a lot of fun. However, on my first few tries I found that most of the time I was underneath the inverted canoe, which tended to dampen my enthusiasm somewhat, but I stuck with it and improved quite a bit.

Like anything else, canoe surfing takes practice, and if there's more than one canoeist in the boat, it takes teamwork. It is important to keep the prow of the boat up by putting most of your weight towards the rear of the center. As with other types of surfing, gathering enough speed ahead of the wave is important and requires some very fast paddling.

Boat surfing can be quite dangerous, for until you become skilled, it is very easy to misjudge the velocity or direction of the waves and have your boat overturned. Sometimes the boat is thrown high in the air by the force of the inrushing wave, and it can descend upon its erstwhile occupants and anyone else who may be in the vicinity.

Lifeguards on many beaches use dories or flat-bottomed rowboats (occasionally canoes) and develop considerable skill at boat surfing. In some places races and other competitions are held which are highly interesting to watch.

It is never safe to boatsurf close to other surfers or swimmers.

Choosing A Board

There are four legal ways to get your first surfboard:
1. Buy it used from a friend, another surfer, or from a surf shop. This is usually your least expensive route.
2. Buy it new, ready-made by a good manufacturer.
3. Have it made for you by a professional surfboard builder.
5. Build your own.

Of the above alternatives, No. 3 is usually considered best by most experienced, serious surfers. You should expect to pay at least $100. If you can't come up with that much bread, then consider No. 2. Price surfboards in a good, estalished surf shop (not the local discount store), and if you still have trouble meeting the tab, then No. 1 must be your answer. However, when you buy a used surfboard, look it over very carefully, check to see how many times it has been repaired (unless very well done, you can usually spot the "patches"), check to see if the surface is cracked, look for chips, gashes, etc. Check the fin to make sure it is intact and that it is still securely fastened to the board. Get the advice of a more experienced surfer.

Right now, at the outset of your interest in this enjoyable water sport, it is a good idea to join a club. Inquire at the local surf shop or ask other surfers.

Beginning surfers who have yet to learn the code of behavior followed by good surfers are termed "Gremmies" in surfese. The term describes an inexperienced, rash surfboard rider who has little regard for other surfers or for his own safety. You can avoid being dubbed a Gremmie by learning all you can about surfing, surfboards, surf and surfing safety and becoming reasonably proficient as quickly as possible.

First, you must understand your equipment, the surfboard, before you make your initial purchase. Naturally, the front end is called the nose and the rear the tail; the sides are known as the left and right "rails." The board curves upward slightly at both ends so that the surface of the board from nose to tail is concave. This hollow is known as the "scoop" or "rocker" and is essential to the design and engineering of every modern surfboard. At the tail there is a fin projecting downward from the center. This is usually called the "skeg." The top surface of the board is the "deck"; the underside the "belly."

Surfboards vary from about eight feet long up to a maximum of about twelve feet. Boards of the latter length are rarely used today except by very heavy surfers and for certain specialized surfing on very heavy surf. The longer boards provide good stability, but they are not very maneuverable, are difficult to transport and hard to paddle out through the waves. You may on occasion see even longer boards around—up to eighteen or twenty feet—but these are paddleboards and not intended for surf riding.

If you decide to go the custom-made route right at the beginning, the surfboard manufacturer will specify the right length, width and style of surfboard for your own weight and needs. Until you become an experienced surfer and have developed your own special style and tried out a few different models, it is not a good idea for you to specify any particular shape but rather to let the board builder do it for you. Rely on his experience and expertise. The only exception to this, I would say, would be if you have a knowledgeable, adept surfer who is going to teach you—in this case you may want to follow his advice and request the type of surfboard he recommends.

For about half the cost of a good board or less, you can buy a kit with complete instructions and build your own IF you are experienced at working with fiberglass and resins and have a safe place to work.

Put It In The Water . . . If It Floats, Ride It

Before launching, the deck of your board should be well waxed. Wax will reduce the slipperiness of a wet surfboard and help you stay on board. Parafin wax is as good as anything and cheapest, although there are a variety of surfboard waxes on the market. Many surfers wax the soles of their feet also, and some wax their feet instead of waxing the entire deck of the surfboard in order to conserve wax.

If you cover your body with a good suntan oil before you go surfing you will probably get either a bad sunburn or a beautiful tan; however, you will not do much surfboard riding, because any oil or grease on the smooth surface of your board will dump you in no time flat.

Next examine the sea bottom for rocks, junk, shells, coral and anything else that may cause injury either to your feet when wading in with your board, to your board as you ride back in, or to your own body when you "wipe-out" (fall off). If you are in water frequented by sea urchins, extra care is advised for these spiny little creatures can cause you a lot of pain if you step on them or touch them. They usually lie among coral or rocks, so unless you are on this type of beach in warm water you are not likely to be bothered by sea urchins. Sting rays like to lie on sandy bottom in fairly shallow water and should definitely be avoided, as should stinging jellyfish. In a few areas (mostly Australia and the West Indies) sharks present a possible surfing hazard. Other surfers will usually tell you of any problems of this kind. Occasionally you must watch out for sea lions, seals and whales—not because they might attack but because they get in your way. Kelp (seaweed) may be great on a health diet but a hindrance on some beaches.

As you wade into the water, carry your surfboard upside down to keep the skeg or fin from hitting the bottom. Keep the nose up, for if a wave hits it as you are wading in you may lose your grip and possibly your board—especially if it is slammed on rocks.

Once you get out in the water, paddle out to where the waves are breaking and try your first surfboard ride. Lie on the board on your belly, chin up, shoulders back, with most of your weight on the lower part of your body. Reach as far forward as you can and as your hand enters the water cup your fingers and pull back strongly and swiftly to propel yourself through the water as quickly as possible. After a while, when you feel at home on your surfboard, you will want to try paddling in the kneeling position. This makes it easier to change your point of balance and direction. If you keep most of your weight just rear of the center of the board as you paddle out, you reduce the possibility of "pearling" caused by the nose pointing downward and digging in the water, sending up a spray of "pearls." This slows you down or stops you and will probably cause you to "wipe-out". A third paddling position is sitting astride your board—a position used mostly for paddling short distances out to the smaller waves.

Be a wave watcher—study the water, what it does, how it moves, where and how the waves break. Don't force your way out through "soup" (white foam on the crest of the wave) unless you have to . . . look for a way around the wave break. This way you use up far less energy and get out there faster and you avoid the possibility of being clobbered by a maverick surfboard some other surfer has lost. Also, you are less likely to impede the progress of surfers riding in.

In addition to watching the waves, you should also watch the other surfers—not just the shapliest ones of the opposite sex, either. Don't watch the ones who are the obvious experts just yet—the "hotdog-gers" (surfers who ride the nose of their boards with toes usually curled over the leading edge, a very difficult technique). Don't bother watching the tandem surfers (two on a board, etc.). At this stage you will learn little from these accomplished surfers. Keep your eye instead on the average or intermediate surfers who are trying to learn and improve rather than prove their skill or test their courage.

As a wave travels toward shore, pushed by winds often far out to sea and by other waves, they get higher as they gather more water until they reach the "break point"—the point at which the top of the wave begins to fall off the body. What is happening is that the bottom of the sea is creating friction drag on the lower portion of the inrushing wave so that the top of the wave—the crest—being subjected to less friction drag, begins traveling faster than the bottom part. The top or crest therefore begins to curl over, since there's nothing to hold it up, which creates a hollowed-out effect between the surface of the main body of water and the crest of the faster-moving wave. This hollow is called the "trough" or when very pronounced, the "tube." When you hear a surfer talk about sliding down the trough or shooting the tube, he is referring to riding on the surface of this hollow body of water.

As the crest of the wave falls forward into this trough, surf forms, and this is just what you and other surfers have been waiting for. Quickly position your board with its nose at a ninety-degree angle to the direction of the approaching wave; lie on it so that the nose points slightly upward and paddle fast. If you have timed it right you will feel the incoming wave raise you up and move you along with it at its own speed. When you have ridden the waves a few times in this position, try kneeling on your board. Then move up to the real stuff—riding the surfboard on your feet. The proper standing position is with your left foot ahead of the right, your body weight slightly to the rear of the center of gravity. This should keep your board "in trim"—straight and level. Try to avoid having the nose dip or you will pearl and wipe-out.

From here on you will progress according to how hard you work at it, the instructional help you can get, types of surf you ride, type of board you use, the degree of your coordination, balance, and other factors.

Help Is Available

Membership in a surfing club would be a good bet for you as would professional instruction. Each club has at least one good surfer who acts as instructor and helps bring the new members along to proficiency. Some surf shops offer skilled instruction and surfing schools are becoming more widespread—especially in California. In some areas, the local YMCA conducts surfing classes and workshop sessions are held from time to time on popular surfing beaches by the United States Surfing Association, which you should certainly join. There are two divisions—the Western Surfing Association, PO Box 905, Aptos, CA 95003 and the Eastern Surfing Association, c/o Colin Couture, 400 Brookline Ave., Boston, MA 02115. The associations have done a great deal for the sport of surfing, for surfing enthusiasts, and for the surfing industry and for motion picture companies and others. Membership costs only $3.00 a year for surfers 17 and under; $5.00 for those over 17.

As a member you will receive your membership card, an automobile decal, an embroidered patch for trunks or windbreaker, and the association's newsletter. You may attend meetings, vote, help elect officers and perhaps serve as an officer of the association yourself.

The United States Surfing Association, through its Western and Eastern divisions, conducts a number of positive, continuing programs from which you and all surfers will benefit. Broadly, these cover the following:

- Activities directed toward saving present surfing locations.
- Endeavors aimed at reopening surfing areas which have been closed to surfers.
- Efforts to obtain new surfing areas (a) for all surfers and (b) special efforts to obtain new areas for USSA members spefically.
- Standardization and continuing improvement of surfing contests.
- Educational efforts toward improved surfing safety.
- Effective representation on city, county, state and federal government levels.
- Dissemination of factual, positive information about surfing to the press, legislators, authors, etc.

Where Surf Is Up

The cry "Surf's Up" is eagerly awaited by surfboard riders hanging around the beach, the local surfshop, or perhaps waxing their boards and rapping on the tailgates of their station wagons or vans. Usually at least one surfer will be watching the water and testing the waves. As soon as he deems the surf suitable for effective surfing, he notifies the others and they run, rarely walk, to the water.

Aloha, Surfers!

Ridable surf is found in dozens of countries across the globe at various times and at hundreds of locations throughout the USA. Many well-known surfers have traveled the world seeking surf and reported their findings to the USSA, publications and others.

Still considered best by most serious surfers are the Hawaiian Islands, the Mecca of the American surfing fraternity. The main island, Hawaii, offers at least a dozen good surfing areas although hotels and developers have gobbled up many great beaches which are therefore off limits to surfers unless they are staying in the hotel or living in a development that owns one of these beaches. It is a pity that there is not a law that keeps every inch of America's coastline for a couple of hundred yards free of buildings and private speculation and available to all the citizens of the country, instead of being reserved exclusively for the rich, greedy few.

The west side of Hawaii, called the Kona Coast, has quite a number of good surfspots, and there are more on the opposite side of the island. However, the big island is not as popular with surfers as are Oahu and Maui.

The island of Oahu's northern shore offers some really huge waves especially in the winter. Makaha Beach, on Oahu's west coast, has good surf most of the year but especially in the winter months. In the summer months, Yokahama provides challenging surf; Laniakea is becoming very popular among north shore surfers because of the variety of its surf. Ala Moana, on the south coast, is a hot dogger's paradise, and Waikiki Beach, immortalized in many movies, is still the most popular surf area in the Islands—in terms of numbers of surfers.

Sunset Beach, close to the northernmost point of Oahu, is known for its challenging, big surf—ridden successfully and safely only by the surfing masters. It is said waves on Sunset Beach never break twice in the same place, and careful judgment and the utmost control are essential. Rip currents can carry you away from shore when you wipe out but can be helpful to those who understand them in paddling out to the breaks. Even for the inexperienced, it is worth a visit to this beach just to watch the real surf wizards.

Maui, Hawaii's second largest island, offers a number of fine surfing areas—notably Lahaina at the northern end where the harbor entrance provides good, though not spectacular, surf . . . especially valuable to the inexperienced surfer. At Maui's northern tip is Honolau Bay which at certain times of the year challenges the best. Kahului Bay, also up north, has well-formed waves with usually predictable breaks.

There are other islands in the Hawaii group where some surfers seek the elusive perfect wave. Transportation problems have retarded their popularity in many cases, some have been visited by surfers via helicopter.

Probably the best book written or likely to be written for a very long time on the subject of where to find surf is Peter L. Dixon's *Where The Surfers Are* (Coward-McCann Inc., NY). Dixon, whose book *The Complete Book of Surfing* is virtually a standard text book on the subject, covers surfing areas all over the world and writes with authority on each.

Golden California

In this book, space limitations permit only brief mentions of some of the better beaches in the USA. According to Dixon, California alone offers over 300 known, well-surfed beaches. Because of the preponderance of surfers in California, where U.S. mainland surfing began, and because there are probably more accessible, good surfing areas in that state than in any other, I will cover some of them briefly.

Taking it from the top—extreme northern California—between Crescent City (close to the Oregon border) south to the Golden Gate Bridge, there are few really good surfing beaches, and those that exist are often inaccessible except to surfers fond of long hikes. The water temperature along this coast is very discouraging. In the Bay area, however, there are some excellent, much-frequented surfing areas. Kelly's Cove with its ten and twelve footers is best known. Pedro Point shows some lively surf—ten-foot waves are common here, just below Kelly's.

Going south there are several excellent areas between San Francisco and Santa Cruz—Ano Nuevo Point, in particular. Then there's great Santa Cruz, one of the best big-wave surf spots anywhere. Steamer Lane and other beaches in this area offer excellent surfing, where waves up to twenty feet have been known—not surfed much, but known. Rip currents, rocks, sudden fogs, and other surfers are among the hazards to be watched for here.

Continuing south, there is surf at Monterey and at nearby Carmel— generally good areas for surfers who haven't too much experience behind them yet, although the water is still very cold and deters all except the most hardy surfers in winter.

Big Sur is the next attraction as you head into warmer waters, with waves that are sometimes too big for most surfers. San Simeon does not attract big crowds, but there are a couple of likely spots for the surfer who wants to improve his techniques. Farther south the Morro Bay area is quite popular because of its smooth swells and predictable breaks. Avila Beach, Pismo Beach and Jalama Beach, all offer interesting surf at times with some good point breaks.

Gaviota Beach, south of Point Concepcion, and Refugio Beach State Park (where surfing is permitted) are popular because of the long rides possible on the rolling swells. El Capitan Beach State Park, good at high tide, is another of many state parks where surfing is permitted.

Proceeding down the coast towards Los Angeles there are many good surfing beaches, most of which are well-populated by surfers. Carpinteria Beach is especially good with a fine break out on the reef, and nearby Rincon Del Mar is highly rated by surfers for its long, well-formed swells with predictable breaks. A beach called The Overhead, near Ventura, provides some very challenging surf, particularly during the winter months. Several fair to good surfing beaches dot the coast down to the Los Angeles area which has over thirty surfing spots throughout the Santa Monica Bay area. Most of these are heavily frequented.

Some of the popular board-riding beaches in the general Los Angeles area are:

Arroyo Sequit in the Leo Carrillo State Park which usually runs surf four or five-feet high and offers good sport summer and winter.

Malibu, an almost magical name for surfers with its long waves and predictable breaks, offers excellent summer surfing and at times big, challenging waves.

Los Angeles' Sunset Beach is popular with learners; Malaga Cove has enjoyed some good surfing crowds in the past but seems to be losing popularity. On the other hand, although it offers some fine surfing, especially in the winter, it is not the kind of beach that encourages the fierce loyalties surfers show some other areas.

Paddleboard Cove, Lunada Bay and Cabrillo Beach Park, all fair surfing spots, attract both experienced surfers and novices.

Huntington Beach, where the annual United States Surfing Championships are held each Fall, boasts consistently good surf in four separate areas. The Huntington Beach State Park is safe and popular with beginners.

Newport Bay and its impressive surfing area known as "The Wedge" attract skilled surfers, for the most part because of its challenging surf. Rip currents are quite dangerous here.

Approaching Mr. Nixon's retreat we hit the Laguna Beach area where novices and experts mix freely, and San Clemente Beach State Park is popular and usually crowded.

Heading toward the Mexican border, San Onofre and Oceanside beaches attract a growing number of surfers each year and Carlsbad, La Costa, Leucadia and Moonlight Beach all offer good surfing much of the year. Seacliffe Roadside Park at Encinitas—called "Swami's" because of the "Self-Realization" temple at the turnoff—offers particularly good surfing on long, well-formed swells. Winter waves here hit ten feet on occasion.

La Jolla, just north of San Diego, runs some good swells along its lengthy beach, and a surfing club called WindanSea maintains a fine surfing beach to the south of La Jolla, where big waves often break consistently.

Around San Diego are a number of surfing beaches—a few of which seem to get particularly crowded—Mission Beach, Ocean Beach, Pacific Beach and Imperial Beach.

South of the border, on Baja California's Pacific Coast, there are surfing areas aplenty—most of them still waiting to be discovered. But that's another story.

Oregon Offers More Than Apples

Famous as Oregon is for its fine fruit, surfers know it best for its 350 miles of coastline which includes some very fine surfing areas rarely

crowded to the degree that the better California beaches often are.
Here are some of the best of the Oregon surfing spots:

Whaleshead Beach and Gold Beach, a few miles north of California,
have surf that caters to beginners and master alike. A few miles farther
north are Hubbard Creek and Battle Rock, offering good breaks and
fine surfing most of the year.

Coos Bay, with its Bastendorf Beach State Park and several other
state-operated surfing areas, shows some big surf and well-formed
smaller waves.

Farther north in the Newport area, are Agate Beach, Newport Beach
and Otter Rock—all popular spots with both local and visiting surfers.

Of special note in Oregon is Seaside Cove, the top spot in the state
all year 'round. Strongest surf is in winter with ten foot waves
common.

Juan de Fuca and All That

In Washington, Long Beach and Westport are good, though little
used, surfing areas offering high swells, good breaks and spectacular
scenery. A word of caution—much of the land along this part of the
Washington coast belongs to the Indians and lies in their reservation.
They will permit you to cross it and use the beaches, but it is wise and
good surfing manners to ask first.

Farther along this state's 200-plus miles of coastline, there are a
number of areas where surfing could be popular. But the extremely
cold water, plus access difficulties, tends to keep most surfers away.
In any case, wet suits are essential. Most noteworthy are Point
Grenville and Shipwreck Point, both in an Indian reservation. The
Indians do not bother considerate surfers, who remember to ask
people who own the property before crossing it. There's good surf
here, strong, well-shaped waves, with breaks running in both
directions.

Florida Tries Harder

California is the mainland's No. 1 surfing state and likely to remain
so, but the increase of surfers on Florida beaches in the past few years
is truly phenomenal. The warmer air and much warmer water play a
large part in the orange-juice state's increasing popularity. Plus some
truly fine surf spots on both east and west coasts of the peninsula. In
northern Florida, on the Atlantic coast just north of Jacksonville, is
the fine Fernandina Beach, with a long, shallow shelf making for well-
formed, well-behaved waves offering long rides. Neptune Beach and
Jacksonville Beach offer first-class breaks. Just north of Daytona
Beach are Flagler Beach and a fine surfspot near Ormond-By-The-Sea.
Daytona itself offers some interesting surfland; New Smyrna Beach
farther south is fast becoming a favorite of surfers of all levels of

experience.

Coca Beach, The Ramp, Patrick Pier, Shark Pit—all in the Cape Kennedy area—have blossomed as surfing resorts, and the Fort Pierce Jetty, at Fort Pierce, has a great many devotees.

Other good surfing areas down the Atlantic coast of Florida include Riviera Beach near West Palm Beach, Del Ray Beach and Boca Raton. There are many more beaches, some privately owned, where the surf is definitely up on occasions,but they are too numerous to mention. Miami and Miami Beach have surf, if you can get at it through the thick crowds.

On the Gulf of Mexico side of Florida are many surfing areas; some great, some average, some barely worth visiting. Between Pensacola and Panama City there are any number of beaches where surfers may be seen trying their luck, and doubtless many more beaches will see surfboards in the next year or two along the East Coast.

Lone Star Surf

One of the many things Texas has going for it is that its eastern coast fronts on several hundred miles of the Gulf of Mexico, providing many good surfspots. Warm air, warm water. Spring and winter months are best at most of the Texas Gulf surfing areas. Galveston Island provides good surf along its many breakwaters and jetties.

A fine, popular surfing area is at the southern tip of Matagorda, a peninsula offering strong winter swells and very ridable surf much of the year. Going south toward Corpus Christi is Port Aransas Beach at Aransas Pass. All along Padre Island south of Brownsville, surf may be found at certain times.

Go North, Young Surfer

In their search for surf, board-riders have scoured the East Coast and in North and South Carolina have found Kill Devil Hills, Nags Head, Kitty Hawk Pier, Waves, Hatteras, Atlantic Beach, Surf City, Carolina Beach, Myrtle Beach, Pawleys Island, Folly Beach, Hunting Island, and many more. Still more good surfing areas probably remain to be discovered all along the sunny coast of the Carolinas.

On the Virginia Coast is the eastern Mecca for surfers—Virginia Beach, at the southern end of the state where the East Coast Surfing Championships are held. Along the Delaware and Maryland coasts surfers are finding good breaks at Indian River, Ocean City, Rehoboth Beach, Dewey Beach, Slaughter Beach, Ocean City, and other spots.

New Jersey beaches attract a surprising number of surfers. Jetties, piers and breakwaters create some excellent surf at times on such beaches as Asbury Park, Belmar, Point Pleasant, Seaside Heights, Seaside Park, Barnegat Inlet, Beach Haven, and several others in the Atlantic City area. Some good surf is to be found on many Long Island,

New York, beaches.

Farther north in New England, Horseneck Beach in Massachusetts, close to the Rhode Island border, is very popular because of its well-defined breaks and quite large waves. Cape Cod offers many excellent surfing areas, but the combination of cool air and quite cold water keeps many surfers away.

In New Hampshire, surfers like Rye Beach and Hampton Beach best because of their good beach breaks and because there aren't that many beaches in New Hampshire in any case.

Maine has surf, all right, but what a price you have to pay in goose pimples and blue noses! Among the good spots are Ogunquit, York Beach, Wells Beach, Drake Island, and Old Orchard Beach.

Tiny Rhode Island has some fine surfspots, notably around the Newport and Middletown areas which have well-formed swells. Tuckerman's Reef makes big, rolling swells. A number of new surfing areas have recently been opened, and it is anticipated that more good surfing beaches that are almost deserted much of the time will soon permit surfers to use waves that few others seem to utilize.

Surfboard Builders

The following is a partial list of well-established surfboard builders:
1. Channel Islands Surfboards, 16 Helena St., Santa Barbara, CA 93103.
2. Dyno Surfboards, 109½ Main St., Huntington Beach, CA 92648.
3. Gordon & Smith Surfboards, 5465 Gaines St., San Diego, CA 92110.
4. Hobie Surfboards, P.O. Box 216, Dana Point, CA 92629.
5. Jacobs, 422 Pacific Coast Hwy., Hermosa Beach, CA 90254.
6. Lightning Bolt, P.O. Box EH, Dana Point, CA 92629.
7. Tom Morey & Co. Inc., 184 Chestnut Ave., Carlsbad, CA 92008.
8. Sunshire House, 3501 S. Atlantic Ave., Cocoa Beach, FL 32931.
9. Sunset Surfboards, 940 First St., Encinitas, CA 92024.
10. Surf Line Hawaii, 508 Piikoi St., Honolulu, HI.

Your Surfing Library

Here are some books you may want to borrow from your friends, or from your school, college or public library, or purchase:
The Art of Bodysurfing, by Robert Gardner.
Surfing—A Handbook, by William Desmond Nelson.
Waves and Beaches, by Willard Bascom.
All three of the above books are published by Surfer Publications, Inc., Dana Point, CA.
The Complete Book of Surfing, by Peter L. Dixon.
The Complete Book of Water Sports, by Arthur Liebers.
Where the Surfers Are, by Peter L. Dixon.

All three above books are published by Coward-McCann & Geoghan, Inc., New York City, NY.

The Young Sportsman's Guide to Surfing, by Ross Olney, published by Thomas Newlson & Sons, New York City, NY.

The Surfboard Builder's Manual, by Steve Shaw, published by Products Unlimited, La Mesa, CA.

Inside and Out, a handbook on mental and physical conditioning for surfing, by R. E. Abreu, published by Mr. Abreu in Huntington Beach, CA.

SURFER Magazine is published by Surfer Publications, Inc., P.O. Box 1028, Dana Point, CA 92629 and is usually available on newsstands in surfing areas. The company also publishes books, produces and sells surfing films, and offers a wide range of surfing posters and murals.

Windsurfing—New Watersport

Californian Hoyle Schwitzer has done for the new sport of windsurfing what Duke Kahanamoku did for surfing. Actually, development of Windsurfing gear was the mutual brainchild of Hoyle (now president of Windsurfer International, the world's largest producer of the units), and two friends—Fred Payne and Jim Drake.

Although this growing sport is called windsurfing (named for Sweitzer's craft), it is sailing in its purest form. It is also a bit like waterskiing and something like surfing (the main similarity is in the board which is the "hull" of your sailing rig). It is, in fact, direct involvement with the wind.

The Windsurfer unit consists of only what is essential for gathering power and directing it efficiently. There's a board and one very simple sail assembly . . . mast, sail, and twin control booms all neatly linked into one pivoting unit, eliminating everything which would separate you from feeling the wind directly.

When you windsurf you rotate this assembly in all directions, positioning the sail exactly where the wind's drive is greatest. At the same time you move your weight forward or backward and from side to side . . . trimming the hull, banking or flattening its plane across the ever-changing shapes of the sea. Because the Windsurfer's mast and hull work independently of each other, you move welded to the wind's power giving and taking . . . "feeling" your way along with each subtle change in pressure . . .

As a result, your speed is great and your actions become instinctively correct from the beginning. Because your learning is based on intimately real experiences, you learn fast and a true mastery of sailing has become possible.

Before taking your first lesson your Windsurfer, it is necessary to understand the equipment. This is not a surfboard with a sail stuck in the middle. It is a boat and you sail it as you would a boat. But it is much easier and much more fun. With a Windsurfer, your personal involvement with the wind is considerably greater than with any other type of sailing craft.

The board, or hull, is made of polyurethane form core covered with polyethylene. Beneath the board at the rear is a fin or skeg to give it its surfing name. Slightly to the rear of the board's center is a second, larger fin known as the daggerboard. The tapered mast is made of lightweight epoxy fiberglass weighing only four and one-half pounds. It is held in place by a universal joint. When rigged, on either side of the mast and sail is a boom by means of which you hand-control your craft, adding body "English" for steering (there is no rudder). These booms are made of teak, hand-laminated in Bangkok. Sail is dacron. The foam-filled, cross-link hull is so light that it seems to accelerate instantly with the slightest increase in wind. The entire craft folds together neatly and weighing only about sixty pounds can be carried in a stationwagon or van, on top of a car (even a VW), towed on a one-wheeled trailer behind a bicycle, or carried on a brawny young shoulder. The manufacturer claims the Windsurfer can be rigged for the water in thirty seconds. It took me just over one minute, but then, I am all thumbs. After considerable practice, half a minute would probably not seem out of line.

In addition to the manufacturing facility in California, Windsurfer craft are now being made in Holland and Japan. Clubs (called fleets) are rapidly growing in number both in the USA and abroad, and there is an international controlling body known as the Windsurfing Association, 317 Beirut Ave., Pacific Palisades, CA. Competitions for these fast-moving craft are held on both east and west coasts and on lakes across the country. A World Championship is held annually—in 1974 it took place on Lake Ontario in Canada. Incidentally, Windsurfers have been clocked in excess of twenty knots.

Step Aboard and Race the Wind!

If there is one basic rule to remember if you want to become a proficient Windsurfer it is this: *always keep your back to the wind.* As you get into the sport, you will soon understand why.

Putting your rig together is so simple that even an adult can do it. Before putting the craft in the water, insert the mast tip into the small mast end and the universal mounting in the large mast end. Then slip the mast into the sock of the sail and secure the sail to the universal mast base with the downhaul line through a sail grommet. Next step is to slip the twin booms over the mast so that they "embrace" the sail—the booms are secured with a clove-hitch in a 3/16" line that comes with the kit; the clove hitch stops the booms from sliding down the mast. If you are using your Windsurfer fairly regularly, it is wise to keep the mast, sail and booms assembled as outlined above.

Take the board and sail assembly into water that's about waist deep. Ask a friend or stranger to hold the nose (prow) end of the board while you pull on the uphaul line to get the sail up the mast. Climb aboard and stand with one foot on either side of the mast, with one hand on

Keep your back to the wind and the boom end clear of the water.
(Photo courtesy Windsurfing International, Inc.)

each boom and with your back to the wind, facing the prow of your little boat. Pull on the right boom to make the nose of the board turn counter-clockwise and on the left boom to move clockwise. Once you have the feel of the board, turn in a 360° circle, by pulling with either the right or left boom hand. As the board begins to move, slowly and with tiny steps, walk around the mast *keeping your back to the wind!* This is an important maneuver to do well for this is how you aim the Windsurfer in the desired direction. Remember too, that the mast should be kept upright with the boom ends out of the water. To sail offwind, use the right hand on the boom, slightly behind the mast and tilt the mast forward along the centerline of your board. With the left hand, slowly sheet the sail in. Tilt the mast approximately 15° off center and do not sheet the sail in too much at this point for too much wind in the sail can pull it right out of your hand. If you feel you are going to spill, let go with your left hand and hold onto the mast with your right. Your sail will start flopping around ("luffing") and you can try again.

To sail upwind, the mast is tilted forward again but with the sail sheeted in more. Control the mast by means of the boom in your right hand and sheet in with the left hand for a starboard tack, the reverse for a port tack, explained later.

Once you are underway, rake the mast to a more upright position to head into the wind and rake it farther forward to head off the wind. You turn your little craft by tacking and jibing. First let us consider the tack. This is accomplished by raking the mast aft past the upright position which will cause the board to head upwind. Once you are aimed into the wind, let the sail luff and walk carefully around to the front of the mast, keeping your back to the wind. Now pull on the boom (left or right as the case may be) to start the opposite tack.

The bugaboo of many beginning sailors with regular sailboats is the jibe. With a Windsurfer this often tricky maneuver becomes fairly simple. Being in a universal joint, the entire sail-mast-boom assembly can be let go forward and then retrimmed on a new jibe. As you rake the assembly forward to head far offwind, let the sail luff. Keeping your back to the wind, walk around the back of the board and tack in the opposite direction as explained above.

This is about all the basic instruction that can be given on paper. The rest is you, your board, sail, the water and the wind. Here are some of the specifications: length—twelve feet, beam—twenty-six inches, draft—two inches, (that's right, two inches) draft-board down—twenty-four inches, weight of hull—forty pounds, sail—fifty-six square inches, mast—fourteen feet, wishbone booms—nine feet each.

At present, the only manufacturer of this craft is Windsurfing International Inc. (President is Hoyle Schweitzer, designer of the craft and patron of the sport), 1038 Princeton Dr., Marina Del Ray, CA 90291.

Harnessing The Wind

This chapter will concentrate on giving you some understanding of the

A good beginner's sail boat is the "Sea Devil" sloop, which sells for around $320 including sails. (Photo courtesy Lockley Manufacturing Co.)

basics so that you can sail a small sailboat. We presume your Boy Scout days taught you how to tie a bowline knot, a reef knot, etc., and we are not going to get into navigating by the stars, sailing the four-masted square rigger, etc. Instead, we are going to get right on with discussing:

How To Sail

The kind of boat you will want to learn to sail first is called a "sloop," a craft with a single mast which supports a large triangular-shaped sail and smaller sail about the same shape, which is called the "jib." Along the bottom of the large sail, known as the mainsail, and attached to the mast by means of a universal joint-type fitting, is the boom. The boom swivels in its fitting which is called a "gooseneck". This movement of the boom (and consequently, the mainsail), coupled with the rudder, gives your sailboat the ability to travel in various directions and to change direction. The edge of the mainsail that is toward the front (facing "forward") is—for some unknown reason—called the "luff." Why it isn't simply called the front edge I can't imagine. But over the years a whole language has been developed by men who go down to the sea in ships, and most of it is completely incomprehensible to the uninitiated. In fact, some sailing schools and instruction books insist on teaching you the nautical language before they start to teach you how to sail—which is what you really want to learn.

In self-defense, if for no other reason, you will learn to call the front edge of a sail the "luff," the rear edge the "leech," the bottom edge the "foot," the lower front corner of your triangular mainsail the "tack"; similarly, the "mainsail line" becomes the main halyard," and a length of rope or line a "sheet."

Sooner or later you will pick up several hundred of these strange, non-descriptive names and terms that sailboat owners wear like an old fraternity pin. If you really want to understand nautical language, get a copy of Joanna Carver Colcord's book *Sea Language Comes Ashore* (Cornell Maritime Press). But just now, let's concentrate on learning to sail instead of learning to talk about it in the yacht club.

What makes a sailboat sail? The wind, obviously. Early sailors were pretty much content to sail before the wind to wherever they were going and then wait for the wind to change direction so that they could sail back. They used quite large steering rudders and eventually learned to use lines to swivel their big square sails at ninety-degrees and later forty-five degree angles to the direction of the wind, which, combined with use of the rudder, enabled them to change course instead of merely sailing straight downwind all the time.

Today, with our knowledge or aerodynamics and better understanding of the forces which come to bear upon a sailboat in the water, we are able to sail into the wind as well as with it and at angles to it.

Off On A New Tack

When sailors talk about "tacking" or "coming about," they mean they wish to change the direction in which a boat is heading. To do this, you change the sail's exposure to the wind from one side of the boat to the other. First, you must have enough speed to enable you to complete this nautical maneuver since for a short moment your sailboat will be heading directly into the wind and if you haven't got enough speed up your sail will "luff" or flap about in the wind and the boat will, in all probability, "wallow" or come to a stop or near stop.

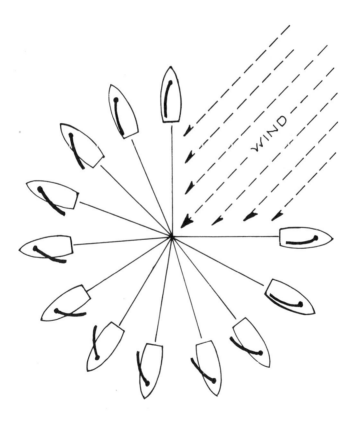

Illustration shows position of mainsail and boom when sailing at various angles to the wind.

Here's how you tack or change direction. First swing the tiller over so that your boat heads directly into the wind; then release the

the jibsheet to free the sail. As you are now heading into the wind and losing speed, the sail will flap about and begin moving to the other side of the boat. The boom will sweep across the deck, carrying the sail to the other side. Watch your head and be sure it doesn't brush you off the boat. You will find that your boat is heading in a new direction when the sail is on the opposite side of the boat.

Changing direction when heading downwind is called "jibing". You start this maneuver with your boat heading away from the wind rather than toward it. As move your tiller, the wind catches the other side of the sail and the boom swings rapidly across the boat's cockpit to the other side. Instead of losing speed as you do when you turn into the wind, your boat is more likely to gain speed when jibing. Remember that your boom and mainsail are extended out from the boat at a much greater angle when sailing downwind than when sailing into the wind. Consequently, as soon as you start the jibe, the mainsail immediately fills with wind and swings the boom across the cockpit much faster than in an upwind tack. Watch your head—many a skull has been cracked and many an inexperienced sailboat owner has been knocked overboard by a fast-moving boom.

Sailing Against the Wind

The keel under the boat helps keep the boat straight, upright, and resist the wind's attempts to push the boat sideways. Meanwhile, the wind's pressure against the *front* of the sail creates a vacuum pressure at the *back* of the sail which "sucks" the boat along through the water. Here's where the smaller triangular sail becomes useful. Located in front of the mainsail, the jib helps direct the approaching wind onto the luff (front edge) of the mainsail creating greater vacuum behind it, helping propel the boat forward. The tricky part is learning how to "trim" the two sails in harmony with each other in order to present the most effective surfaces to the wind.

If the sails are trimmed too tightly they will not present enough area for the wind to act upon and consequently not enough vacuum effect. If you let the sails out too much they will be too loose and flutter—or "luff"—along their front edges. The boat will slow down and eventually stall.

Obtaining the right amount of balance or trim is easy once you know how. Experienced sailors do it almost by instinct but you haven't developed that yet, so do it this way. Let both sails out until they begin to "luff" along their leading edges, then tighten them just enough to eliminate the luffing effect. Because the wind does not blow at a constant, even pressure and because characteristics of the water surface change and you want to change direction, you must stay alert and continually re-trim your sails to obtain the most effective use of wind and vacuum pressure.

Sailing With The Wind

We've tackled the hardest part first—sailing into the wind. Now let's look at an easier side of sailing . . . with the wind directly behind you (provided it isn't too strong). Generally, you need to let out the mainsail as much as possible in order to obtain the most push from the wind and help overcome the resistance to the water offered by the hull of your boat. In other words, when sailing directly with the wind your mainsail is about at right angles to the direction the wind is coming from.

So much for theory. Now you need practice in order to cultivate that "feel" of the wind, the water and your craft, that are so essential if you really want to enjoy sailing without getting into difficulties. The ideal way to develop this "feel" is to get into a calm bay or lake with a *breeze* blowing off shore. Not a strong wind, but a nice, steady breeze. Slacken and tighten the mainsheet (the line controlling the mainsail) and observe the results.

When you are sailing with the wind, with sail fully extended for maximum wind "push" (generally called "running") and wish to turn right (nautically known as a starboard tack), the tiller—which is attached to the rudder and controls the steering—has to be moved over to the left. This brings the rudder—and the prow of your boat—over to the right. To steer left (or tack to port) the procedure is the opposite—you move the tiller over to the right. As you make your turn, you will reach a point where the wind is blowing on both sides of the sail at the same time which inhibits the wind from reaching the rear edge of your mainsail (the "leach"). At this point your sail may luff and your boat will reach stall speed. Careful steering is needed. If you steer too tightly into the direction the wind is blowing—in other words within a theoretical forty-five-degree angle—luffing will probably occur and your boat will stall out. What we have to do is make our turn in such a manner that our sail does not quite luff which means careful steering. The helmsman (the person handling the tiller) has to watch the top front edge of the mainsail for the first signs of luff and make the necessary correction.

On the other hand, if you steer too far off the wind—away from the wind's direction—your boat will probably become sluggish although there is no luff because the sail is too tightly "sheeted" in.

Sailing at Right Angles to the Wind

The easiest sailing direction of all is at right angles to the wind. Boat enthusiasts call this "reaching" although what you're reaching for is never quite clear. I call this sailing at right angles to the wind—a term which I find is fully descriptive and understood by all—even though somewhat condescendingly by some of my experienced boating friends. Let's say you are heading into the wind which is approaching from the north and you want to sail at right angles to it—in an easterly direction. You let your mainsail about halfway out to your right (starboard) the appraoching wind will strike the left (port) side of your hull and your sail which you have let out over the right side of your boat. However, because of the shape of the sail as the wind fills it and because of your application of rudder, your boat will keep moving forward and will not sideslip. another reason is again this vacuum effect which tends to keep your boat straight. The same forces enable you to sail easily in a westerly directlon when the wind approaches from the north.

We have now covered the basic how-to of sailing at angles to the wind, with the wind and into the wind. Now we should look at this in a little more depth without getting too deeply mired down by strange terms and needless amounts of theory—get these later in an advanced course, or absorb them by osmosis as you do more sailing and hang around the marina.

Sail Positions

Let's review the position of your tall, triangular mainsail under various wind conditions. Our illustration shows four situations:
(1) Sailing at an approximate forty-five-degree angle to the direction of the approaching wind is called "beating."
(2) Sailing at ninety-degree angles to the approaching wind is called "reaching."
(3) Sailing directly away from the wind is called "running."
(4) "Luffing" is when the boat is headed directly into the wind and the sail is "fluttering". Luffing can also be the result of letting the mainsail full out while "beating" or "reaching".

When sailing, your crew (even if it is only yourself) should sit on the high or windward side of the boat. The reasons are because the boom is on the lower side and also because your weight is needed on the higher side to balance the boat.

You may have to position your weight foward or aft to fit your particular boat, but be ready to make some fast adjustments. With the mainsail under control, you can adjust the jib (the small sail). You pull the jibsheet (line controlling the jib) to the same side of the boat that the boom is riding on and trim the sail so that the billowing jib is at approximately the same angle as the mainsail. If you draw the jib too tightly it will tend to stop an even flow of air between the jib and the mainsail and will consequently "backwind" the mainsail (cause wind to press on the back of the sail). This will make your boat very sluggish. So you have to achieve the right degree of jib trim, and it doesn't take much experimenting to learn this.

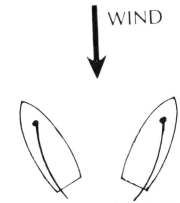

WIND

BEATING - Sail in over the corner of the boat.

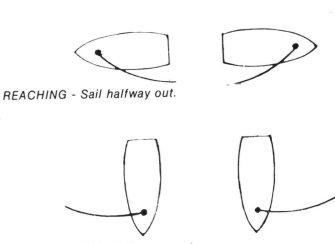

REACHING - Sail halfway out.

RUNNING - Said all the way out.

LUFFING - Boat pointed into the wind. You can also luff while beating or reaching by letting the main sail out.

Tiller and Rudder

The sails, of course, are only part of your craft—the biggest part, from the point of view of motive power, but there's still the hull of the boat, your tiller and the rudder. Learn to use the tiller by sailing a little way out into the bay or lake away from the heavy boat traffic. Leaving the mainsail where it is, push the tiller away from you all the way, and then all the way towards you. Notice how the boat reacts. If your boat lists dangerously (tips over to one side too much) push the tiller away from you to steer into the wind and/or release the mainsheet somewhat. These actions will spill some of the wind out of your sail and bring the mast up straight again.

Righting A Capsized Boat

Since you don't know much about boats, water and wind, chances are you are going to capsize before you have been sailing very long. It happens to almost everyone. In your early sailing efforts, it is advisable not to carry an expensive camera aboard or wear good clothes, etc. Of course, you and your companions, if any, should wear lifejackets. Righting a small sailboat is not difficult. First of all, stay near your boat—don't let current or wind or wake from other boats move your boat away from you or you away from it. Swing the bow around until it is facing into the wind. Make sure the mainsheet is loose. Now put your feet against the keel (also called the "center-board"), grasp the top side (gunwale) of the boat and lean back, pushing with your feet and pulling on the gunwale). It is not hard to right a boat this way and if there's more than one of you, it's easy.

Putting On The Brakes

We have discussed sailing with the wind, against the wind and at angles to the wind. There's one more point we should cover before turning you loose out there with you own sailboat—how do you stop

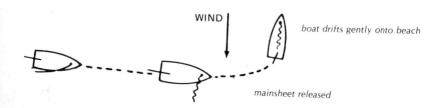

WIND

boat drifts gently onto beach

mainsheet released

Beaching your sailboat.

this thing? Here's how: simply let go of the mainsheet (that line which controls your mainsail) and your boat will coast to a stop. It will not stop on a dime, but it will stop in quite a short distance once the sail begins to luff.

Let's say we've been out sailing happily across the lake or bay and now it's time to come in. Imagine there's an off-shore wind blowing. That's good. Aproach your dock from either the right or left. It is easier for a beginner to approach from the left if you're docking on the left side of the deck, and its easier to approach from the right to dock on the right side. If you are docking at the end of the dock it doesn't much matter which side you approach from.

The following illustrations demonstrate docking procedures and show how letting the mainsail "luff" causes the boat to coast to a stop. Beaching your boat is similar to docking—you come in parallel to the beach, then let out your mainsail so that your boat slowly drifts ashore.

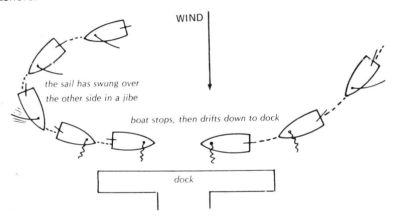

Approaching dock from either side with an off-shore wind.

Not all small sail boats are sloop-rigged—have both mainsail and jib. Some have just one triangular sail, called a lateen rig. Main difference is that this boat is usually a little cheaper than the sloop. It doesn't offer quite the performance of the sloop but still offers endless hours of sailing fun. Also, since you have only the one sail to worry about, the lateener is easier to rig and handle.

Two Hulls, One Mainsail

A catamaran may be just what you need. You can get them in various configurations but if you're a fairly recent arrival at the local marina, try a sloop-rigged catamaran. This boat has twin hulls with a trampo-

Lateen-rigged "Salty Kat" weighs 140 lbs. complete. A good sail boat for the beginner. (Photo courtesy Hollowform, Inc.).

Sloop Rig

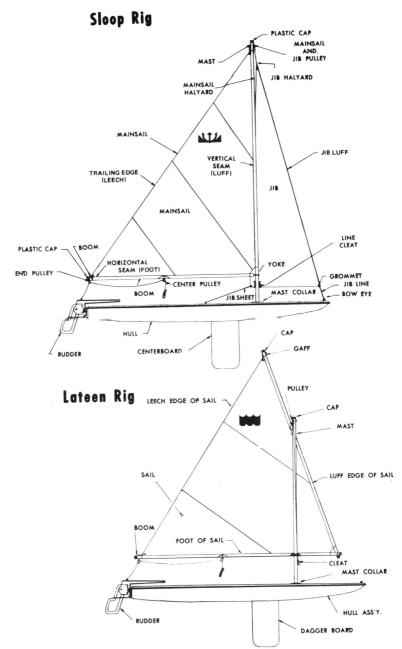

Lateen Rig

Illustrations show sloop and lateen rigs, with proper nautical terms.

The catamaran provides thrills and excitement galore as it reaches 35 m.p.h. in a 11 m.p.h. wind. (Photo courtesy Great Lakes Manufacturing.)

line-type platform of some kind between them—usually canvas on a lightweight aluminum frame. It has only one mainsail and a jib, and it provides you with all the sailing thrills you want—fast response, high speed, stability, maneuverability, easy-handling—the cat has them all.

The twin rudders are siamese-connected by twin tillers connected by a single control bar.

One especially easy to sail and inexpensive (for a catamaran) unit of this type that performs particularly well in a test is the "Sizzler," manufactured and marketed by Great Lakes Sports Manufacturing Inc., 5135 Richmond Rd., Cleveland, OH 44146. Admittedly this is only one of dozens of companies making cats, but the sturdy construction, workmanship and finish are noteworthy. There are four models in the Sizzler line, ranging in price from $1,795 to $2,495 with sails, trampolines, etc. The hydrodynamic and aerodynamic design make Sizzlers among the sleekest-looking cats available. The Sizzler Seafire 18 handles and responds very well even in water so rough that conventional single-hull sailboats stayed in their docks.

Sailing techniques are similar to those of any single-hulled sloop-rigged sailboat—the differences are mainly in the handling and speed attained. To get maximum speed out of your cat on "light" air, you should sit well forward, keeping the transom well clear of the water. This should add at least ten percent to your speed. In heavy air a trapeze is essential. These boats will do easily twenty-five m.p.h. in a fifteen m.p.h. wind and can tow a skier with ease.

The best way to come about in a catamaran is to ease the boat up into the wind, leaving the jib sheet sheeted down as of the last tack until the forestay goes through the eye of the wind and the wind then hits the back side of the jib. This brings the catamaran around rapidly. Then release the jib and sheet down to the other side for the next tack.

Sailing Safety

The best way to learn true sailing safety is to attend a US Power Squadron course in boating safety, which usually is free. Many of the publications covering sailing contain lists of precautions. The most important of all is to wear a life jacket at all times when sailing. If you are a super-strong swimmer, you can probably feel safe with a lifesaver or two (one for each person on board). With a lifejacket, you *know* you're safe.

Always check the weather forecasts before venturing out of sight of land—even on an inland lake, storms can come up very suddenly and inexperienced sailors can easily get into trouble.

Stay with your boat no matter what happens. It floats just about indefinitely—you don't. Sooner or later someone will spot your predicament and help will be at hand.

Never take on winds or water too high, too strong, too turbulent for your craft or for your experience. Watch other boats of the size of yours to see if they are going out or coming in when the weather looks uncertain. If in doubt call your nearest US Coast Guard station, or check with your local yacht or boating club. And you can always ask other, more experienced sailors for their advice . . . nothing wrong with that.

On a hot afternoon, there's just nothing like a nice, cold beer. But take it easy on the beer if you're planning to sail or if you are already asail. You may feel fine casting off but after a while the hot sun and the brew in your belly may suddenly hit you. Then your reactions are slower and you may fumble and use bad judgment at a critical time. Also, like the drunken driver on the highway, you become a menace to others.

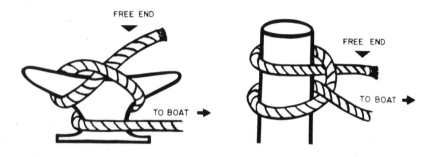

In boating, line is most commonly used for tying-up to a dock. To do the job like a real "salt," Mercury outboard boating authorities suggest that you learn these two simple hitches. Use the knot in the left illustration to tie-up to a cleat. Pass the line around the cleat under both horns, then diagonally across the top of the cleat and under the first horn. Tuck the loose end under the line where it passes across the top. The more pull by the boat, the greater the holding power of the hitch—yet it can be loosened easily by tugging at the free end. Use the other knot, the clove hitch, when tying-up to posts or piles. This hitch consists of two loops with the free end tucked under. Don't use this knot for permanent fastening, since it may eventually slip.

Sailing On Frozen Water

If the art and fun of sailing really grabs you, there's no need to give it up for the winter if you live in an area where the lakes and rivers freeze. Take up ice sailing! A whole new world of speed, adventure and enjoyment await you out there on the ice.

Winter's ice does not stop the real sailing enthusiast. (Photo courtesy Lockley Manufacturing Co.)

There are quite a few ice yachts on the market and they tend to be rather expensive as a rule—$1,000 and more. However, there is a "Volkswagen" among ice sailing craft, called the "Skimmer 45". It is made by the Lockley Recreational Products Division of Lockley Manufacturing Co. Inc., 310 Grove St., New Castle, PA 16103. Lockley's Skimmer 45 sells for $325 (unassembled)—a very realistic price. However, like the VW, this is a well-built, easy-to-operate, high-performance unit. The frame of this ice boat (and some others) is of tubular construction which provides lightweight, high-tensile strength. It measures 106 inches by 72 inches and the body is only 20 inches tall. It weights less than fifty-five pounds (less sail), and its runners are 18½ inches long and one-quarter inch thick. The mast of this "lateener-rigged" iceboat is 14'10" long and the boom measures 7 feet. Forty-five square feet of 3.8-oz. dacron forms the mainsail which can move you across smooth ice at terrific speed.

Before taking your assembled ice boat onto the frozen lake or river, make absolutely sure that the ice is safe. Then "step" your mast, making sure the shrouds are not tangled. Always have the front of your craft heading into the wind with the parking brake under the rudder and the sail free to flutter in the wind. If you don't take these precautions there's every chance your craft will take off before the wind without you. When you are ready to sail her, swing the parking brake up and lift the front of the boat and turn it at right angles to the wind. Get aboard and slouch down so that the boom will clear your head. Pull in the sheet (the line that controls the sail) until the sail fills and the boat starts moving.

Don't try getting up much speed until you have practiced turning and stopping. Control your boat by leaving the sail fairly loose. Stopping is accomplished by turning into the wind and coasting to a stop. Make sure you leave enough space to turn and coast to a stop.

Duck your head when turning because the boom sometimes swings around very fast. After some practice with it and when you have developed a certain "feel" for it, try increasing your speed by pulling in the sail a little tighter. If the boat gathers too much speed or begins to feel unstable as though it may tip, release the sail a bit and you'll slow down.

With a good wind and more experience, try "hiking." That means tilting up on two runners. You can travel great distances this way if you can hold her steady.

Ice Yacht Racing

The International Skimmer 45 Ice Yacht Racing Association is a non-profit, informal organization devoted to promoting competition in ice yacht racing of the Skimmer 445 class boat. The ISIYRA holds a National Championship regatta on the second weekend of February each year. Handsome trophies are presented to the winners. Membership in the association is restricted to owners of this class ice boat and costs $2 per year. For information contact Hank Evans, 330 Mitchell Rd., New Castle, PA 16105.

Safety Precautions

This is a high-speed craft, and you have no protective shield so wear a safety helmet and face shield to protect yourself from spills, from driving snow, flying ice chips, and the cold wind. A ski or snowmobile suit will usually give you all the protection you need against the weather, and lined snowmobile boots are pretty much essential as are good gauntlet-type snowmobile gloves.

Take time to learn how to handle this zippy little craft before you over-extend yourself and start taking spills.

I've tried it, and it beats snowmobiling hands down as an ice sport, although, of course, you are restricted to open frozen surfaces—you cannot sail an iceboat on a road or snowmobile trail. But for the low investment this is my idea of winter fun.

Information and Help

The beginning sailor or boatman would do well to join a club. Such clubs are a great source of boating information and much can be learned by mixing with more experienced sailors. Free literature is often available to club members, and sometimes discounts on boats, accessories and other products. The social side of being a member of a sailing club, yacht club, etc., should not be overlooked by gregarious sailboat enthusiasts.

Yachting magazine usually runs into about 250 pages and is jam-packed with informative articles and boat talk. The magazine covers both power and sail boating. The advertisements form an excellent buyer's guide to craft and accessories. It is available on newsstands everywhere. Published by Yachting Publishing Corporation, 50 W. 44th St., New York, NY 10036.

Sailing for Beginners by Moulton H. Farnham, published by The Macmillan Company, New York.

Royce's Sailing Illustrated, by Patrick M. Royce, Royce Publications, Box 1967, Newport Beach, CA 92663.

The Boatman's Manual, by Carl D. Lane, published by W. W. Norton & Company, New York.

Folklore and the Sea by Horace Beck, Weslyan University Press, Middletown, CN 06457.

A History of Seafaring by George F. Bass, published by Walker & Company, 720 Fifth Ave., NY 10019.

Sailing by Bill Wallace, Golden Press, New York.

Sea Language Comes Ashore by Joanna Carver Colcord, Cornell Maritime Press, Inc., New York.

Hang In There, Cliff Hangers!

Whether you call it hang gliding, hang soaring, sky sailing, sky surfing, kiting, or one of the fancier technical names, you are talking about one of the newest, most thrilling, least expensive and—believe it or not—safest sports in the world. Hang gliding is perhaps the widest-used term, and it is probably the most descriptive since the flyer is suspended below the "wing." Hang-gliding enthusiasts total close to 50,000 in the USA and Canada alone. Some authorities expect the number to double in the next five years. Over 300 firms were manufacturing various types and styles of hang gliders as this book went to press.

Like most sports, in order to learn it properly at the outset and avoid a lot of headaches later on, it is best to start with professional instruction. And a book by Dan Poynter, entitled *Hang Gliding* is perhaps the best. He is the most knowledgeable person alive in terms of hang-gliding history, equipment, progress and technique. He is also a pilot, a parachutist, a hang-glider enthusiast, and most effective communicator. His book is a definitive work and as essential to everyone truly interested in this sport as is the flying wing itself. The book may be purchased at most hang-glider shops and schools or may be obtained by mail from Daniel F. Poynter, 48 Walker St., North Quincy, MA 02171 ($5.95 plus .40 postage). The first step one should take toward becoming proficient at hang gliding is to read Dan's book, cover to cover. A list of other publications dealing with the sport is included at the end of this chapter.

Who Started It?

Among hang-gliding enthusiasts, there is a favorite saying: "If God intended men to stay on the ground, He'd give us roots!" Ever since primitive man first developed a semblance of intelligent thought, he has looked upon the birds with envy. He learned to run fleet of foot, like a deer (though not quite as fast), he taught himself to swim, like the fish (or as near to it as he could get), and developed in his relatively puny body the strength to cope with many larger animals. But when it came to producing eggs and breaking the chains of gravity, man was nowhere. It wasn't inability to lay an egg that bothered him—it was the other.

It didn't take Homo Sapiens long to figure out that the reason he couldn't fly was because he had no wings. Who knows how many of our ancient forebears brought down eagles with well-aimed rocks or spears, removed their wings and, holding them aloft, stepped hopefully off the nearest cliff? We do not know, for they did not live to pass the story down to us.

We do know that long before Leonardo da Vinci began applying scientific principles to his studies of birds in flight, some of the more determined would-be aviators tried capes and sheets and things flapping in the wind. There are ancient temple drawings which still exist as memorials to those adventurous souls. Da Vinci had the right idea, though, and did a lot work on aerodynamics. However, he never developed a practical means of lifting a man off the ground, keeping him aloft for a time and lowering him back to *terra firma* in one piece.

Man continued to eat his heart out over his inability to fly until almost 100 years ago when a German engineer built a glider, held it aloft, ran with it into the wind and actually left the ground for a time. Before his death in 1896, Otto Lilienthal made 2,000 flights, of which 1,999 were completely successful. The bi-plane type glider Otto designed and flew inspired a long series of designs and experiments and even today hang-glider manufacturers are making and selling bi-plane hang gliders that do not look or operate much differently from those made by Otto.

Most patriotic Englishmen like to remember that long before Lilienthal's first flight, Sir George Cayley, who spent much of his life engrossed in the idea of men being able to escape the surly bonds of earth and soar about their estates on wings, had actually gotten his coachman—a man with tremendous obedience but little sense—to step off a hill clutching an early type of hang glider. Apparently Sir George's man not only got up there, but got back down again safely—several times. This was a quarter century before Deutchland's Lilienthal began gliding silently over the German countryside.

A long succession of quickly forgotten names became associated with hang gliding, and finally the Wright brothers wrote their names across the pages of aviation history and into the hearts of modern-day glider pilots with their work in this field. Long before going in for powered flight, Orville and Wilbur built and flew dozens of gliders of various types.

A name fast becoming even more famous with hang glider enthusiasts is that of Francis M. Rogallo, known affectionately to skysurfers today as Rog. This gentleman was an engineer at the Langley Center in Virginia during the late forties. He and his wife took out a number of patents on kites and wings of various types. For some time the

National Aeronautics and Space Administration considered a Rogallo design for a glide-wing to lower space capsules to the surface of the earth. NASA never did use this idea although many experiments were made.

Rogallo-type designs are probably the most popular hang gliders in use today, although dihedral mono and bi-plane gliders have their share of devotees.

Choosing the Right Sail and Instruction

Choosing the sail that is best for you is very simple—you leave it entirely.up to your hang-glider dealer/instructor. He will specify a sail that is correct for your weight. If you try to use one that is too small, you will have difficulty getting airborne and may not be able to leave the ground at all. If you try to use too large a sail, you will have handling and control problems.

Most Rogallo wing-type hang-glider dealers use this table to calculate how much sail you need:

YOUR WEIGHT	(Center Keel) WING LENGTH	WING SPAN	SAIL AREA	(Empty) WING WEIGHT
100-125 lbs.	16 ft.	20.8 ft.	169.8 sq. ft.	32 lbs.
125-155 lbs.	17 ft.	22.1 ft.	192.4 sq. ft.	35 lbs.
155-200 lbs.	18 ft.	23.4 ft.	216.2 sq. ft.	37 lbs.
200-250 lbs.	20 ft.	25.8 ft.	267.6 sq. ft.	42 lbs.

Although you can, armed with the right hang glider and printed instructions, teach yourself skysurfing, it makes far more sense to take hang-glider lessons from a qualified instructor. Especially since the cost is so low—usually varying from about $35 to $100 for the basic course.

One problem is finding qualified hang gliding schools and instructors. Because it is a new sport (dating no farther back than about 1962) which is growing rapidly, it has attracted the usual opportunists who regard it more as a source of profit than a sport. Since hang gliders retail at between $500 and $1,000, it does not take a very big investment to become a hang-glider dealer. An unethical dealer first spends fifty bucks or less on a quicky course, or hires someone else as a salesman who knows how to fly. Then he rents a small store as cheaply as possible and advertises his products and "flying courses." Since there is no such thing as compulsory certification of hang-gliding instructors, it is difficult to know whether or not a dealer is a good instructor.

The best way out of this dilemma is to contact—and join—the United States Hang Gliding Association, PO Box 66306, Los Angeles, CA 90066. Membership cost $10 a year. The USGA has an office at 11312½ Venice Blvd., Los Angeles, CA 90066; telephone (213)

395-4991. The USGA publishes the monthly "Ground Skimmer" which, in addition to interesting and helpful editorials, contains advertisements for various brands of hang gliders. Another organization from which you may be able to receive information on reputable manufacturers of hang gliders is the Hang Glider Manufacturers Association, 137 Oregon St., El Segundo, CA 90245. You can get a list of manufacturers from the HMGA, send for literature, find out which have certified dealers in your area and inquire about instruction. The HGMA sets minimum construction standards its members must follow. A new organization is Glider Sports International which provides a program of certification and flight rating plus instruction and other benefits. Most dealers offer instruction of one standard or another. A good instructor understands the construction and characteristics of the equipment he sells. A partial list of manufacturers and dealers operating hang-gliding schools is included at the end of this chapter.

If you would rather find out whether or not you're going to like hang gliding before you lay out $500 or more for a sail, many dealers have rental programs—some include the rental in the price of the course.

Am I Going To Break My Neck?

The question in the minds of many people who are initially attracted to this fun sport is: "Am I going to break my fool neck just to have some fun?" The answer is, no. Hang gliding is far safer than playing football, driving a car, riding a motorcycle, scuba diving, and many more sports and occupations. The rate of injuries requiring medical treatment for close to 30,000 participants nationwide, in 1974 was .003 per thousand. Most of these were relatively minor injuries—sprains, an occasional broken bone, etc. Yes, there have been some deaths, too—mostly caused by inexperienced hang-glider pilots attempting to go beyond the limits of their capabilities or equipment, failing to follow instructions, neglecting the essential pre-flight equipment check, etc. One quite well-known hang-glider pilot, thirty-year-old Lloyd Short, who had recently won an important competition, was killed when his fold-up experimental kite collapsed. Folding WAS accomplished by removing two pins at the cross-tube/keel junction. One of these pins worked loose during his flight and the other was found in his pocket.

Even experienced hang glider pilots can sometimes forget to carry out a thorough pre-flight inspection of their equipment. Such accidents cannot be blamed on the sport, nor on the equipment. They are the results of human carelessness.

According to Paul Makis and Dave Snook, who operate the Four Winds Sports Sky Gliding School and sky sail dealership in the Chicago area with branch schools in other midwest communities, their instructors gave over 2,500 lessons in one year with only two injuries—dislocations due to students not following takeoff instructions.

Arnie Norum, president of Fire Craft Corporation in Chicago, has taught enthusiasts from 15 to 60 to fly—about a third of whom were women. Arnie says the best first flight he ever witnessed was by a young woman. His school's "drop-out" rate is around 20 - 25 percent.

A typical hang glider flight school offers a 12 to 15-hour course for around $45. The course includes 2½ hours of ground school where students watch films, are instructed on the equipment, learn assembly and pre-flight inspection, receive instructional materials, etc.

Many of the midwest's growing number of hang gliding schools take their students to Warren Dunes, Michigan, on the east shore of the big lake. Conditions here are ideal for hang gliding beginners and students, with near perfect winds coming off the lake and blowing up the ridge providing the right amount of ridge lift.

Warren Dunes is headquarters for the Midwest School of Hang Gliding, under the directorship of recognized authority Wayne Christenson. Interviewed on a television talk show, Wayne summarized his thoughts on hang gliding:

"Provided a person enjoys average physical fitness, hang gliding is a sport for people of both sexes and almost all ages. Why go through life on a two-dimensional plane when a third dimension is available to everyone?"

Wayne believes hang gliding is the fastest-growing participant sport in the midwest and lists his favorite midwest hang gliding locations as Warren Dunes and Frankfurt in Michigan, Nelson in Wisconsin, the Mississippi Palisades near Galena, Illinois and Winona, Minnesota. He and other hang gliding shcool directors are working to get more suitable sites opened for public participation in the sport.

California, New Mexico, Colorado and other western states offer large numbers of suitable hang gliding sites where winds are favorable and the terrain ideal, and on the east coast, sand dunes, cliffs and prevailing winds are attracting great numbers of hang gliding enthusiasts.

On gentle rolling sand dunes a hang gliding student gets his or her first taste of the real thing outside the classroom. After mastering the technique of holding the glider at exactly the right angle, the student runs into the wind to get the feel of the wind in the sail. Next short "bounces" are made on the soft sand. By the end of his course, the average student is enjoying descending flights of half a minute or more.

One hang glider pilot at Warren Dunes flew for two hours and nineteen minutes in November of 1974 after a takeoff from a 150-ft. high sand dune! Another stayed aloft three and a half hours after a takeoff from a 400-foot hill at Sleeping Bear Dunes, Frankfurt, Michigan. These flights are noteworthy not so much in terms of time aloft but because of their low-altitude takeoffs. At this point it may be appropriate to look at how a hang glider flies. First, there are two basic types—the Rogallo which is a delta-shaped wing and the fixed wing which is shaped like an airplane wing. The fixed wing (airplane-like) gliders may be of the monoplane (single wing) type or may be bi-plane type (two wings). Some of the fixed wing hang gliders actually have tail sections with rudders and elevators—a few have wing ailerons. The more popular Rogallo wing is a flexible wing and operates in a manner similar to the sail of a boat. Air trapped underneath keeps it up as it gradually descends due to force of gravity. You take off into the wind from a point higher than the ground ahead of you. The approaching wind fills the sail and as you are gradually being lowered to the ground the wind rushing past you through the sail gives you forward motion, just as on a sailboat. However, with a Rogallo wing you can fly in a no-wind situation—your descent is about one foot for every four feet of forward motion. The stronger the wind the less your glide ratio (rate of descent compared to forward movement) because your rate of descent is slowed by the speed of the approaching wind.

Higher and Higher

As you become more proficient and learn more about winds, air currents, aerodynamics, glider control, you can actually soar, using air currents, thermal boost, ridge lift, updrafts, etc. This way you can climb to higher altitudes. Mark Clarkson, of Mesa, Arizona, took off from 120 feet above sea level and rose to a maximum of 2,800 feet.

Rudy Kishazy, of Pontiac, Michigan in October 1973, flew a hang glider at an altitude over 13,000 feet, at Mount Blanc, France. He flew a distance of over eleven miles and was aloft for thirty-five minutes. Californian Bob Wills stayed aloft more than eight hours by gliding off the great crater of Haleakala, Hawaii. Another Californian, Bill Bennett, launched his Rogallo wing from Dantes View in Death Valley and landed lightly eleven minutes later, having flown over six miles and descended over 5,700 feet. Some of these accomplishments have been improved upon and the duration record is now well over 14 hours for a single flight.

Prepare for Take-Off

Because of differences in construction of various Rogallo wing-type gliders, assembly instructions vary. The following step-by-step directions are typical of the assembly of many Rogallo-design wings.

1. Lay sail on ground with nose pointing into the wind.
2. Separate front, side and rear wires (front wires are shorter than

rear wires).

3. Attach control bar, making sure bolt is completely through the hole and nut is firmly attached with threads showing beyond the nut.
4. Attach lower rigging to control bar with U-brackets and bolts and nuts provided.
5. Place sail in upright position, nose down and still facing wind.
6. Rotate cross bar.
7. Raise king post and attach rear upper wire.
8. Turn rear turnbuckle so that approximately one to one and one-half inches of upward flex occurs when sighting down the keel tube.
9. Unfold each wing out to end of crossbar.
10. With wings open, install wires from control bar and king posts.

The entire assembly procedure takes approximately ten minutes. A little less when you have more assembly experience. Most reputable schools insist on a pre-flight safety check, of which the minimal requirements are:

1. Check all bolts for signs of wear and make sure they are tight, allowing for no play.
2. Run your hand along all tubes making sure they are free of dents and bends.
3. Check wires for signs of wear.
4. Check for upward reflex in keel tube (center of keel should be lower than at nose and tail).
5. Check swing lines for wear and make sure harness and swing seat are securely fastened.
6. Check all of sail for signs of fraying or tearing.

O.K., Let's Try It

The steps to become airborne are considerably simpler than those for preparation. If there is no hang glider flight school or instructor near you, begin as follows:

Start on level ground or a very gentle slope with a relatively soft surface such as sand, snow or grass. Grip the control bar. Run as fast as you can into the wind. Although you will not lift off you will feel your sail become lighter to hold and it will lift until you are running with it at arms' length above your head.

Now progress to a good slope—not a steep hill or a cliff—about a three-to-one ratio descent. Run into the wind, downhill. If the wind is not blowing straight up the hill, run diagonally down into the wind. It is a good idea to start near the bottom of the slope and gradually progress to the top. The combination of your running speed, wind velocity and the degree of the slope will cause you to lift-off. Until you are sure you are an experienced pilot, never try to fly higher than you feel

World Altitude Holder (for foot-launched aircraft) Rudy Kishazy, carrying his glider up the dunes at Frankfurt, Michigan. (Photo courtesy Four Winds Hang Gliding Schools.)

you could safely fall.

The first few times you try sky surfing you will be content with flights of up to half a minute or so and will be too busy concentrating on staying a few feet off the ground to concern yourself with attempting to soar (gain altitude by utilizing thermal activity, updrafts and air currents). Nevertheless, it is important to avoid stalling, for if you do, you and your wings will drop rather rapidly to the ground, which can be quite bumpy and possibly cause injury. Since you are probably but a few feet from the ground with a reasonably soft surface below, you are not likely to get seriously hurt.

Some sky surfers have been killed by stalling at altitudes high enough for the fall to be fatal but not high enough to allow time for recovery from the stall. The hang glider is *not* a delta-shaped parachute. It is a flexible aircraft and you must fly it. If you stop flying it chances are you will lose airspeed, stall and drop.

Increasing Speed

Once you are clear of the ground, pull back on the control bar in order to lower the nose of your glider and pick up speed. If you are flying directly into the wind you will increase your speed relative to the approaching wind by dropping the nose slightly. You will *not* nosedive into the ground. However, don't let the nose drop too radically or you could nose-in or "luff" as in water sailing when the wind velocity is the same on both sides of the sail and the sail merely flaps in the wind.

Turning

Maintaining flying speed is especially important in a turn, which is accomplished by a combination of shifting your body weight in the direction you wish to turn and by pushing the control bar away in the opposite direction. In other words, if you want to make a right turn and have sufficient altitude and airspeed, you push the bar out to the left and your body to the right. Make sure your airspeed is sufficient for a turning maneuver by pulling back a little on the control bar just prior to starting your turn, this will give you a little more airspeed. Always turn into the wind and, of course, make sure you have enough altitude to permit a turn.

Landing

What goes up must come back down again, and you are no exception. As you get ready to land, keep your glider headed directly into the wind and maintain flying speed. Then, by pulling the control bar back, lower the nose of your glider into the wind. Now gradually push the bar forward as your feet are about ready to touch the ground. Finally, push the bar far forward to raise the nose and stall your wing and you should glide in and land lightly on your feet, running a few steps forward to maintain balance. As gracefully as a seagull. Once you have landed, immediately tip the glider onto its nose and unhook your harness or a strong wind may tip your wing and you go over backwards which is not only undignified but may be injurious.

It is well to remember that when making a landing with a hang glider you usually do not get a second chance at it. It is not like learning to pilot an airplane—if your landing speed and attitude are not right your instructor tells you to throttle back and pull up for another try. You are too close to the ground for that when coming in on a hang glider. Not that you are likely to get seriously hurt if you don't make a perfect landing every time, but since you are attempting bird-like flight you want to try to land gently and gracefully, as does a bird. Generally, when your feet touch the ground it is like stepping off an eight or ten-inch stair. It is not at all like landing with a parachute when you hit the deck with about the same amount of force you would experience by jumping off

Rudy Kishazy flying a hang glider of his own design over the dunes on Lake Michigan's eastern shore. (Photo courtesy Four Winds Hang Gliding Schools.)

a six-foot wall.

At The End Of Your Tether—Kiting

Over a quarter century ago a water skier whose name has been forgotten, built a large kite, put on his skis, grabbed the end of a ski-tow rope behind a motorboat and rose into the air as the boat gathered speed. Then he let go of the rope and glided to the surface of the water amid applause from shapely sun-bathers, small boys building sand castles, boaters and fishermen.

Other air-minded adventurers tried various kite configurations until the Delta and Rogallo wings came along. About 500 feet of tow rope is used by the experts, plus very fast motor boats. After attaining maximum altitude, the kitist releases the rope and slowly glides down to the water making turns, performing figure eights, skimming over or under bridges, leaping tall ships in a single bound, etc. Kite championships are held annually at Cypress Gardens, Florida and competitions take place in various other locations.

Kiting water skier signals to tow boat crew as he crosses a jump on Lake Pleasant, Arizona. (Photo courtesy James Tallon).

Beginners start with a short tow rope, just enough speed to allow for liftoff, and a lot of optimism. The control bar *must* be held back as you climb to the full extent of the rope so that your wing's nose is pointing slightly downward so that instead of falling you will fly down, should the rope break or become disconnected.

Accidents occur much more frequently in towed kiting than in free flight with hang gliders. One cause of accidents is that kitists sometimes become over-confident (which is easy considering the feeling of exhilaration you experience). They allow the tow boat to exceed speeds safe for kiting. This can result in three problems:

1. The kite is probably not stressed to withstand the strain applied by excessive speed.
2. If you release your rope at a very high rate of speed, you may not have sufficient stability to maintain a flying attitude.
3. You may veer out too much from the line of travel which can cause severe sideslip from which you may not be able to recover. Needless to say you should wear a life vest and attach floating devices to your glider.

Automobiles are sometimes used for land kiting. The danger possibilities inherent in this type of kiting are numerous. Winches have been used for kite towing as they are regularly used to tow standard gliders (sailplanes), and a recent innovation in the sport has been the use of snowmobiles to tow skiers who are hang-gliding enthusiasts. Some skiers like to ski partway down a hill to get enough speed and then fly the rest of the way down. In some areas, ski jumps are used for this variation of the sport.

Para-Sailing

Para-sailing is a cross between hang gliding, tow-kiting and parachuting. A parachute-type configuration is used although there are variations currently in use and being tested. The pilot is towed aloft by boat or car and literally sails back to the ground or water. Sportsmen like to see how much distance they can cover during descent, how small a target they can land on, how many turns and intricate maneuvers they can accomplish, etc.

Where Do We Go From Here?

Hang-gliding enthusiasts and commercial interests have been experimenting with powered hang-glider flight and small jet engines for this purpose are being marketed by EMG Engineering Company, 18518 S. Broadway, Gardena, CA. 90248 and Thermo-Jet, Inc., PO Box 1528, Kerrville, TX. 78028.

Unquestionably we shall see further advances and variations of hang gliding in both equipment and technique. Automotive vehicles and supplies of all kinds have been moved by hang glider or variations thereof. One can visualize the day when flexible wings will be offered

Para-kiter and assistant hold para-sail until tow rope tightens and pilot climbs into the sky to sail back to earth (or water) after releasing the tow rope. (Photo courtesy James Tallon).

as optional equipment on smaller cars, turning them into powered gliders (aircraft would be more accurate, although such vehicles would probably be able to make unpowered descents). Boats, too, may become airborne in the future, and snowmobiles. Families living in the mountains may use multi-passenger hang gliders with small take-off motors to provide an economical, fun way to visit friends in the valley. Of course, getting back home may not be quite as easy. Perhaps big game hunters will swoop silently over their hunting areas, spotting game like hawks spot mice. Airborne ball games might be fun. Hang glider warfare? Let's not get carried away! Anyway, suggest a few possibilities to your friends and if they tell you you're full of hot air, say: "That's good—I need the thermal!"

The following glossary of terms was prepared by noted hang gliding authority Donald J. Stern and Wayne Christenson, Director of the Midwest School of Hang Gliding.

Acceleration: Add to the speed of a sky sail. Normally related to dive mode until drag stabilizes the dive speed and attitude. Pilot experiences lightness as his body creates more drag than the sky sail.

Angle of attack: The attitude or pitch of a sail as it rotates on the lateral axis.

Aspect ratio: Relationship between the length or span of a wing and its chord length (L/C).

Bank: The lateral inward tilt of a sky sail. As a 45° bank will require 60% greater speed to prevent stalling, a pilot must maintain centripetal force (sufficient air speed).

Blow back: The failure of the nose of a sail prior to the failure of the tail section. Normally accompanied by extreme bar pressure and can cause inversion.

Blow down: The flattening of a flexible canopy when a sail accelerates beyond recommended flying speeds.

Camber: The convexity of the curve of an airfoil from its chord. As applied to a sky sail, the relative convexity (or curve) of the outer or leading edges to the root.

Center of gravity: The center of all flight movements. A point which, by its location, aids positive stability.

Center of lift: The center of the negative pressure envelope for upper lift. The center of induced drag for lower lift on a sky sail.

Centrifugal force: The force that tends to impel a thing or parts of a thing outward from a center of rotation. A product of inertia. The body attached to a sky sail experiences centrifugal force in a turn.

Centripetal force: The force that tends to impel a thing or parts of a thing inward toward a center of rotation. A controlled use of inertia. A directed sky sail forms a centripetal force.

Chord length: Average distance between leading and trailing edge.

Counter balance: To oppose with equal weight or force. Applies to pilot body movement which does not transfer weight. If dynamic energy is applied, a change still can be induced.

Cupping: The negative elevator effect of a bolt roped trailing edge during a dive. This can also cause inversion.

Deflection: The change of shape inward, outward or upward of any spar member.

Dihedral: The angle between an aircraft supporting surface and a horizontal transverse line.

Dive: The nose is down, or at a low angle of attack. It is performed by pulling the control bar in toward the stomach and shifting the weight forward toward the nose to speed up and increase stability. A dive is useful to penetrate into a strong wind, to set up for a landing or gain stable flight in turbulent air. Diving does not mean a loss of altitude as speed increases lift.

Drag: The retarding force acting on a sky sail moving through the air parallel and opposite to the direction of motion.

Dynamic or inertial weight transfer: A powerful, quick weight transfer in which energy is applied.

Flat spin: To turn rapidly downward. The wing stalls in a flat plane while inertia plays a part in continuing the wing rotation.

Flare: The nose is up, or at a high angle of attack. A flare is performed by pusing the control bar away from the body, causing the pilot's weight to shift to the back of the sail. Under certain conditions the flare causes the sail to slow down, gain altitude, or approach a stall or conditions in which the wing no longer develops lift.

Glide ratio: The relative distance traveled forward in feet for each foot of altitude lost.

Hammerhead stall: A stall in which the sail rotates on its lateral axis as it drops its nose into a dive.

L/D: Lift divided by drag to determine performance.

Lateral control: Controlled utilization of both yaw and roll axis in a turn.

Leverage: The mechanical advantage gained by a long lever and a fulcrum. As the control bar is a lever, length affects the energy required as well as the distance of weight transfer needed for control.

Lift: The component of the total aerodynamic force acting on a wing or airfoil that is perpendicular to the relative wind which, for this wing, constitutes the upward force that opposes the pull of gravity.

Lower lift: The parachuting capability of a sky sail. Drag induced from a horizontal dropping sail which slows its descent.

Maximum control: Maximum movement and energy required to change motion already introduced.

Negative dihedral: A downwardly inclined wing from a horizontal transverse line.

Negative recurve: The downward bowing of the keel at the tail causing less longitudinal or pitch stability, less drag, and greater acceleration. Sometimes called cathedral shaping.

Negative stability: The property of a wing that causes it, when disturbed from a condition of equilibrium, to continue in the direction initiated.

Penetration: To enter by overcoming resistance; in sky sailing to move through an airmass with positive ground speed.

Performance: Highest lift with minimum drag.

Pitch: To revolve around a lateral axis, located at the c. g. of a sky sail and normally directed through a straight cross bar.

Positive dihedral: An upwardly inclined wing from a horizontal transverse line.

Positive stability: The property of a wing that causes it, when disturbed from a condition of equilibrium or steady motion, to develop forces or movements that restore the original condition.

Recurve: Positive reflex: The upward bowing of the keel at the tail. Increases longitudinal or pitch stability, and drag. Reduces acceleration.

Roll: To revolve on the longitudinal axis of a sky sail. Flight maneuver in which a complete revolution about the longitudinal axis is made with the horizontal direction of flight being approximately maintained.

Roll-out: The act of reversing a roll.

Root: The essential core. As applied to sky sails, it refers to the center of the wing along the longitudinal axis.

Root cylindrical: A combination of both conical and cylindrical with the cylindrical plan form occuring at the root of the sail.

Skid: To slide without rotating, to slide sideways away from the center of curvature when turning a sky sail.

Slip: To slide out of place or away from support. A slip occurs in a banked turn when centrifugal and centripetal forces are no longer in effect, usually resulting in the last half of a hammerhead stall and inducing a spiral.

Spar members: Any of the prime frame pieces including keel, wing tubes, and cross bar.

Spiral: To turn rapidly downward in a nose-down flying mode.

Stall: The condition of an airfoil operating at an angle of attack so that there is a flow breakdown and a loss of upper lift with a tendency to drop. In a sky sail, one can observe the lower center of lift move forward along with the upper center of lift until the angle of attack is too great for air flow to continue over the top of the wing. A bubble forms at the nose as the sail loses the upper lift envelope and then drops.

Tail steering: The rudder effect of the sky sail's tail caused when applying maximum control in a roll out. The control wire tightened acts to bow the keel away from the desired direction. This effect is amplified in a nose-high, tail-low sail.

Thrust: To push or drive with force. The forward directed reaction force produced by air discharged rearwards from a Rogallo-type wing.

Tripping: The property causing a drop in a wing. Usually relates to negative dihedral and negative stability.

Turn: To cause to move around an axis or center, to cause to move around so as to effect a desired end. As related to sky sails, a weight shift changes the wing loading so that the weighted wing has less lift and a bank is induced. Centripetal force is applied as a skid appears and before a slip occurs.

Unweighting: The reduction of or elimination of the pilot's weight and effective control by weight transfer. Usually experienced during acceleration.

Upper lift: Lift caused on the upper part of a wing due to a negative pressure envelope generated by acceleration of relative wind over the upper surface causing a venturi effect.

Venturi effect: The fact that as the velocity of flow of air increases over the surface of a wing, the pressure decreases.

Wash out: The change of camber on a leading edge. Normally causing the washed out wing to lose lift.

Weight: Force of gravity acting upon pilot and airplane.

Weight transfer: The movement of weight in a manner which changes its relationship to the C. G.

Wing tip vortices: Twisting trail of air flow generated at outside edge of a wing.

Yaw: To turn by angular motion about the vertical axis.

Publications to Help You

Hang Gliding, by Dan Poynter, basic handbook of skysurfing. Published by Daniel F. Poynter, 48 Walker St., North Quincy, MASS. 02171. If you buy no other book on hang gliding, at least buy this one. Cost $4.95 + .40 postage.

The Complete Book of Sky Sailing, by Rick Carrier. McGraw-Hill Book Co., Inc. N.Y. 10036. Cost $7.95.

Hang Glider Market Study, by Group 3, c/o Professor Norris Love, Advanced Management Institute, Lake Forest College, Lake Forest, IL. 60045. Cost $35 per copy. Intended primarily for those who have a commercial interest in the sport.

How to Fly-With Wings, by John Weiss. Available from Sport Wings, 22 N. 2nd St., Box 1647, Lafayette, IN. 47902.

True Flight, by Herman Rice. Available from True Flight, 1719 Hillsdale Ave., San Jose, CA. 95124. Cost $5 per copy. Covers materials, construction and flying.

Guide to Rogallo Flight-Basic, by Bob Skinner and Rich Finley. Available from Flight Realities, 1945 Adams Ave., San Diego, CA. 92116. Cost $2.50.

Hang Flight, an instructional manual, available from Eco-Nautics, PO

Box 1154, Redland, CA. 92373. Cost $3.25.
Simplified Performance Testing for Hang Gliders, by Jack Park. Available from Jack Park, 15237 Lakeside, Sylmar, CA. 91342. A useful book at only $2.
Ground Skimmer Magazine, published for members by the United States Hang Gliding Association. PO Box 66306, Los Angeles, CA. 90066. Membership dues are $10 including subscription.
Man Flight Magazine, published monthly by Whitney Enterprises, PO Box 90762, Los Angeles, CA. 90009. $7.50 per year.
Delta Kite Flyer News, PO Box 483, Van Nuys, CA. 91408.

Hang Glider Associations and Clubs

United States Hang Gliding Association, PO Box 66306, Los Angeles, CA. 90066. Membership $5 per year.
North Texas Hang Glider Society, Mark Hicks, President, 1716 Jasmine Lane, Plano, TX. 75074.
Boston Sky Club, Box 375, Marlboro, MA. 01752.
Pacific Tradewind Skysailors, Mike Dorn, President, 3142 Hinano St., Honolulu, HI. 96815.
Southern Ontario Hang Glider Association, John D. Farnan, President, c/o MiniSport, 10 Gobernor's Rd., Dundas, Ontario, Canada.
Ultralite Flyers Organization of San Diego, PO Box 81665, San Diego, CA. 92138.
Hang Glider Manufacturers Association, 137 Oregon St., El Sugundo, CA. 90245.
New England Ridge Riders, 274 Bishops Terrace, Hyannis, MA. 02601.
Capitol Hang Glider Association, c/o Vic Powell, 7358 Shenandoah Ave., Annandale, VA. 22003.
Delta Birdmen, c/o Lance Leonard, 147 N. Wilcox Ave., Los Angeles, CA. 90038.
Eastern Washington Hang Gliders Association, c/o George Greger, 1425 Marshall, Richland, WA. 99352.
Eastern Pennsylvania Hang Glider Association, c/o J. M. McTammany, 620 Walnut St., Reading, PA. 19601.
Escape Country Sky Surfing Club, Trabuco Canyon, CA. 92678.
Inland Empire Aeronauts, c/o Bill Johnson, PO Box 2009, Missoula, MT. 59801.
Kydid Flyer Club, 323 N. Euclid, Santa Anna, CA. 92703.
North American Sky Sailing Association, c/o Chandelle Corp., 511 Orchard St., Golden, CO. 80401.
Michigan Sky Surfers, c/o Mark Richards, 1361 Oregon, Pontiac, MI. 48054.
Midwest Hang Glider Association, 11959 Glen Valley Drive, Maryland Heights, MO. 63043.

The Mississippi Valley Air Surfers Association, Ron Lovejoy, President, 501 W. View Drive, Hasting, MN. 55033.
Northwestern Hang Gliders Association, c/o Fred Tiemens III, 212 15th Ave., South, Minneapolis, MN. 55404.
Ohio Hang Glider Association, c/o Tony Mittelo, 26875 Bagley Rd., Olmsted Falls, OH. 44138.
Orange County Sky Sailing Club, c/o Gail Montgomery, 916 Delaware, Huntington Beach, CA. 92648.
Pacific Northwest Hang Glider Association, c/o Pete Rutherford, 417 Harvard Ave., Seattle, WA. 98102.
Tidewater Hang Glider Club, c/o Otto F. Horton, Jr., 5624 Hampshire Lane, Virginia Beach, VA. 23462.
Self Soar Association, PO Box 1860, Santa Monica, CA. 90406.
Wings of Rogallo, c/o Gary Warren, 502 Barkentine Lane, Redwood City, CA. 94065.

In the Hang Gliding Business

AA Flight System, 10 N. Barton, New Buffalo, MI. 49117.
Alpine Haus, 628 S. College, Ft. Collins, CO. 80524.
Apollo Skycraft, 222 Waukegan Rd., Glenview, IL. 60025. (312) 729-7990.
Apollo Skycraft, 700 E. Higgins Rd., Schaumburg, IL. 60172 (312) 885-0958.
Base Camp, 121 W. San Francisco St., Santa Fe, NM. 87501.
Cloudmen Glidercraft Co., 905 Church St., Nashville, TN. 34203. (615) 256-6221.
Colorado Flight Safety, Boulder Municipal Airport, Boulder, CO. 80302.
Delta Wing Ski Kites & Gliders, Inc., PO Box 483, Van Nuys, CA. 91408. (213) 785-2474. 787-6600.
DSK Aircraft Corp., 12676 Pierce St., Pacoima, CA. 91331.
EMG Engineering Company, 18518 S. Broadway, Gardena, CA. 90248.
Eipper-Formance, PO Box 246, Lomita, CA. 90717. Midwest Headquarters, c/o Midwest School of Hang Gliders, Inc., 11522 Red Arrow Hwy., Bridgmen, MI. 40106. Outlets in a number of cities.
Firecraft Corp., 4904 N. Pulaski Rd., Chicago, IL. 60630. (312) 736-7050.
Flight Realities, 1945 Adams Ave., San Diego, CA. 92116. (714) 298-1962.
Four Winds Sports, Inc., 109 W. Prospect, Mount Prospect, IL. 60056.
Get High, Inc., PO Box 4551, Aspen, CO. 81661.
Gorsuch Inc., PO Box 1508, Vail, CO. 81657.
Hi Performance, Palo Alto, CA.
Hummingbird Sales, 2217 Grand Blve., Waterloo, IA. 50701.

Kenniker Supplies, 1000 E. Platt, Maquoketa, IA. 52060.
Kitty Hawk Hang Gliders & Sky Kites, 230 W. McDaniel, Springfield, MO. 65806.
Kitty Hawk Hang Gliders & Sky Kites, 5202 San Mateo NE, Albuquerque, NM. 87110.
Kondor Kite Co., PO Box 603, Lewisville, TX. 75067. (214) 434-1646.
Manta Wings, 1647 E. 14th St., Oakland, CA. 94606. (415) 536-1500.
Man-Flight Systems Inc., PO Box 375, Marlboro, MASS. 01752.
MiniSport Canada, 10 Governor's Rd., Dundas, ONT., Canada (416) 627-0672.
New Mexico Sky Sails School, 625 Amherst N.E., Albuquerque, NM. 87106.
Oak Ridge Sports, 1360 Central, Dubuque, IA. 52001.
Olympic Sports, Telluride, CO. 81435.
Oxbow Air Sports Center, RR1, Box 323 A, Elkhart, IN. 46514.
Pacific Gull, 1321 Calle Valde, San Clemente, CA. 92672. (714) 492-0670.
Phantom Wing Inc., PO Box 6044, Concord, CA. 94524. (415) 798-7350.
Rocky Mountain Marine, 5411 Leetsdale Drive, Denver, CO. 80222.
Sailbird Flying Machines, 3123 N. El Paso, Colorado Springs, CO. 80907. (303) 475-8639.
Sailwing Sky School, PO Box 1413, Torrance, CA. 90505. (213) 378-3060.
Sailwing Sky School, 2631 Rancho Rd., Redding, CA. 96001. (916) 241-1105.
Skycraft Inc., 615 Ruberta Ave., Glendale, CA. 91201. (213) 240-9475.
Sky Sails of Michigan, 1611 Woodward, Birmingham, MI.
Sky Sports, Inc., PO Box 441, Whitman, MA. (617) 447-3773.
Solo Flight, 930 W. Hoover Ave., Orange, CA. 92667. (714) 538-9768.
Sport Kites Inc., 1202 C E. Walnut, Santa Ana, CA. 92701. (714) 547-1344, 547-6366, 544-0445.
Sunbird Gliders, 21420 Chase St., Canoga Park, CA. 91304. (213) 882-3177.
True Flight, 1719 Hillsdale Ave., San Jose, CA. 95124. (408) 267-0692.
Ultralite Products, 137 Oregon St., El Segundo, CA. 90245. (213) 322-7121.
Valderrain & Company, PO Box 314, Lomita, CA. 90717. (213) 325-2960.
Volmer Aircraft, PO Box 5222, Glendale, CA. 91201.
Werner's Storm Hut, Steamboat Springs, CO. 80477.
Whitney Enterprises, PO Box 90762, Los Angeles, CA. 90009. (213) 641-5303.
Max Tufts, PO Box 166, Warrenton, VA. 22186.

LIST OF EIPPER-FORMANCE DEALERSHIPS AND HANG GLIDING SCHOOLS

Alaska
Falcon Air
4049 Mallard
Fairbanks, AK 99701

Alaska Baloon Ascensions
P.O. Box 78
Palmer, AK 99645

California
Head Office:
Eipper-Formance, Inc.
1840 Oak Street
Torrance, CA 90501
(213) 328-9100

Flight Realities
1945 Adams Avenue
San Diego, CA 91226

Flight Realities
2414 Parkway
Bakersfield, CA 93304

The Hang Glider Shoppe
P.O. BAox 1860
Santa Monica, CA 90406

The Hang Glider Shop
1351 S. Beach Blvd.
La Habra, CA 90631

Windsong
27 N. Garden
Ventura, CA 93001

Sail Wing Sales & Service
2631 A Rancho Road
Redding, CA 96001

Free Flight Systems
848 W. 9th Street
Chico, CA 95926

Quicksilver Mountain
1022 Mangrove
Chico, CA 95926

Jim Greene
136 E. Olive
Fresno, CA 93728

Angel Wing Kite Sales
236-A Santa Cruz Avenue
Aptos, CA 95003

Colorado
Get High, Inc.
P.O. Box 4551
Aspen, CO 81611

Rocky Mountain Marine
5411 Leetsdale Drive
Denver, CO 80222

Naturally High Flight Systems
P.O. Box 5218
Steamboat Springs, CO 80499

Mike Larson
c/o 775 Merry Lane
Boulder, CO 80302

Coal Creek Sky Sail Co.
General Delivery
Crested Butte, CO 81224

Hawaii
Air Performance Hawaii
217 Prospect
Honolulu, HI 96813

Idaho
Upward Bound South
110 North Second Street
Pacotello, ID 83201

Walker Recreational Products
1230 N. Skyline Drive
Idaho Fall, ID 83401

Illinois
Raymond W. Fleischman
516 Lowell Avenue
Glen Ellyn, IL 60137

Kansas
Benny Jumper
422 B East 9th
Hay, KS 67601

Voyager's Pack & Portage Shop
5935 Merriam Drive
Merriam, KS 66203

Prairie Skimmer Hang Gliders
308 E. Pine Apt. 3
Wichita, KA 67214

Maine
Portland Bicycle Exchange
396 Fore Street
Portland, ME 04111

Maryland
Sport Flight
3305 Ferndale Street
Kensington, MD 20795

Massachusetts
Sky Sports
P.O. Box 441
Whitman, MA 02382

Ultralight Wings
Kenmore Station
Box 384
Boston, MA 02215

Michigan
Ski and Sail
7949 W. Grand River
Brighton, MI 48116

St. Joe Tool Company

11521 Red Arrow Highway
Bridgman, MI 49106

The Midwest School
of Hang Gliding
11522 Red Arrow Highway
Bridgman, MI 40106

Minnesota
Jeff Pink
11516 Friar Lane
Hopkins, MN 55343

Montana
Track and Trail
(Rex Nebel)
701 Dunham Avenue
Billings, MT 59102

Upward Bound North
(Bill Johnson)
P.O. Box 2009
Missoula, MIT 59801

Nevada
Wings
(Bill Duca)
318 E. Hoover
Las Vega, NV 89105

New Mexico
Sky Sailors
4521 Central N. E.
Albuquerque, NM 87108

New York
Thomas W. Frutiger
74 E. Park Road
Pittsford, NY 14534

North Carolina
Kitty Hawk Kites, Inc.
P.O. Box 386, Bypass 158
Nags Head, NC 27959

Oregon
Billy B. Beamway's
  Flying Machine Shop
1260 Hilyard
Eugene, OR 97401

Pennsylvania
Y. B. M. Cycle Sails
572 W. Lancaster Avenue
Bryn Mawr, PA 19010

Tennessee
Butterfly Industries, Inc.
1911 3/4 W. Cumberland
Knoxville, TN 37916

Texas
Crow Flite
1802 Branard
Houston, TX 77006

Washington
Delta Wing Kites, Inc.
3003 112th S. E.
Auburn, WA 98002

Free Light Enterprises
1425 Marshall
Richland, WA 99325

Wisconsin
H.H. Petrie's Sporting Goods
P.O. Box 5427
Madison, WI 73705

Canada
Hi Flight
R. R. No. 1
Elko, B. C.
Canada

Riding On Air

Since no one has yet been able to manufacture, promote and market hovercraft in the USA on a profitable basis, the best way to obtain one of these fascinating little vehicles is to build it yourself. Besides, it's a lot cheaper.

You need two engines—one to drive a huge fan beneath the unit which blasts air downward at the ground or water and provides the cushion of air the vehicle "floats" on and a second engine to drive a rear-mounted pusher propeller which gives your craft forward motion.

The craft's skeleton framework is shaped something like an egg fried by unskilled hands. It's covered by an inflatable plastic covering surrounded by a "skirt" containing the air cushion. The craft also needs an inflatable seat, mounts for the engines and propellers, engine screens, additional flotation chambers (old inner tubes will do nicely), a fuel tank and controls for the engine. You can add a windshield, electric starter and battery, a couple of instruments and a canopy, if you want to go *deluxe*.

There are various plans available to help you construct any of a number of types of hovercraft, or, if you keep your eyes open, you may be able to purchase a hovercraft built by someone else, or one made by one of the few companies that have tried to manufacture and sell these interesting units. When you do find one for sale its price usually seems way out of line for what you get.

The English are much farther advanced in the hovercraft field than we are on this side of the Atlantic. Being surrounded entirely by water and crisscrossed and honeycombed with rivers, canals, lakes, ponds and swamps, our British cousins seem to be fascinated with various types of craft that travel through, under and across water.

Take Sir Donald Malcolm Campbell, for instance, who spent most of his life obsessed with the idea of crossing water faster then anyone else. For the most part he succeeded. In 1967 he actually drove a turbo-engined two and one-quarter-ton "boat" called the Bluebird K7 at a speed of 328 m.p.h. This feat, although a world record at the time, could not be deemed entirely sucessful since it cost Sir Malcolm his life.

We have only to look at Britain's progress in the field of huge, fast luxury liners, at their development of the world's first turbine ship back in 1894 and many other nautical accomplishments to be convinced that here is a nation severely hung-up on water.

The British got into hovercraft in 1910 with an invention by Christopher Cockerell after an air cushion design by another Englishman which dated back to 1877. However, hovercraft never got off the ground or the water until 1959 when the four and one-half-ton Saunders Roe crossed a body of water at the south of England without getting its occupants wet (beyond a splash or two, that is).

Today, Britain operates a number of very fast, very profitable ferry services using hovercraft—across lakes, river mouths, the English Channel, strips of water separating the mainland from off-shore islands, etc. One of their big ones is the seventy-seven-knot Westland SR-N4, weighing 185 tons which carries 174 passengers and 34 automobiles as well as miscellaneous freight.

On a smaller scale, hovercrafting is a rapidly growing sport in the British Isles and national hovercraft championships are held annually. Although a great many of the hovercraft entered in these competitions are home built, more and more commercial concerns are using the events as a proving ground for craft they plan to market not only in the United Kingdom but all over the world. British-built hovercraft are already in use in flooded areas of Africa, Pakistan, India, Australia and many more countries. Medicines, food and other emergency supplies are able to reach small communities completely cut off by floods and swamps. They are also used by several African countries for river patrols, wild life protection, pest control, to keep down smuggling activities, for exploration and many other uses, so hovercraft are by no means mere toys.

One British company, Pindair Ltd., is actively exporting hovercraft to the United States as well as to South America, Canada and other countries. This company's hovercraft, the most successful yet from a commercial standpoint, have given impressive demonstrations in the United States over water, ice, snow, sand, grass, cement, swamps and other surfaces. Called the Skima, Pindair hovercraft in two and four-man models, start at almost $3,000, which is higher than even the more expensive snowmobiles. Speaking of snowmobiles, the two Skima engines, both running at full throttle, are about as loud in the driver's ears as is the engine of a powerful snowmobile. Newer-type mufflers are beginning to quiet the units somewhat, and we shall no doubt see further progress in this direction, atlhough the silent or near-silent hovercraft is a long, long way off.

Wearing a safety helmet when driving or riding in a hovercraft not only offers protection in the event of a spill and from low-hanging branches, short-sighted woodpeckers, etc., but also helps make the engine noise more bearable. Earplugs also help, and a slight tendency toward deafness is not all that bad when you're in a hovercraft.

Smooth water or wake, the Skima hovercraft travels straight and level. (Photo courtesy Pindair Ltd.)

The two-man Skima weighs around 200 pounds and can be carried by its side handles by two strong men. Deflated, the unit can be collapsed for easier portage and storage. Movie goers and television viewers saw a Skima star in a spectacular chase sequence in the film "Dr. No." The Skima is capable of thirty m.p.h. or better and some British hovercraft can travel considerably faster than that over smooth water. Hovering about six inches from the surface, Skima will clear obstacles up to foot high. Used on a beach it passes over the prone bodies of courageous volunteers with damage neither to the bodies nor to the craft. Short slopes of forty-five degrees present no special problem or challenge to this versatile craft and longer slopes of about thirty degrees are all in a day's work for the Skima.

A Skima showed its amphibious paces on the Potomac river at Gravelly Point, amid great interest from the press, the military and civil servants who were supposed to be working. The intriguing demonstration was followed next day by a demonstration in the rotunda of the British embassy in Washington, D.C., which included hovering down the embassy's front steps to Massachusetts avenue.

If you decide to build your own, the best configuration for most effective balance seems to be with the thrust engine mounted at the rear, driver and passenger directly in front and approximately in the center of the unit, and the lift enging just forward of the occupant's

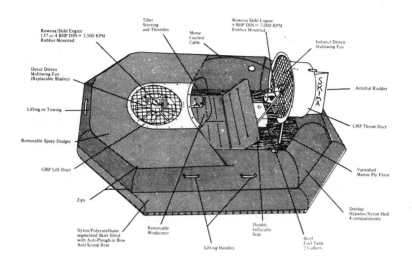

Rowena/Sthl Engine 137 cc 4 BHP DIN @ 3,500 RPM Rubber Mounted

Tiller Steering and Throttles

Morse Control Cable

Rowena Sthl Engine 9 BHP DIN @ 7,000 RPM Rubber Mounted

Indirect Driven Multiwing Fan

Direct Driven Multiwing Fan (Replacable Blades)

Aerofoil Rudder

Lifting or Towing

GRP Thrust Duct

Removable Spray Dodger

GRP Lift Duct

Varnished Marine Ply Floor

Zips

Dunlop Hypalon/Nylon Hull 4 compartments

Nylon/Polyeurethane segmented Skirt fitted with Anti-Plough-in Bow Anti-Scoop Rear

Removable Windscreen

Double Inflatable Seat

Steel Fuel Tank 2 Gallons

Lifting Handles

seat. Balance is an all-important factor in this type of craft. If the occupants lean too much toward the rear, for instance, or carry too much weight behind the seat, there is a tendency for the rear skirt to drag in the water which results in a loss of steering capability. The Skima, like other small hovercraft, has a considerably greater width/length ratio to provide increased stability. The two engines used on Skima units were originally German-built chain-saw motors and offer excellent power-to-weight factors.

Driving A Hovercraft

One of the most persistent problems with which the hovercraft owner must contend is what the British call "hump." With a normal water craft there is a certain speed which, when reached, tends to lift the hull somewhat to produce a planing effect. A hovercraft experiences a similar effect as it lifts clear of the turbulence its own engine creates. Below this "hump" speed the craft tends to be sluggish and difficult to control effectively because it is, in effect, riding in a "basin." This means that maneuvering in tight areas at low speed is very difficult. The factors that affect "hump" are: lift pressure, thrust speed, length of craft, total payload and wind speed.

Many hovercraft designers have come up with many different types of controls. Most common, perhaps, is the tiller or joystick type of control lever, as used in the Skima. It is located in the center of the crew area and pivoted from the duct of the lift fan. Two separate hand throttles control the speeds of the two engines. Once your craft is

moving at its lift limit (about six inches) the slide throttle controlling
the lift engine is usually left fully open in order to maintain maximum
lift.
    To steer to your left you push the joystick over to the left and the
reverse to steer to the right. You can help steer by shifting your body
weight from side to side as when steering a toboggan, snowmobile,
etc. Leaning the body weight to one side tends to dip the skirt on that
side slightly into the water, presenting drag which helps the steering
action. "Body English" can also be used to achieve "trim." The combination of bursts of throttle, plus the sideways slip of the craft as you
push the joystick over, plus the shifting of your body weight (when
judiciously applied in the right combinations at the right time) enable
you to make really tight turns. In Britain, hovercraft enthusiasts
develop their steering coordination on a marked slalom course. When
steering, it is always important to apply full throttle to gain maximum
control since the air jet thrust is directly over the rudder. To stop, you
merely cut both motors and your craft drops the six inches onto the
water or ground. In this manner it is possible to come to a complete
stop from thirty mph in a distance of less than thirty feet. On water you
can use the thrust motor only and use your hovercraft as an inflatable
powered dinghy. On other surfaces you cannot achieve forward movement without lift except with probably damage to your craft. As with
all water-going craft, drivers and passengers should always wear life
jackets when driving or riding in a hovercraft over water.

Need Information?

    If you would like information regarding Pindair Ltd., and its Skima
hovercraft, write to Pindair Ltd., 16 Broom Lock, Teddington,
TW119Q0, Middlesex, England.
    For information regarding the importation of hovercraft from Great
Britain, contact Merrick Baker-Bates, Information Department, British
Embassy, 3100 Massachusetts Avenue, NW, Washington, DC 20008.
    For plans on how to build your own hovercraft, check back issues of
such publications as *Popular Science, Popular Mechanics, Mechanix
Illustrated,* and similar "how to" publications. You may be able to pur-
chase plans from the Experimental Aircraft Association, Hales
Corners, Wisconsin.

Cycling For Fun, Exercise and Transportation

A bicycle, having only two wheels, has a natural inclination to fall over. This tendency is, of course, even more pronounced with a unicycle, which has only one wheel. Tricycles, three-wheeled pedal-powered units, are able to stand up for themselves.

The first step in riding either a one or two-wheeled cycle, then, is to keep it upright and resist its desire to keel over and deposit you in an ungraceful heap on the ground. It's a question of balance and motion. Once you have boarded the thing and got it moving in a forward direction, it will not fall unless you stop, develop an extreme wobble, or hit something.

Unicycles Are Not Just For Clowns

The unicycle is not nearly as difficult to ride as it looks. Since there are no handlebars, as on a bicycle, you can use your arms to achieve and maintain balance, although once you have mastered the art of unicycling, it is no longer necessary to flail about with the arms like an inebriated seagull. On the campus of Northwestern University in Evanston (near Chicago) I recently watched a student pedaling his unicycle between buildings while studying a textbook; and I have seen circus clowns perform juggling feats with complete *elan* while unicycling all over the circus ring.

It is important to start with the right size unicycle. When making a selection, have the salesman help you keep balance while you straddle a unicycle and sit on the saddle. The saddle height should permit your foot to rest firmly on the pedal when the leg is comfortably extended and the pedal is at its lowest position.

Unicycles come in a number of sizes intended for different use. The Schwinn Bicycle Company makes unicycles in two sizes—a twenty-inch wheel and a twenty-four-inch wheel. The smaller wheel is easier to maneuver and is best for tricks; the larger wheel is better for traveling because the larger wheel enables you to go farther with less effort. When selecting a unicycle for a youngster who is still growing, the

Riding a unicycle is easy; even a child can do it. Adults may have a little more trouble.

growth factor should be considered. A minimum of two and one-half inches of seat post must be inserted into the frame at all times, so buy your unicycle with consideration for this fact and for the owner's growth factor.

The next step, of course, is to ride. To mount, the unicycle must be held stationary by another person, by blocking the wheel at the back, or by using a groove to steady the wheel, etc.

Stand behind the unicycle with the left pedal forward, the right pedal to the rear and the front of the seat in your right hand.

Using the left hand to hold onto something or someone, place your right foot on the right pedal toward the outer edge and slide the seat under you. Then place the left foot on the left pedal toward the outer edge and slide the seat under you.

Still using the left hand, hold for a moment while you get the feel of it. Now with the wheel held steady by the wooden block or whatever, apply pressure to the left pedal and move forward, keeping your back straight.

Lean slightly forward and keep all your weight on the saddle, not on the pedals. Don't wobble, don't look down—keep going! Balance yourself with your arms and turn by twisting your body and moving your weight.

The unicycle has what is known as a "fixed" hub—it can turn in either direction depending on whether you are pedaling forward or backward. Likewise, when you stop pedaling, the unicycle stops moving and you will have to dismount.

Although most people regard the one-wheeled unit as merely part of a circus clown's bag of tricks, unicycles are gaining popularity and are now sold in many bicycle shops and department stores. They have several advantages over conventional two-wheelers. They take up very little storage space, can be easily carried with one hand, can be stored in the average car's trunk or back seat or front seat of a sports car, and for getting about a campus or resort they provide an interesting and faster alternative to walking. In addition, unicycles provide excellent exercise.

Two Wheels Are Better Than One

Now that we have mastered the unicycle let's proceed to its big brother—the bicycle. Most people manage to learn to ride a bicycle in a few minutes and once learned, this skill is supposedly never forgotten.

It is best to start with a roadster-type bicycle—i.e., one with upright handlebars. If you have never ridden a bicycle before, you may find the racing-type (or "drop") handlebars rather awkward; although once a cyclist has learned to ride with racing handlebars, most enthusiasts prefer this type, especially for long distances. The upright handlebars are best for city driving since they permit a better view of the road and traffic ahead.

Actually, there are two methods of mounting a bicycle. The first is by straddling a stationary bicycle. At first you may find it necessary to have someone hold the bicycle until you've gained your balance. Straddle the bicycle, placing the right pedal in the forward position. To move the bicycle forward, apply pressure with your right foot and place your left foot on its pedal. Once you have your balance and are moving, your helper must let go of course. Keep pedaling and steering with the handlebars and you're a cyclist.

The second way to mount a bicycle seems to be the most popular and the easiest with those who have already learned to ride. However, because it is not considered by cycling authorities as safe as the first method described, it is generally not to be recommended. People at safety-conscious Schwinn Bicycle Company, for instance, are adamant in their efforts to discourage any cycling practices which they consider unsafe. Nevertheless, the author has used the second method of mounting a bicycle exclusively for a great many years, and so have countless others; so without recommending it here is another method for mounting a bicycle.

Take a firm grip on each of the handlebars, place the left foot on the pedal which should be toward its lowest point. You are facing the front and your right foot is immediately behind the left. Press down on the left pedal, shove-off with the right foot and—with all your weight now on the left pedal—swing the right leg behind and up over the saddle and place the right foot upon the right pedal.

Keep pedaling and hold the bicycle on course with the handlebars. No need to look down at your feet, the pedals, the wheels or the ground immediately under the bicycle—just look ahead as you do when walking. The faster you pedal the easier it is to keep going; if you slow down to the point where you have little forward motion, the cycle will stop, and you will either have to get off or you will fall off. Within a few minutes you will find yourself cycling away as though you had done it all your life. Actually, you are moving along by placing one foot in front of the other, just like walking; cycling is almost as natural. When cycling at a fairly low speed, balancing is accomplished simply by turning the handlebars to left or right. As you become more experienced, you will find that you can maintain your balance by merely leaning to one side or the other.

Now that we've got you going, it is just possible that sooner or later you may want to stop, so let's discuss brakes. There are two kinds— coaster (or foot) brakes and hand brakes. The coaster-type bicycle is built with a fixed wheel hub so that when you stop pedaling the bicycle stops going forward. By suddenly backstepping on the pedals, you can virtually "stop on a dime." As the bicycle stops, gravity takes over and you must remove one foot from the pedal to catch yourself and the bicycle before you fall over. Bear in mind it takes a lot of practice to stop a bicycle "on a dime" when moving at any reasonable speed and still keep the machine and yourself under control.

Handbrakes, of which there are two basic styles—caliper brakes and hub brakes—operate by means of cables which, when you apply the handbrake levers on the handlebars, transmit this movement to the wheels. Caliper or rim brakes use rubber or synthetic rubber pads to grip the wheel rims; hub brakes operate by gripping the wheel at the hub. If properly adjusted and operated, boty types of handbrakes cause the bicycle to stop safely. Naturally, you have to stop pedaling at the same time you apply the brakes, otherwise it becomes a duel of strength between your legs and the brakes.

Generally speaking it is best to use the rear wheel brakes more than the front wheel brakes. If the front brakes are properly adjusted and the pads are fairly new, by suddenly and forcefully applying the front wheel brake alone while traveling at a good rate of speed, you stand the risk of being thrown over the handlebars. This is no fun—I had the gravel scars for months when I first did this at a rather tender age. Applying the rear brake first and then, if necessary, the front brake, to bring your bicycle to a safe, quick stop is best under most conditions. This way, the braking is more or less equalized; however, you can usually get all the stopping power you need from the rear brake alone provided the rear brake pads are not unduly worn and the brake is properly adjusted.

Into High Gear

These days it is almost as difficult to find a bicycle without variable-speed gears as it is to purchase a car with a manual transmission. So many people have seriously taken up bicycling, and with increasing fuel shortages the bicycle is assuming such importance as a means of commuting, shopping, getting to school, etc., that variable-speed gears are almost a necessity. Bicycles are currently available in a wide range of variable-speed models, but for the average cyclist three-speed, five-speed or ten-speed units offer all the variations needed. For most, the three-speed rear wheel hub provides sufficient variation. Gear selection is controlled by a hand lever mounted on the handlebars or frame of the bicycle. The control lever has three positions corresponding to the three gear ratios. First gear is low gear and is helpful when pedaling uphill, against the wind, or when you are getting tired. Second gear is the middle gear and is usually direct drive—just as if you were riding a bicycle without variable-speed gears. This is the gear you normally use most when cycling on fairly level ground with little or no head wind and when you are not particularly tired. Third gear is high gear and is very helpful when pedaling downhill, with the wind, or on level ground if you feel energetic or are in a hurry. When you shift from one gear to the next, keep your pedals turning without forcing them—ease up your pressure on the pedals and move the gear lever to the next position. Never try to change from one to three or from three to one or jump any intermediate gears. Five and ten-speed gears operate on the same principal as the three-speed except that they offer a wider range of gear variations.

Oil, Rag and Wrench

A bicycle is a piece of mechanical eqiupment. It needs adjusting, oiling, cleaning, tightening and regular inspection like most other mechanical things. Parts that require adjusting are the seat (or saddle), the handlebars, the brakes, and the gears if your bicycle has

PROPER
FRAME FIT

Rider MUST be able to straddle bicycle when standing

Proper frame fit is essential for optimum cylcing enjoyment and per- formance. Basically, the proper frame is the largest one the rider can straddle comfortably. Ladies may use the men's style frame to deter- mine the spproximate size of the corresponding ladie's model. (An alternate method is to subtract 10 inces from the crotch-to-floor dis- tance while standing in stocking feet. People six feet may need to subtract a greater distance for the proper frame size.)

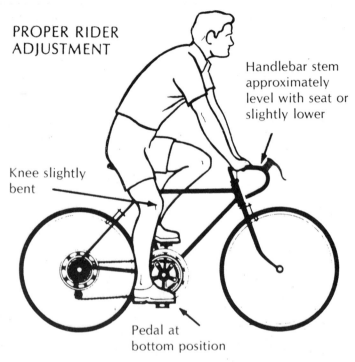

PROPER RIDER ADJUSTMENT

Handlebar stem approximately level with seat or slightly lower

Knee slightly bent

Pedal at bottom position

The saddle is correctly adjusted when the rider's heel in stocking feet rests on the pedal with the leg fully extended (no bend at the knee). When the ball of the foot is placed into the pedal and toe clip, the leg will assume a slightly bent position as shown in the illustration. The handlebars should be approximately level with the saddle or slightly lower. At least 2 inches of the seatpost and stem should remain inside the frame for maximum safety.

variable-speed gears.

Adjusting the seat to the most comfortable height is especially important when you are learning to ride. Most manufacturers recommend the following as the best method of determining proper seat height:

Have someone hold the bicycle firmly, straddle it, place the right pedal in its lowest position and place your foot on the pedal. The ball of the foot should rest comfortably on the pedal, and the leg should be not quite straight—a slight bend in the knee should be evident. Many learners prefer to adjust the seat so that they may place one foot on the ground, until they are more proficient.

Seat height adjustment is made by means of a hexagonal nut on the frame at the point where the seat post enters the frame. Loosen this nut with the wrench provided with the bicycle, wiggle the saddle to the desired height and firmly tighten the nut. At least two inches of the post must remain inside its frame. The angle of the seat is adjustable also by means of a hexagonal nut at the base of the saddle. Loosen this nut and adjust the saddle angle by tipping.

Next thing to adjust is the handlebars. This is accomplished by means of a small hexagonal nut in the center of the handlebars and a larger hexagonal nut lower down on the column. Handlebars may be adjusted up and down and may be tipped, as can the seat. Most authorities agree that for everyday cycling the handlebars should be level with the saddle. It is important to make sure that adjusting nuts are thoroughly tightened after adjustment; otherwise your bicycle is not safe to ride since the seat may move unexpectedly or the handlebars may work loose and prevent proper steering, either of which can be hazardous.

Join The Crowd

Now that we have mastered the bicycle we have joined over seventy million cyclists, according to the Bicycle Institute of America, Inc., whose headquarters are at 122 E. 42nd St., New York City, NY 10017. The Institute has available all kinds of information about bicycles, their manufacture, sale and use. There are more than 1,000 organized cycling clubs in the USA and thousands more in other countries throughout the world.

The leading organization for bicycle users in the USA is the League of American Wheelmen, with headquarters at 19 S. Bothwell, Palatine, IL 60067. This not-for-profit organization has been helping the sport of cycling for many years—since the 1880s, in fact. Membership in this fine group is $5 per year, or $8 for a family membership. The LAW has actively encouraged and promoted the construction of bikeways and has established marked bike routes. It sponsors all kinds of bicycle events, gives tour planning assistance and direction, and champions the right of bicyclists to use the roads just as other vehicles. LAW has successfully fought anti-bicycle legislation on many occasions, encourages sensible non-discriminatory legislation approaches, and promotes cycling safety. LAW publishes an annual directory which lists all members, LAW officials and all affiliated bicycle clubs throughout the country. It is a good way to find out what clubs are near you, if you enjoy group activities.

More and more cities are now providing cycle ways, bikeways, bicycle paths—there are a number of terms. Chicago is outstanding in this regard since it not only provides excellent cycle paths through its many miles of lake shore park, but has specially marked-off cycle ways on city streets to help bicycle commuters. Some motorists and most taxicab drivers seem to ignore these bicycle "safe" zones, but as the use of bicycles by commuters increases, with active encouragement by City Hall, this problem should lessen.

Executives, secretaries, doctors and nurses and many others may be seen during fair weather commuting through city streets to work in Chicago, thus cutting down on pollution from automobiles, traffic congestion, and parking problems, while saving valuable gasoline. Near the city are many forest preserve areas, some within city limits, where bicyclists may enjoy this healthful, fun sport.

Sights like this are common today in national and state parks, forest preserves, and on country roads. (Photo courtesy The Schwinn Company.)

Wisconsin's 300 miles of bikeways lead through cities and along country roads where cyclists may enjoy pleasant scenery and clean air. Florida and California provide suntans, palm trees, glimpses of beautiful beaches and oceans, and many miles of cycleways. In New York City as many as 10,000 bicyclists enjoy the bikeways of Central

Park on a Sunday in good weather, but in 1879, the New York Board of Commissioners banned bicycles from Central Park. The League of American Wheelmen fought this decision in the courts for over eight years and finally won.

Probably the best-known manufacturer of quality bicycles in the USA is The Schwinn Bicycle Company, headquarted in Chicago. This company produces around 6,000 units per day—1.5 million per year. However, there are several companies in the country larger than Schwinn, including American Machine & Foundry, Columbia Manufacturing Co., Huffman, and Murray-Ohio. The world's largest bicycle manufacturer in terms of units is Murray-Ohio, producing some two and one-half million bicycles a year.

There are over 150 brands of bicycles sold in the U.S.A. Some of them are well-known, others are known only to a small segment of the cycling public—Azuki, AMF, Bianchi, Bottechia, Campagnola, Corsa, Columbia, Dawes, Detto-Pietro, Drake, Falcon, Fuji, Frejus, Garlatti, Gitane, Hudson, Huffy, Hubbard, Jeunet, Lambert, Legnano, La Pierre, Masi, Murray-Ohio, Mercier, Motobecane, Nishiki, Peugtot, Ranger, Raleigh, Ross, Sekine, Schwinn, Suntour, Stronglight, Triumph.

These are but a few of the many brand names now available in bicycle, department, discount and sporting goods stores across the country. Addresses of these and other manufacturers may be obtained from the Bicycle Institute of America Inc., 122 E. 42nd St., New York, NY 10017.

The Bicycle Duet

Back in the earlier days of bicycling, tandem bicycles became very popular—the bicycle built for two was even immortalized in a popular song. There was something very romantic in those days, about two young people riding the same bicycle. Usually the man took the front seat, steered, did most of the hard pedaling and was prepared to meet any obstacle head-on. His young ladyfriend, in her long skirt and sunhat tied prettily over her lavish curls with a colorful scarf or ribbons, pretended she was pedaling, but we know better. What she was doing was allowing the pedals to carry her feet in their high-buttoned shoes around while she coyly smiled at all the admiring young swains.

As part of the current nostalgia kick—which is really a rebellion against the computerized dehumanization and gadgetry of modern American life—the tandem bicycle is back. A California couple, in the summer of 1974, rode a tandem bike from the northernmost part of California to its most southern extreme and back again, to the accompaniment of nine flat tires, three accidents, and one incident of getting stuck in fresh cement.

Tandem bicycles are available in most established bicycle shops

Double your fun by sharing a tandem bicycle with an attractive friend.
(Photo courtesy The Schwinn Company.)

and in some department stores. Provided you both agree on where you are going, the teamwork that goes into riding a tandem bicycle is said by tandem bike manufacturers to promote "togetherness." It is, in my view, twice as much fun as riding singly. Try it—you'll probably like it.

Free-Wheeling Three Wheelers

Three-wheeled cycles, known as tricycles, are growing in popularity and are losing their former reputation as the exclusive property of little old ladies in senior citizens' developments. These units offer certain advantages not provided by the standard bicycle. Because they are larger and can accommodate a good-sized luggage holder behind the seat across the two rear wheels, they can carry more freight, picnic paraphernalia, text books, artist's materials, etc. Also, with a tricycle you don't have to worry about balance or maintaining forward motion . . . you can stop and not lose your seat. They are more stable in motion and with three-speed gears are easy to pedal even on moderate hills. Most cycle shops carry tricycles or will order one for you.

Tricycles are useful and easy to ride. (Photo courtesy The Schwinn Company.)

Some of the optional equipment currently available for bicycles and tricycles includes luggage and book holders for the rear, rear wheel saddle bags, front basket, bells, horns (manual or battery), transistor radios, rear-view mirrors, carriers for water bottles and food, pumps (foot and hand), speedometers, odometers, front and rear lamps (battery or generator operated), reflectors, safety flags, locks and chains, tire and tube repair kits, cycle covers, and more. While a transistor radio can be a pleasant accompaniment when cycling in the park or the country, it is not recommended in city traffic where the fullest concentration and attention to traffic are of the utmost importance.

Be A Safe Cyclist

A few words about safety. In order to avoid discriminatory legislation and to encourage the continued development of bikeways in towns and cities across the country, cyclists must show a reasonable sense of responsibility, from small children on up to senior citizens. As a bicyclist, you are the operator of a road vehicle; therefore, you must follow and obey the rules of the road. If you don't, you can be ticketed, taken to court and fined, just like a motorist. Also, you can create a hazard to other users of the road and increase your chances of being involved in an accident that can cause you personal injury—in extreme cases, death. Here are eight basic Rules of the Road published by the Bicycle Institute of America:

1. Always ride on the right-hand side of the road, with traffic, as close as possible to the curb. In larger cities, on one-way streets, cyclists are sometimes permitted to travel in the left-hand lane. I prefer to stay clear of buses, trucks and other vehicles that normally use the right-hand lane. While some authorities recommend staying behind buses in city traffic for a measure of protection from other traffic, I don't.
2. Always ride single-file when cycling with others.
3. Obey all traffic signals—traffic lights, stop signs, cautionary signs, one-way street signs, traffic officer's signals, signals of school crossing guards, construction zone guards, etc.
4. Cross an intersection before making a left-hand turn and walk your bicycle across if necessary. Look back over your shoulder frequently; be alert when passing driveways, shopping center parking lots, school yards, etc.
5. Yield to cars and pedestrians. Don't try to "beat the other guy;" you may wind up "deadbeat."
6. Always use hand signals to indicate turns and a stop.
7. When riding after dark, you just have a light on the front of your bicycle and a light or a reflector in the rear. American-made bicycles, identified with a BMA/6 decal, are factory-equipped with large rear reflectors, reflectorized pedals and other reflective devices. Wear light-colored clothing; for added safety, apply reflective tape to your poncho, backs of shoes, hat, etc.
8. Never weave in and out of traffic and never carry a passenger or a large load that may interfere with the safe operation of your bicycle, such as large baskets, packs, shopping bags, etc.

The Schwinn Bicycle Company issues a set of twelve Bicycle Safety Rules of the Road which contains, in addition to the rules listed above, the following:
Watch out for drain grates, soft shoulders, deep puddles and other road hazards. Watch out for car doors being opened and for cars pulling from a parked position into the traffic. NEVER hitch a ride by holding onto the back of a vehicle of any kind. Drive a safe bicycle—have it regularly inspected and adjusted to keep it in good and safe condition. Drive defensively—always watch out for the other rider or driver who may not have as much road sense as you have.
Schwinn also adds these common sense tips to help you enjoy using your bicycle in safety: Carry an inexpensive tube/tire repair kit and know how to use it. If you are going on a fairly long trip, carry the kit and a spare tube. Keep tires inflated to the correct, recommended pressure—always carry a pressure gauge with you.
A bell or horn or other sounding device is mandatory for all bicycles in all states. Many different types are on the market—the louder the better. A rear-view mirror is helpful in traffic; mirrors are inexpensive and easily mounted.
To help reduce chances of having your cycle stolen, always lock it up when you are leaving it even for a moment of two. Use a case-hardened chain and a strong padlock—you can get them at all cycle shops, at hardware stores, etc. It is best to pass the chain through both wheels and then around some immovable object such as a light pole or iron railing. Lock your bicycle up in a place where there are lots of people and traffic. Don't lock it up and leave it in an alley or quiet side street. Never leave it outside at night, even locked. You can purchase an insurance policy or a rider to a property owner's policy—usually about $10 - $15 a year for a bicycle costing around $100 and higher for more expensive bikes. One company insuring bicycles is the National Bicycle Insurance Brokers, PO Box 7954, Rincon Annex, San Francisco, CA 94120.

Two-Wheeled Records

Man's inherent desire to compete with his fellows is strongly evident in the sport of bicycling. According to the *Guinness Book of World Records*, the first recorded cycle race took place in 1888 over a 1.24 mile course. The publication gives the highest speed ever attained on a bicycle as just over 127 miles per hour by a Frenchman, Jose Meifrett, in July 1972. He used a 275-inch gear and rode behind a windshield mounted on a racing car. Bicycling has been part of the Olympic competitions since 1896. Marcus Hurley, an American cyclist, won four gold medals in 1904, a feat that has never since been equaled.

However, even Olympic races seem tame compared to the World duration record set, according to Guinness, in 1964 by Syed Muhammed Nawab of India. He cycled on a track for 168 hours, or seven days, continuously. An Englishman, Ray Reece, circumnavigated the globe by bicycle—13,000 miles in 143 days. In August, 1973, a Dr. Allan V. Abbott of California, is reported to have ridden a bicycle at 138.674 mph.

The vast majority of people who take up bicycling will never set any records, but will enjoy the convenience, economy, healthful exercise, companionship and pleasure that riding a bicycle can give.

Here are a few more addresses you may find useful as a bicycling member of the public:

American Youth Hostels, 20 W. 17th St., New York, NY. They organize US and foreign tours and give assistance to groups of cyclists wishing to form a hostel chapter or club.

The International Bicycle Touring Society, 846 Prospect St., La Jolla, CA 92037. This group organizes long-distance tours in the USA.

Amateur Bicycle League, 137 Brunswick Rd., Cedar Grove, NJ 07009. This group's activities are in the area of competitive and Olympic competition.

U.S. Bicycle Polo Association, PO Box 565, FDR Station, New York, NY 10022. They will give you information about polo games played on bicycles.

American Unicycling Society, c/o Wm. Jenack, 67 Lion Ln., Westbury, NY—for information pertaining to unicycling.

The Wheelmen, c/o Robt. E. McNair, 32 Dartmouth Circle, Swathmore, PA 19081—for information about antique bicycles and bygone era bicycling.

Books about Bicycling, PO Box 208, Nevada City, CA 95959, for a folder listing bicycle publications.

You can contact any city or town's department of recreation or bureau of streets for information about bicycle routes.

Books On Cycling

The Complete Book of Bicycling, by Eugene A. Sloane, published by Simon and Schuster and available in bookshops everywhere, is the modern cyclist's "bible". It covers buying a bicycle of the proper size and fit, presents concise riding instruction, discusses the health aspects, gets deeply into the subject of gears, covers bicycle touring, racing, etc., care of the bicycle, and many other subjects of interest to the serious cyclist.

DeLong's Guide To Bicycles and Bicycling—The Art and Science, by Fred Delong, published by Chilton Book Co., Radnor, PA. A definitive publication authored by an acknowledged bicycle authority.

Anybody's Bike Book, by Tom Cuthbertson, published by Ten Speed

Press, is essentially a maintenance and repair guide. But it is so explicit and well-written that it is an interesting book to read even if you don't own a bicycle.

The Great Escape is an anthology of fun things to do and contains several interesting articles on bicyling. The book may be purchased on newsstands and in bookshops. Address is The Great Escape, 150 Shoreline Highway, Mill Valley, CA 94941.

Cycling Magazines

Bicycle Spokesman, published bi-monthly April through December, by Hub Publishing Co., Palatine, Illinois 60067, is a family magazine for those interested in riding. Contains features on touring, camping, safety, new equipment available, technical information, etc.

Bicycling! published monthly by Capital Management Publications, San Rafael, CA 94903. Features unusual bicycle adventures, family cycle trips, health, bicycle commuting, bicycle history, etc.

Bike World, published bi-monthly by World Publications, Mountain View, CA 94040. Covers maintenance, tours, races, personalities, equipment, events, etc.

You Don't Have To Be Evel Knievel

If you want to save a lot of money over your regular transportation costs, get wherever you want to go when you want, and have unlimited fun all at the same time, you're ready for your first motorcycle. You are also ready to join more than fifteen million responsible Americans who ride motorcycles, and fifteen million people can't all be wrong.

Pretty motorcyclist finds a public park an ideal place to clean up her machine. (Photo courtesy Yamaha.)

First lets look at the economical aspects of motorcycling. Almost all, except for a few large, specially equipped bikes, cost considerably less to buy than a car—new or used. Then there's the matter of

operating costs . . . there really isn't any comparison. A 125cc motorcycle can give you seventy-five miles to the gallon or more at forty
m.p.h., whereas the average American passenger car delivers less
than fifteen m.p.g. Motorcycle repairs generally cost considerably
less than repairs on most automobiles. Parking a motorcycle is
usually easier and cheaper than parking a car; many parking garages
give motorcycles a lower rate because they take up less room than
cars.

In a one-car garage there is almost always room for a motorcycle
too, and a great many motorcyclists who have no garages, push their
bikes onto patios for the night or cover them, lock them and leave them
in their driveways, on their front lawns or in the backyard.

On most road surfaces and under all but the very worst weather conditions, a motorcycle is more maneuverable than the average car.

Aside from pocket-book considerations, there is the unique enjoyment of riding in the open, with the breeze blowing in your face—the
feeling that you are part of the outdoors, of the sky, the wind, the land-
scape. There's the feeling of speed and power controlled by your own
hands and feet . . . the feeling that your body is part of the machine,
that the machine is part of you. And there's the competition aspect—
far more competitive events are staged for motorcycle owners than for
car owners. Whatever your tastes, you can compete on a motorcycle
. . . from motocross (cross country racing) to road racing, from enduro
(endurance racing) to hill climbing and dirt racing.

Yet, owning and driving a motorcycle has certain disadvantages,
like anything else. For one thing, in the event you hit a car, truck, wall
or other unmovable object, there's nothing between you and Kingdom
Come except your safety helmet. So you'd better wear one at all times,
whether or not it is a law in your state.

On your motorcycle, you can carry only one passenger, unlike the
family car into which you can cram your wife, kids, dog, and miscel-
lany. So if you really want to figure out the economics of motorcycle
ownership you must take the mileage a motorcycle is likely to give for
one or two people and compare that with the mileage a car gives for the
number of people it carries. In other words, say your motorcycle gives
you 60 m.p.g. with yourself and one passenger (two people), you must
compare this with the mileage a family car would produce (perhaps 14
m.p.g.) with five occupants. Don't bother figuring it out—you're still
way ahead on the motorcycle, but remember this is with two people at
most. Similarly, to obtain a true comparison, you would have to
consider purchase price, repair costs, maintenance, etc., divided
among all members of the family. So if economics are your chief moti-
vation for purchasing a motorcycle, these are things to consider seriously. If you are by yourself, or there's just you and she, vice versa, or
your brother, or pal, then from the money-saving point of view you

shouldn't hesitate for a minute—get to your nearest motorcycle dealer right away.

Let's look at another of the negatives . . . unless you live in a geographical area where the weather is fair almost all the time, you have to consider the weeks or even months when you just won't use your motorcycle much. This is money tied up, sitting in your garage. Another point is that to be a safe, effective motorcycle rider you need to be better at it than the average car driver is at handling his vehicle. You need to pay stricter attention when you're on the road, especially in heavy traffic—your eyes must not wander to the scenery, the girl or guy on the corner, etc.

On a motorcycle you are less visible to other road users than if you were driving a car. There are fewer metal surfaces to reflect light to catch another driver's eye and, of course, you on your bike are a lot smaller than the driver in the station wagon or other vehicle. You have only to look at the accident statistics to realize that accidents involving motorcycles are rising at an alarming rate. The answer to this problem lies with the motorcyclist. What are needed are better initial instruction and a more responsible approach to riding on the part of the motorcyclist. Your life is in your own hands; guard it well.

How to Ride a Motorcycle

There are several ways of learning to ride a motorcycle. The hardest, least safe and least effective of all methods is to teach yourself how to do it. How can you teach yourself how to do it when you don't know how in the first place? If you are teaching yourself, who stops you when you're doing something wrong? Who corrects you? Who encourages you when you do it right? No one, that's who. And that's why this is not a good way to learn.

The best way is through a proper course of instruction, conducted by a competent instructor. By far the best motorcycle riding courses are conducted by the Motorcycle Safety Foundation, Inc., 6755 Elk Ridge Landing Road, Linthicum, MA 21090 which is associated with the Motorcycle Industry Council, Inc. The council's main office is at Suite 101, 4100 Birch St., Newport Beach, CA. Contact your State's Department of Education or local high schools or other community groups concerned with motorcycle safety.

A great many high schools and colleges are either now offering the foundation's excellent course or have plans to do so. If you send $2.50 to the foundation, you will receive a fully illustrated 64-page Beginning Rider Course book and a Student Workbook. These are publications you can study at home and then attend a class with at least a fair knowledge of the subject.

Learning to ride a motorcycle is in a great many ways like learning to fly a small airplane—quite a bit of classroom instruction is necessary

Britisher Gordon Farley, member of Suzuki's professional racing and trials team, gives a rough-riding demonstration. (Photo courtesy Suzuki.)

before you get behind those controls. Some motorcycle dealers are offering the Foundation's Rider Course. It's a good idea to check around before you make other arrangements.

A second way of learning to ride a motorcycle is through a manufacturer's instruction program. Yamaha International Corporation's *Learn To Ride Safety Program* is outstanding in thoroughness and effectiveness. Motor vehicle departments in most states look with great favor upon carefully developed and conducted courses like these.

A third way of getting some riding instruction is from the dealer where you purchase your bike. Most dealers have experienced motorcyclists on their staffs. In a great many cases you will find ex-champions and former professional riders either operating or working at motorcycle dealerships. Usually, if you buy a motorcycle from a recognized, responsible dealer, they will give you free riding instruction as well as pre-riding check-out.

Going down the line, a fourth way of learning to ride your bike is to have a friend who rides teach you. However, he may be a good experienced rider himself, but is he a good communicator and effective teacher? But in any case, this is better than trying to teach yourself without any instruction.

Know The Law

Most motorcycle enthusiasts know that they are required by law to wear a safety helmet when riding a motorcycle on public roads in most states. All motorcyclists with intelligence wear one whether it is re-

Motocross champion Pierre Karsmakers demonstrates proper cornering technique at Yamaha Dirt Days conducted in Tamp-St. Petersburg area, Florida (Photo courtesy Yamaha.)

quired or not. As this book goes to press, the only states where helmets are *not* legally required are California, Illinois and Iowa. Only ten states do not presently require special driver licenses for motorcyclists. They are Alabama, Arkansas, Florida, Idaho, Indiana, Mississippi, Montana, North Carolina, Oklahoma, and West Virginia.

Did you know that in Arkansas you are required by law to keep your headlights on in daylight when riding a motorcycle? And Arkansas isn't the only state with this law—there's Florida, Georgia, Illinois, Indiana, Montana, New Mexico, North Carolina, Oregon, Rhode

Island, Wisconsin, and Wyoming. Some other laws you should check so that you don't find yourself in violation as soon as you start enjoying your new bike apply to the wearing of eye protectors (goggles or face shields), proper seat and foot rests for a passenger, the requirement for rearview mirrors, periodic state safety inspections and others.

In some states riding two abreast is illegal. Some roads are closed to motorcycles of all kinds and some ban motorcycles of less than a certain cubic centimeter displacement or below a given horsepower. Reflective material on the bike and on the riders' helmets is required in some states, so you can be quite legal in one state and in violation as soon as you cross the state line. If you take an approved course, such as that offered by the Motorcycle Safety Foundation, you will learn these laws for your own protection.

Know Your Machine

To be a safe, skilled motorcyclist, you must have a thorough knowledge of your motorcycle and of motorcycles in general. The machine has limitations, idiosyncracies, special features. You must learn all of them. This bike becomes almost a part of you and you of it so know its anatomy and physiology. Find out, in other words, exactly what makes it tick. And what may make it not tick. If there seems to be undue vibration or wobble, find out why. Is it you or the machine? Whichever it is, it must be corrected.

Make sure your motorcycle is properly equipped, has all the necessary safety devices on it. Remember, every time you get on that machine you are virtually laying your life on the line.

Learn where every control is located so that you can operate it almost by instinct without looking, feeling, fumbling. And be sure you know what each control does and how it does it. These things are far more important in riding a motorcycle than they are in driving a car; this is one of motorcycling's similarities to flying.

Let's look at a typical motorcycle. Your machine is equipped with hand and foot controls on both sides. The throttle is controlled by the right handlebar grip. Turning it supplies more or less gasoline to your engine to increase or decrease its speed. Twisting the throttle toward you pours it on, twisting it away from you cuts it down. Your left handlebar grip is just that and nothing more. But located just above or below the left grip is the clutch lever. The clutch is disengaged by squeezing this lever toward the handlebar grip. This disengages the drive to the rear wheel and enables you to change gears. After changing, you smoothly release the clutch lever and the clutch engages.

The turn-signal light switch is usually on the left handlebar. Just in front of the left handlebar grip is the horn button. Your rearview mirror should be mounted just ahead of the horn control. The righthand rear-view mirror is in a corresponding position on the right handlebar ahead of the "kill' switch—a button just in front of the grip which immediately stops your engine in emergencies.

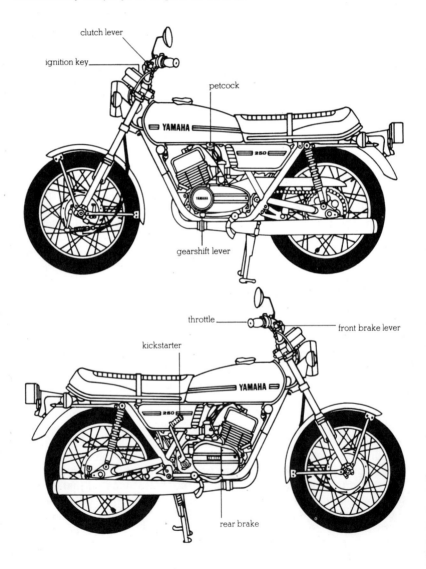

Mounted in front of your handlebars, in the center, are your tachometer and speedometer and just in front of them are your left and right front turn signal lights. Your headlight is in the center, directly over your front fork.

Mounted just above your right handlebar grip is a vitally important control—your front wheel brake lever. It is operated by squeezing the lever toward the grip.

Headlight and taillight switches may be located on the handlebars, on the headlight housing or combined with the ignition switch.

Working back along your machine there's the gasoline tank with its filler cap on top. Just about directly beneath the gas filler cap and underneath the left side of your tank is the ignition switch (sometimes it is located near the center of the handlebars). The choke control is usually mounted directly on the carburetor to the front of the engine, or it may be mounted on the handlebars, depending on manufacture and type of bike. You have to use the choke to start the engine when the engine is cold. As it warms up you must remember to return the choke control to it's OFF position.

On most bikes the gear change lever is a pedal on the left side of the machine in front of the foot rest. You operate the gear change lever with the toe part of the left boot. There are usually four or five gears and a NEUTRAL position.

Opposite your gear change lever on the right side of your bike is the rear wheel brake pedal. You normally use both this rear foot-operated brake and the front hand-operated brake simultaneously to bring your motorcycle to complete, safe stop.

Behind the foot brake is the right foot rest and to the rear of the foot rest is the kick starter (unless your bike has an electric start button on the handlebars). This pedal usually folds back up when not in use. To operate the kick starter, after turning on your ignition switch, making sure your bike is in neutral, apply the choke, straddle your machine and using a little muscle power, stamp the pedal all the way down to the end of its stroke. After starting, fold the kick pedal in again. again.

Continuing toward the rear of your machine you will find two more pedals one on either side. These are foot rests for your passenger. At the rear, on either side of the rear fender are your rear turn signal lights and on the extreme end of your rear fender are your tail light and brake light.

These are typical motorcycle controls in their most common locations. Additional equipment and accessories may necessitate additional controls, and as we have already mentioned, the positions of the controls do vary slightly with different makes and models.

Life Protection Equipment

At the age of 23, Carl, a young neighbor of mine—who had been riding motorcycles for over five years—got a phone call one evening from his buddy in another town a few miles away. His friend was having mechanical trouble with his new motorcycle. Carl hopped on his motorcycle and went off to aid his friend. He never got there. He was carried unconscious on a stretcher into the emergency ward of the hospital. Every day of his life since then, Carl has sat in a wheelchair, staring into space—he is little more than a vegetable. His young life has just been wasted away. He and his family would be better off if he had killed himself that night when he forgot, for once, to put his safety helmet on before going to aid his buddy.

Please don't do it—don't even get on your bike without your helmet. Ever. Our sport needs every enthusiast it has and we can't afford to lose you. And you don't want to end up like Carl. Besides, when people see you on your bike wearing your safety helmet they think—"Now there's a REAL motorcyclist!" They do, take my word for it! Modern motorcycle helmets are comfortable, and they give you a high-performance, experienced look. And they keep your hair in place. Break an arm or leg if you have to, but for God's sake don't smash up your brain—it cannot be set in plaster to heal.

If you have more than one pair of eyes then it's O.K., I guess, for you to ride your motorcycle without protective goggles or a face shield. Should you be limited to just one pair, however, use one or both of the two protection devices mentioned, in addition to your windshield. Some of the following things can blind you for life—sand, road chemicals, flying rocks, insects, mud, dust, bright sunlight, snow, hail, oil from a vehicle ahead of you, and all kinds of other junk.

Are you the type person who enjoys skinned knuckles and squashed fingers? If not, then good, strong leather gloves are for you. Not stiff gloves—your fingers must be flexible inside them.

Here's why you need them. First, they improve your grip; second, they keep your hands warm; third, they protect your hands from the same flying debris that goggles and face shield keep off your face; fourth, if you should take a spill, your gloves will save your skin being scraped off by gravel or hardtop. If you're a girl, they also help protect your nail polish.

Protect your feet, too, with good, leather, lace-up boots or high boots that at least cover your ankles. Boots do the same for your feet that gloves do for your hands.

There's a part of you between your helmet and your boots that should also be protected—your body. Leather clothing, preferably in bright colors is the next best thing to a suit of chain mail armor (and you can't hardly get that no more!). If you are thrown off your bike and slide along the road, which is quite a common occurrence, the leather will protect you from cuts and bruises.

Riding the Motorcycle

The first thing to learn, obviously, is how to mount and sit your machine. Your instructor will help you and show you how to start by standing on the left side of your cycle and holding both handlebars firmly. Then he'll tell you to lean the machine toward you slightly, raise your right leg over the saddle and assume a half-standing/half-sitting position. Next thing he will surely tell you to do is adjust both rearview mirrors. When you've done this a few times you'll have no trouble mounting.

Next step is to turn the fuel valve to ON, make sure your gear lever is in NEUTRAL and your "kill" switch ON. Use the choke if the engine is cold, and then open the throttle just a little. Keep your cycle leaning slightly to the left, turn on your ignition switch and stamp down on the kick starter (or press the electric start button). When the engine starts, close the throttle and let it warm up. Now disengage your clutch with the lever at your left hand and put it into first gear. Release the clutch lever smoothly and you're on your way.

The Rupp Centaur single-seat tri-wheeler can be used as a street bike or for off-road riding. (Photo courtesy Rupp.)

146   DuPre

Here's how to stop. First, put the gear lever into the NEUTRAL position. Second, turn the ignition key off and then shift into first gear to help stop your bike from rolling. Dismount and place your bike on its kickstand. Turn the gas supply valve OFF. Remove your ignition key, turn the front wheel to one side and turn the key in the fork or steering lock. When parking, don't park close to a car if you can avoid it. The car driver may not see your bike behind him, and he may back up before pulling out.

When riding, obey all traffic laws and remember you and your motorcycle constitute a vehicle on the road just as a car does. You are not exempted from any laws. You may not ride between lanes of traffic, cut in and out without warning, ride on the shoulder, ride the center line, ride too close to the vehicle ahead of you, ride faster than the legal speed limit, etc.

Everything else is a question of practice and of reading instructional books and magazine articles and learning from more qualified and experienced drivers, particularly from authorized instructors.

The following are some of the better known motorcycles now available in the U.S.A.:
Benelli, BMW, BSA, Bultaco, Can-Am, Ducati, Exalter (three-wheeler), Explorer, Harley-Davidson, Hodaka, Honda, Husqvarna, Indian, Kawasaki, Maico, Laverda, Montesa, Moto Guzzi, Norton, Penton, Ossa, Rokon, Rupp (Centaur 3-wheeler), Suzuki, Triumph, Tri-Sport.

Reading Material

Buyers' and Riders' Guide to Motorcycles, by Al Griffin, published by Henry Regnery Co., Chicago, IL.

The Great Escape contains several good articles on various aspects of motorcycling. Published by Bantam Book Inc., NY.

Yamaha Horizons, bi-monthly magazine published for Yamaha owners by Yamaha International Corporation, PO Box 6600, Buena Park, CA 90620. Sample copy free.

AMA News, published by American Motorcycle Association, Westerville, OH 43081.

The following periodicals are usually available on most newsstands:
Dirt Bike Magazine, Motorcyclist, Popular Cycling, Cycle News, Cycle Guide, Big Bike Magazine, Cycle Magazine, Illinois Cycle News (available only in Illinois; publisher Herzberg & Kramer Inc., Niles, Illinois.)

You Really 'Auto' Learn To Drive

The best way to learn to drive an automobile is with a reputable driving school or a high school driving course. Your relatives and friends may be experienced, good drivers, but are they expert teachers? Driving schools usually employ people who are not only good, professional drivers, but who also are trained to teach you. Many marriages have been imperiled through angry words exchanged while one partner was trying to teach the other how to drive. There actually have been divorce petitions based on differences which have arisen as a result of a "domestic driving course." Another disadvantage of having a non-professional driving teacher is that you will probably learn his or her bad driving habits.

So don't take a chance. Learn to drive with a qualified, professional instructor. This chapter is not intended as a driving course; it merely presents basic theoretical information that can be of value to you when you start your driving course. At least you will have some idea of what the driving instructor is talking about in advance and an idea of the functions of the driving controls.

Operating The "Gate"

Most people these days learn to drive on a car with automatic transmission, since the majority of cars built in the USA today are so equipped. But you never know when you may be called upon to drive a car with standard transmission.

As the terminology suggests, manual transmissions are operated by hand, automatic transmissions work automatically. To understand the operation of a manual transmission automobile, we must look at the controls. The gear lever is mounted on the steering column, just below the steering wheel. Sometimes it is mounted on the floor (especially in sports cars). It is always operated by the right hand (except in English-built cars intended for domestic use). The gear lever is connected by means of shafts to the gears in the gear box. It does the same kind of thing as a three-speed gear on a bicycle; it changes the transmission's gear ratio and also the engine speed. The gears transmit driving power from the engine to the wheels. The main reason we need gears or a transmission is that it takes more power to move a vehicle from a standstill than it does to keep it moving once it has attained normal running speed. The ground offers resistance to the wheels of your car, and this resistance must be lessened in order to move the vehicle. When the car is moving there is still some resistance presented by the ground, called "rolling resistance." When a car's engine is turned off and the gears are disengaged while on level ground, rolling resistance will eventually cause the vehicle to come to a stop, even if you do not apply the brakes. In addition, there is more rolling resistance when traveling uphill than when traveling downhill. These are the reasons why we have various gears.

In a car with manual transmission there are three foot pedals—the accelerator or gas pedal on the right, the foot brake in the center and the clutch pedal on the left. Some cars have a fourth pedal at the extreme left. This operates the emergency brake (many cars have hand levers to control this brake). The right foot operates the accelerator and the brake; the left foot operates the clutch.

Obviously, the gas pedal enables you to give the engine more gas so that it will run faster and the foot brake impedes the wheels to slow you down and stop you. But the clutch does not "clutch" anything. In fact it releases something—the gears. Depressing the clutch is therefore called "de-clutching." When you depress the clutch pedal the drivetrain is disconnected so that the engine is not powering the wheels. To illustrate this point, let's say while the car is standing still you depress the clutch pedal and the gas pedal, the engine will roar and produce a lot of noise and exhaust fumes, but the car will not move because the drivetrain from the engine to the gears has been disconnected. If the gears are not turning, then the drive shaft from the gear box to the rear wheels is not turning. Which means the rear wheels are not turning and the car is not moving.

Now that we understand what the clutch does, the next question to be answered is, why? If there was no clutch, the second you started the engine the car would lunge forward since the engine turns the driveshaft through the gear box to the rear wheels. Another thing that would happen if you had no clutch would be that it would be almost impossible to change gears—to get two gears to mesh into each other while they are spinning at a high rate of speed.

Let us now consider the gear lever—most cars have three forward speeds or gears and a reverse gear. Some—especially sports cars and trucks—have four forward gears and a reverse. The way the gear lever operates is the same on most cars—domestic and foreign, sports cars, sedans, and pickup trucks. And the positions for the gear lever for the forward gears are usually the same. Consider the floor-mounted gear lever. It has four or five positions, depending on whether the car has three forward speeds or four forward speeds. The gear positions are called collectively the "gate." In a four-forward-speed gearbox the forward gear pattern is in the shape of a letter H (see illustration). The horizontal bar between the two vertical bars of the H is the neutral zone—when the gear lever is in this position, the car is in "neutral." None of the gears is engaged. The three-speed gearbox (more common in conventional standard-shift cars) usually has the first gear in the position of the second gear on a four-speed gear box, the second gear in the third position and the third gear in the fourth position. Reverse gear is outside the H (see illustration) and is reached by pressing down on the gear lever and then pushing it into the reverse position. This is a safety precaution to prevent you from accidentally slipping the car into reverse when putting it into first gear.

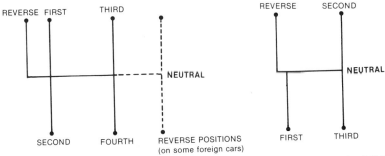

REVERSE FIRST   THIRD

NEUTRAL

SECOND   FOURTH   REVERSE POSITIONS
                        (on some foreign cars)

TYPICAL FOUR-SPEED GEAR SHIFT

REVERSE   SECOND

NEUTRAL

FIRST   THIRD

TYPICAL THREE-SPEED GEAR SHIFT

• PARK
• **NEUTRAL**
• DRIVE
• LOW
• REVERSE

P   N   D   L   R

COMMON POSITIONS OFFERED
BY AUTOMATIC TRANSMISSION

• PARK
• **NEUTRAL**
• REVERSE
• DRIVE
• LOW

P   N   R   D   L

ALTERNATE POSITIONING
ON SOME CARS

Get It Into Gear and Move It

Now that we have some idea of what the clutch and gear lever do and why, let us cover the basic procedure for starting the car, moving off and driving along.

Sit behind the wheel for a moment or two and get the feel of it. Check your seat adjustment and position the seat so that your feet can comfortably depress the control pedals. The left foot must be able to depress the clutch pedal all the way to the floor. Next thing to check is visibility. Remove anything—packages, for sale signs, stuffed or live animals or other obstructions that might restrict your visibility from the dash, rear shelf, rear or side windows or windshield. Next check your rear-view mirror and adjust it so that you have a clear view at the road and traffic behind you. Make sure that windshield and windows are clean.
clean.

Before doing anything else, securely fasten your seat belt. Take a couple of deep breaths and feel yourself alert but quite relaxed. Now depress the clutch pedal and "feel" the gear lever into the neutral position. It should move freely from left to right.

The first step in the actual driving procedure is to switch on the ignition by turning the key, keeping the clutch fully depressed with the left foot. A red light should appear on the dashboard, which merely indicates that the ignition is on.

Turning the key further to the right—clockwise—operates the starter; the engine kicks over and, hopefully, starts. Use the gas pedal, give the engine just enough gas to keep it running and prevent stalling. Release the handbrake.

Now look carefully in all directions to make certain that the coast is absolutely clear—if you hit someone on your first time out, it can be discouraging. Especially to the one whom you have hit. Completely clear? Good.
gear position. The car will still not move forward, however, because you have disconnected the engine from the rear wheels by holding the clutch pedal down. Now you *slowly* and *smoothly* let out the clutch pedal while simultaneously applying just enough gas to allow the car to crawl slowly forward. Again, making sure the way is absolutely clear, turn the steering wheel if necessary to get your car clear of the curb or edge of your driveway or whatever, and gradually, smoothly apply more gas until you are moving along at maybe ten miles an your and change into second (recommended gear-changing speeds vary with different types of automobiles). As you gather speed in second gear, depress the clutch pedal and change to third, then fourth, if you have a four-forward speed gearbox), and away you go.

Look Ma, No Clutch

A vehicle with automatic transmission has no clutch and no gear change lever as such. Instead it has a "gear selection lever" (or in some cases push buttons) offering (usually) five positions—PARK, NEUTRAL, DRIVE, LOW and REVERSE. There is no "gate"—the positions are all in a single line. The PARK position is used only when the car is stationary; NEUTRAL for idling; DRIVE is used for normal driving; LOW provides an extra low gear for very steep hills, for use in rough terrain, soft sand, snow, etc. This gear is also helpful when crawling in heavy traffic for protracted periods since in the lower gear the engine is running faster, thus circulating coolant faster and receiving greater cooling power from the radiator fan. Except in these circumstances, low gear should not be used; all your driving is done in the DRIVE position. REVERSE, of course, is used exclusively for backing up.

Automatic transmissions use engine power and special transmission fluid to shift the gear for you. Since there is no clutch, when you are ready to move the car you move the gear selection lever from PARK to DRIVE (usually marked D), take your foot off the brake, and you are moving foward in low gear. As you gather speed, your car changes gear automatically into high (DRIVE or D). When you need extra power for passing or when driving uphill, you depress the gas pedal farther and change automatically into the lower gear—you do not have to touch the gear selection lever.

However, should you need the "extra low" gear marked LOW or L, you must move the lever to that position, but you must be either stopped or moving at low speed to do this in order to avoid possible transmission damage that can occur if you move the lever into LOW gear while traveling at a high rate of speed.

When you park, before switching the engine off, put the lever in the PARK or P position, apply your emergency brake (some are hand operated, some operate by foot pressure), then switch off and remove the key from the ignition.

A Chimp Can Steer a Car

Steering even the largest automobile and many trucks, equipped with modern, power-assisted steering, is as easy as stirring a pot of stew. Two and three-year old children steer pedal cars through shopping crowds with no trouble at all, and most of us have seen a circus chimpanzee steer a small car around the ring.

The difference between manual and power steering is that on a car with the manual type, the front wheels are turned entirely by your own hands on the steering wheel, through a system of gears, whereas so-called power steering uses engine power and a fluid to help your front wheels turn as you turn the steering wheel. Power steering does not steer the car any *more* than does manual steering—the only difference is that the power assistance enables you to turn the wheels with less effort. Reducing driving effort results in less fatigue and consequently more alert driving. Power steering is especially helpful when parallel parking, particularly in tight parking areas.

When power steering first appeared, many automobile drivers considered it dangerous. A letter to the editor of a Detroit newspaper complained that with power steering "you merely had to sneeze or blink your eyes and you were off the road." Power-assisted steering is now so commonplace that drivers have become completely accustomed to it, and most find it helpful and considerably easier than manual steering. Many drivers on the roads today have never driven a vehicle without it. Prior to the advent of power steering, it often required considerable muscular effort to steer the larger automobiles. Women, physically less strong in most cases than men, and many older people, found the new power-steering method a real boon. Manufacturers' research carried out in the first two years of power steering showed that women automobile buyers were overwhelmingly showing preference for this system. Soon most men specified power steering when buying a car, and today it is standard equipment on most American vehicles.

Parking

When parking a car on a downhill road, always turn your steering wheel so that the front of your front wheel tire nearest the curb is turned into the curb, which will act as an additional safety brake. Put the gear lever in the PARK position and set your handbrake. When parking on an uphill road, turn your steering wheel so that the rear of the front tire closest to the curb is turned into the curb. Apply parking brake and put gear lever in PARK.

Parallel parking gives even experienced drivers trouble at times. Yet it is by no means difficult once you have learned the basics. First, you must make sure your car will fit into the space in which you would like to park. It is surprising the number of drivers who attempt to park cars in spaces too short for their cars. Drive up to the parking spot you have selected until your front bumper seems to be in line with the rear bumper of the car ahead of the desired parking space. Now look back—get out of your car to do this if necessary, provided you are not causing a traffic hazard. Note where your rear bumper is. If it is within three feet of the front bumper of the car back of the empty space, then forget it—you are not going to get your car in there. Find a larger space. If there is at least three feet of space between your rear bumper and the front bumper of the car behind the space, you're O.K. Now

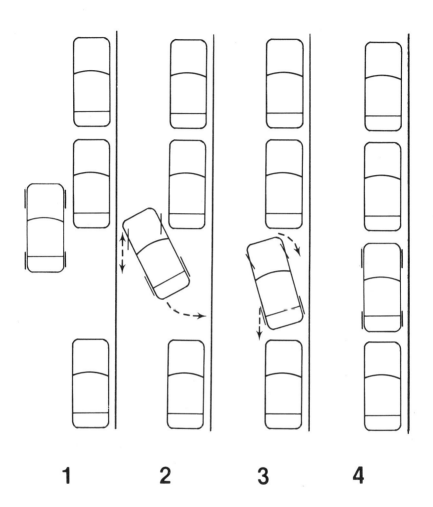

1   2   3   4

HOW TO PARK

draw forward until the front car's rear bumper is in line with the center of your car—in other words, you have drawn forward half a car's length. Now cut your steering wheel all the way and gradually ease back into the space. As soon as your front bumper is clear of the car ahead, cut your wheels the other way, then straighten up and continue back (and forward if necessary) until your car is centered in the space with no more than 18 inches between your car and the curb.

Power Brakes Are Safer

Broadly, when you depress the brake pedal, fluid is forced into cylinders at each wheel, causing brake "shoes" to grip the wheel drums or discs, thus slowing down and stopping the vehicle. Power brakes, like power steering, are acutally power-assisted. You still depress the brake pedal which results in the brake shoes gripping your wheel drums or discs, stopping your car. However, little effort is required with power brakes. Power brake fluid does much of the work for you. In effect, the power of your foot on the brake is multiplied by the hydraulic system. As with power steering, power-assisted brake systems had their detractors when they were first offered on American cars. Many drivers thought that if they pressed too hard on the brake pedal they would wind up smeared all over the hood, surrounded by broken windshield glass. This sentiment was voiced by many a car buyer, and a couple of magazine articles appeared expressing serious doubts about the true safety of power-assisted brakes. Today there can be no question that power brakes are indeed safer. They require less effort and consequently stop a vehicle in less time, in most cases, than do conventional brakes. A car sold with "full power" or "fully powered" has automatic transmission, power steering and power brakes. Additional automatic features that may be found on today's automobiles include electrically-operated windows, electric door locks, alarm and anti-theft systems, electric seat adjustments, automatic rear window defoggers and defrosters, etc.

Auto Talk

Driving a car or other vehicle can be exciting; it can be tedious and boring. It can be a pleasant relaxation; it can be great fun. It can be work—for the professional driver. It can be just about whatever you make of it, which will depend on many factors—your driving experience, the kind of person you are, the circumstances under which you are driving, the type of terrain over which you are driving, the scenery, whether or not you are tired, upset, underfed, overfed, . . . these and many more factors determine what you will get out of driving.

There are currently more than one hundred million passenger cars and over twenty-three million trucks and buses now on the roads (not all at once, fortunately). These figures do not include motorcycles but do include motorhomes (self-propelled camping vehicles) which are rapidly increasing in numbers—the total now in use approaches six-hundred thousand. Of almost four thousand different automobile brand names that have appeared on the market over the years, less than one hundred are sold today.

It is interesting to note that the very first American-made

This 1903 model was the first production Cadillac. (Photo courtesy Motor Vehicle Manufacturers Association of the United States.)

automobile ever sold was also this country's first gasoline-powered vehicle—a Duryea, built in 1896 by the Duryea Motor Wagon Company.

In 1912, production of US passenger cars reached one million. Sixty years later, by 1972, total production of all US motor vehicles had reached three-hundred million and 1973 saw the addition of another twelve and one-half million.

One of the country's smallest associations in terms of members but among the largest in terms of its impact on the national economy and on American life is the Motor Vehicle Manufacturers Association of the United States, Inc. The group's nine members are: American Motors Corporation; Checker Motors Corporation; Chrysler Corporation; Duplex Division of Warner & Swasey Company Inc.; Ford Motor Company, Inc.; General Motors Corporation; International Harvester Company Inc.; Walter Motor Truck Company, Inc., and White Motor Corporation.

The association compiles an impressive array of statistics and facts annually concerning motor vehicles. The MVMA has offices at 320 New Center Building, Detroit, MI 48202; 1909 K. Street, N.W., Washington, DC 20006, and 366 Madison Avenue, New York, NY 10017, plus six regional offices in other major cities.

regional offices in other major cities.

1975 Cadillac Coupe deVille (Photo courtesy Cadillac.)

Myth: "All Yankees Drive New Cars"

The idea seems prevalent that most Americans drive new cars; however, the average age of US passenger cars currently in use is a surprising 5.7 years. Only about thirty percent of the automobiles on the roads in this country are less than three years old. Twenty-five percent are eight years old or older and another twenty-five percent are three to four years old. At least twelve percent of all the cars in use in America are ten years old or older. The MVMA estimates that the average American-made passenger car sold new today has a life expectancy of 9.8 years, with reasonable care.

If your household does not own at least one car you are very much in the minority because eight out of ten US households own a car and one family in three owns two or more. For every ten new cars bought, Americans buy seventeen used automobiles.

Each year around eight million motor vehicles are "retired" from use. Of these, four out of every five enter a system of collection and recycling to emerge as raw material for the metals industries. The remaining twenty percent are abandoned by their owners on public and private property or end up in auto "graveyards," posing a serious disposal problem. For the welfare of us all, it is important that motor vehicles that have outlived their usefulness, be disposed of properly— i.e., taken to an automobile wrecking yard or metal reclamation center.

The Triple A—Your Own Club

Membership fees in the American Automobile Association's affiliated clubs are so low and services provided to its members are so valuable and numerous that it seems incredible that membership rosters are not larger than they are. One reason may be that a great many American automobile owners just do not understand the many advantages of belonging to the AAA clubs.

Founded in 1902, the Triple A is actually a federation of clubs for automobile owners, with close to 900 clubs and branches throughout the USA (including Hawaii and Alaska) and in Canada. The scope and operations of the AAA encompass a dual role—first, providing specialized services to more than sixteen million members and second, conducting public service activities on behalf of all motorists and all who travel this country's millions of miles of streets, roads, highways and tollways. It's a fully tax paying, non-profit organization all revenue goes toward serving its members and improving road travel conditions. AAA is currently leading the fight against legislation that would allow larger, heavier trucks on the highways. It continually works for improved roads and fair distribution of the taxes needed to support them. In 1973 US motorists paid over $18 billion in taxes, and 123 million drivers and operators licenses were in force.

Being a member of a Triple A Club has many advantages. One that most members take advantage of at some time is the emergency road service. Whether you break down on the highway or can't get your car started right in your own driveway, if you're a Triple A member you merely call the nearest of over twenty-four thousand service stations under contract to AAA. Need a booster start? Run out of gas? Locked your keys in the car? Got a flat and can't get your jack to work? The nearest AAA club, which you can find in the phone book or if your AAA Emergency Road Service Directory, will provide road service at no charge.

Of course, there are exceptions—the AAA service people will not do any major repairs free, nor install your snow tires or chains or spend more than half an hour trying to get you going. It is an emergency service and it alone is well worth your total membership fee for the year. Your AAA club also offers members many other valuable services. Each year AAA representatives inspect thousands of restaurants and accommodations. Many of the one-in-seven which meet AAA requirements display the "AAA-Approved" emblem. The club will assist you with hotel-motel reservations anywhere in the world; travel counselors will prepare a "Triptik" for you with specially marked maps and directions for your motor journeys. Campgrounds, points of interest, lists of lodgings—these and much more information are contained in various AAA publications available to members.

Emergency bail bonds, auto financing, insurance, overseas travel help, notary service, license plate service are some of the many benefits of AAA membership. To learn how to become a member, call your nearest AAA Club headquarters.

For The Record

Automobile competitions began in 1887 with a twenty-mile race from Paris to Versailles and back. Average speed realized by the winner, Georges Bouton (driving a steam quadricycle), was 22.16 mph. This speed has since been slightly improved upon—notably by the American Gary Gabelich who in October, 1970 streaked somewhat more than 627 mph in a rocket-engined vehicle powered by liquid natural gas/hydrogen peroxide developing a maximum static thrust of twenty-two thousand pounds. (See *Guinnes Book of World Records*).

The fastest road race in the world is the one thousand-kilometer sports car event held annually in Belgium—the record time to date is 4 hours, 1 minute, 9.7 seconds for an average speed of 154.765 mph, (a record held by Pedro Rodrigues, Mexico and Jackie Oliver, Great Britain, driving a flat-12 Porche 917K).

Stock car races are held on raceways in many cities, large and small, across the country. Many top racing drivers developed much of their driving skills on the stock car circuits. Stock and sports car rallies and road races are held throughout America and in many foreign countries, for both professional and amateur drivers. Serious young automobile enthusiasts can win fame and fortune in various types of automobile competition. But most people who learn to drive are content to experience the enjoyment and convenience that comes with owning and driving any kind of automotive vehicle.

Publications

Mankind On The Move by Christy Borth. History of roads and the never-ending interplay between roads and vehicles down through the centuries. Published by the Automotive Safety Foundation, Washington, D.C.

The Road and The Car In American Life by John B. Rae. A survey and analysis of the influence of motorized highway transportation on American social and economic life. The road and the auto as an integrated transportation mode. Published by the MIT Press, Cambridge, Massachusetts.

Automobiles of America prepared by Ralph Buick for the Motor Vehicle Manufacturers Association of the United States Inc., published by

Wayne State University Press, Detroit, Michigan. Traces development and production of US passenger cars from 1893 to 1974 with photographs and text.

Historic Motor Racing by Anthony Pritchard, published by Weidenfeld and Nicholson, London, Enland. Traces history and development of automobile racing.

What's It Like Out There? by Mario Andretti and Bob Collins, published by Bantam Books Inc., New York. Lifestory of one of auto racing's all-time greats.

Great Racing Drivers edited by David Hodges, published by Arco Publishing Co., Inc., New York. Introductions to some of racing's big names and what made them tick.

Fast and Furious by Richard Garrett, published by Arco Publishing Co., Inc., New York.

Building and Racing The Gravity Car

One day in 1933, a newspaper photographer named Myron E. Scott, was sent by his paper, the Dayton *Daily News*, to find a human interest story. He saw a group of boys racing soap boxes with baby carriage wheels down a sloping back street. He took photographs and later persuaded the editor to sponsor a neighborhood race of boy-built and driven gravity-propelled buggies. They called it "The Soap Box Derby" and it soon became a annual national event, sponsored by Chevrolet. The young photographer who started it was soon employed full-time by Chevrolet for the sole purpose of running this yearly race for kids and their "soap box" cars.

Scott moved the Derby over to Akron because of its better slopes and central location. Fifty thousand people watched the second All-American Soap Box Derby, including such notables of the day as Captain Eddie Rickenbacker and famed movie cowboy Tom Mix. It is an interesting comment on our changing economy to recall that the winning boy got a 12,000 scholarship while the second and third place winner received *only* brand new Chevrolet automobiles.

The Million-Dollar Derby

A special track was built on Akron's east side near the airport which, following postwar renovation (the race was suspended for the duration), has been used ever since. Today the race is no longer sponsored by Chevrolet—the company relinquished the world's biggest amateur race in 1973 after footing the bill since 1934. The race is now run under the auspices of the Jaycees of Akron; it brings an estimated one million dollars annually into the Rubber City.

The All-American Soap Box Derby is now open also to contestants from other countries, and a number of participants in recent years have come to Akron from various parts of the world. One year the NAACP complained that the race was "lily white" although no black competitor had ever been refused or discouraged. The Women's Liberation movement got into the act by threatening to obtain a federal court injunction to halt the race unless the words "all eligible girls" were added to the rules. This in spite of the fact that a young girl had competed and finished in the top seventeen in the very first official Derby in Dayton. Although the word "boys" was used, girls had never been banned from entering the race. In 1972 a young lady named Priscilla Freeman posted the fastest time of the day and finished in the top three.

Under the close watch of starting line officials, finalists in the 37th All-American Soap Box Derby at Derby Downs in Akron, Ohio, make final preparations for the championship heat. (Photo courtesy All-American Soap Box Derby.)

There have been many cries of "cheating" over the years—mostly without any foundation. However, young Jim Gronen, of Boulder, Colorado, gave himself a slight advantage in 1973 by ingeniously concealing an electromagnet in his car's nose which caused the car to stick to the steel starting plate until the plate dropped, giving him a little extra push. Jim was disqualified.

Steps have been taken to eliminate any irregularities that might further sully the name of the All-American Soap Box Derby and interest in the annual event is again on the increase. In fact, it has become necessary to hold local and regional run-offs.

Building An Approved "Soap box"

The following is an abbreviated list of rules pertaining to the construction of a gravity car acceptable to the Derby Committee.

1. Cost must not exceed $75 exclusive of wheels, axles, steering assembly and paint. Fiberglass is considered a covering, not paint.
2. Entrant must submit itemized list of all materials and parts used in the car with purchase price of each item. Every item must have a fair value even if obtained free.
3. Car must not exceed thirty-four and three-quarters inches wide but must be at least twelve inches wide. Length cannot be greater than eighty-four inches (no minimum), height must not exceed twenty-eight inches but must be at least fourteen inches. Intent here is to make the cross section of each racer a minimum of twelve inches x fourteen inches. Height and width measurements must be taken at same locations. Concave curves in the body cross section within the twelve inches x fourteen inch area are not permitted.
4. Weight of car and driver may not exceed 260 lbs.
5. Car must have minimum road clearance of three inches below lowest point, including break facing with driver in car.
6. Wheelbase must not be less than fifty-two inches.
7. Only "official" unaltered Soap Box Derby wheels, tires and axles may be used. Car must run on all four wheels.
8. Axles must be removable for inspection or have removable covers so entire axle may be inspected.
9. Ready-made steering wheels and shafts are permitted.
10. No "altering" of wheels, tires or bearings is permitted—i.e., buffing, crimping, etc.
11. All work on car construction must be carried out by the contestant who may be required to demonstrate that he has the necessary skill and knowledge to have built the racer.

A full set of the numerous All-American Soap Box Derby rules (which some say are better understood by a qualified automotive engineer than by the average 13-year-old), may be obtained by writing the All-American Soap Box Derby Committee, 175 Main St., Akron, OH 44313. Age limits seem to change frequently. As this publication went to press, the main Derby was restricted to youngsters (both sexes, any color, creed, etc.) over eleven years old and under sixteen. Local Derbys operated under the same general rules are run in two age group classifications.

How To Win The "Gravity Grand Prix"

Naturally, the winning car is the one which gets to the bottom of the

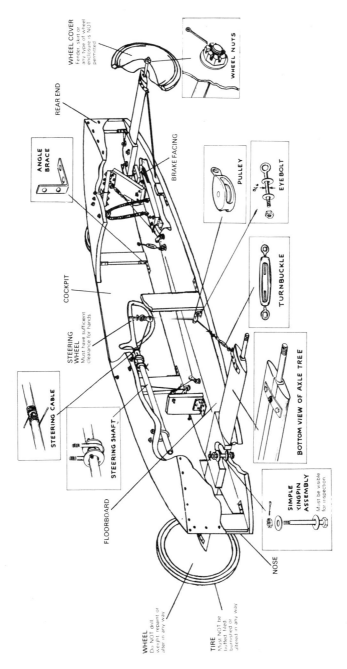

(Courtesy All-American Soap Box Derby.)

inclined course and across the finish line faster than all the others. Photo-finish and electronic timing equipment are used to insure the top prize does indeed go to the first car across the line. Various design and construction methods, within the rigid limits set forth by the Committee, have been tried out on the course in efforts to lessen wind, air and ground friction and thus achieve greater speeds. Streamlining has reached a point that it seems ludicrous to refer to these gravity racing mahcines as "soapboxes".

Fred Lake, of South Bend, Indiana, figured he would have an extra advantage in 1960. He was only four feet, ten inches tall and weighed only eighty-two pounds—the smallest contestant ever. He won.

In 1970, Gilbert Klecan, of San Diego, tried to lessen air friction by "greasing" his car and himself with fine graphite. Perhaps the graphite grease job did help—he beat all the other contestants and 80,000 spectators watched him do it.

Ex-Soapbox Derby champions seem unanimous in advising new contestants to: 1. Keep your head down as much as possible while watching the track ahead. This helps lower wind drag. 2. Steering as straight a course as possible. 3. Avoid colliding with other cars. 4. Concentrate your entire thoughts on winning.

There are two styles of cars used in modern Soap Box Derby competition—one in which the driver sits at the wheel and one which allows the driver to lie almost suppine. The 1974 winner, Curt Yarborough of Elk Grove, California, used the sitting style while the third-place finisher used the reclining style. (Curt's brother Bret won the event in 1973.)

Prizes are given to more than just the winner—there have been prizes given for best time in a single heat, best overall design, best construction, best upholstered, best braking system, etc. The prize structure has changed over the years and will probably change further in the years ahead faced by the All-American Soap Box Derby without its long-time Chevrolet sponsorship.

Funds contributed by local businesses and individuals in the area help keep the All-American Soap Box Derby alive, well, and thriving in Akron, Ohio.

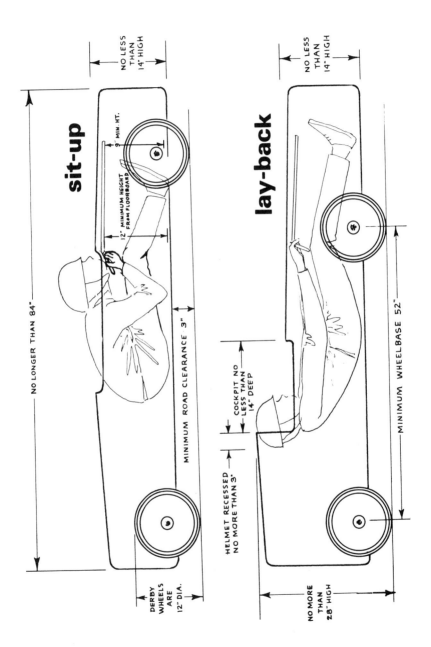

Labels on figure (sit-up):
- NO LESS THAN 14" HIGH
- sit-up
- 9" MIN. HT.
- 12" MINIMUM HEIGHT FROM FLOORBOARD
- NO LONGER THAN 84"
- MINIMUM ROAD CLEARANCE 3"
- DERBY WHEELS ARE 12" DIA.

Labels on figure (lay-back):
- NO LESS THAN 14" HIGH
- lay-back
- MINIMUM WHEELBASE 52"
- COCKPIT NO LESS THAN 14" DEEP
- HELMET RECESSED NO MORE THAN 3"
- NO MORE THAN 28" HIGH

(Courtesy All-American Soap Box Derby.)

Curt Yarborough, an 11-year-old from Elk Grove, California, outraced other champions from communities throughout the United States and from three foreign countries to win the 37th All-American Soap Box Derby at Derby Downs in Akron, Ohio, on August 17, 1974. Curt received a $13,000-college scholarship and the champion's trophy from Derby General Manager Ronald D. Baker (center) while his happy family looks on. His brother Bret (at left) was the 1973 winner. (Photo courtesy All-American Soap Box Derby.)

Riding The Thumb

Note: This chapter was contributed in its entirety by the author's son, Phillip A. DuPre.)

Riding the thumb, or hitchhiking, is known to the large number of aficionados in the USA and Canada as "Hitchen" or "Thumb Ryden." Here we are considering hitch hiking in a much broader perspective than getting a ride a few miles home from school or college or work. In our dimension, hitchen is much more than a means of getting from Pacific Beach, California to Wolf Creek, Oregon . . . more, even, than merely thumb ryden across the continent.

You do it more to occupy yourself and pass the time while you work out your own head than to get from one place to another. This is the best way to examine yourself introspectively, consider your fears and phobias, dissect your hangups, get rid of those resentments that have been building up inside you lately, review your progress or activities of the past, plan for the future, or just plain dream . . . .

It is also a good opportunity to observe human nature, watch a swallow scribe an arc in the evening sky, count the number of cars passing a given point in a given length of time, compose a few heart-felt verses to send to "her" when you return (of course, you never send them) and listen to the world catching its often frantic breath.

You don't pay rent on the road so when you can no longer take what you are doing—be it school studies or a job or living with someone who has really started to bug you—don't quit. Store your possessions (if you can't bring yourself to give them all away, which is far better), dig out your sleeping bag and back pack, stick out your thumb and away you go. Even if you don't know anyone in Wolf Creek, Oregon.

How To Do It Right

As with almost everything else, there's a right way and a wrong way to hitchhike. For one thing, hitchhiking is illegal in many states and communities. That in itself does not mean you absolutely cannot do it—driving above the speed limit is illegal everywhere, but probably nine out of ten drivers do it. However, it is wise to be aware of the law and of those entrusted to enforce it.

In some places where hitchen is illegal, all you will get is a friendly wave from the state trooper as he drives past. In others you may be told to get off the freeway but you won't get "busted" (correct thumb ryden terminology for "arrested"). Then there are those tiresome communities where the police and the petty little local judges get their jollies from harassing young people and, if you are hitchen, they have a perfect excuse.

Harrassment by the law takes many forms. Sometimes it includes manhandling, being stuck in the pokey for a day or two (often without food and drink), shakedown by the cop who picks you up (if he suspects you may have a few bucks on you) and other nasty unpleasantness by means of which some local authorities like to "Show you who's boss around here, Creep!" What they actually show you, of course, is what really small creatures they are, despite their brawny arms and beer bellies. But never curse the police, either outwardly or inwardly. Pity those few who have to behave this way to prove their authority to themselves.

My own hitchen experience covers many thousands of miles of the good old USA, Canada and Mexico. I have had good experiences and some not so good, but all of them valuable. So far I have not had the opportunity to hitchhike across Europe, Africa, or Asia, but I know many young people of both sexes who have. Of course, you are far safer hitchhiking almost anywhere in the world than in the USA. One friend of mine thumbed it from Paris, France, to Khabul, Afganistan, in twenty-five days. Among the hitchen fraternity, that is considered darned good time. I have never personally established any records that I know of, but I once rode from Escondido in Southern California, to Chicago in two days and two hours with only two rides. Once I was driving north along the West Coast and picked up a dude at Grant's Pass, Oregon, who had traveled that far from Yucatan with just one ride. I took him on to his destination, Seattle, and it wouldn't surprise me to learn that he had established some kind of world record for hitchen from the Yucatan to Seattle with only two rides. According to the *Guinness Book of World Records*, Devon Smith thumbed a total of 291,000 miles over a twenty-four-year period. By comparison I am a mere novice!

As far as I know from personal experience and via the hitchen grapevine, Lodi—in the California wine country—is one of the country's worst places to catch a ride on the thumb. I once stood for over five days before getting a ride here. At Jansen Beach, Portland, Oregon, I waited two days. On another occasion I did thirteen hours worth of sorting out my head while trying to get a ride at Salinas, California, eighteen hours at Signal Hill, Long Beach, California. These are exceptions, however, and I have obtained many needed rides within minutes of manning my highway post.

Hitchen Gear

Before getting into a discussion of hitchen techniques, it is important to consider the gear needed for anything like a lengthy trip. Not every experienced hitchhiker will agree entirely with my equipment check list . . . the list is based on my own personal experiences and tastes. Also I do not believe in being unnecessarily uncomfortable, since hitchen is primarily for the pure joy of it, not for punishment.

THE BODY—Wear Levis most of the year; cutoffs are ok in hot weather. For a coat, a denim jacket is probably best. Any type of shirt is ok as long as it has long sleeves—they can be rolled up when it's hot, and you will be glad to be able to roll them down when it gets cool. Naturally, you will wear good, comfortable, sweat-absorbing underwear. And a little deodorant may be appreciated by the driver who shares his car with you.

THE FEET—Lace-up boots or good, sturdy walking shoes. Tennis shoes are not advised for long trips. Sandals are ok when hitchen in warm, dry localities. Barefoot is out, no good at all.

THE EYES—Sunglasses are a must. Heavy wire frames that wrap around your ears are best because they don't fall off easily, and they usually bend rather than break when you sleep on them. The combination of sun, wind, dust and exhaust fumes usually prompts me to stick a small dispenser of eye drops in my pocket. They are especially helpful when you've gone without sleep a night or two, and you feel as though your eyeballs have been sandpapered.

THE HEAD—On a long trip in hot climates you will need a hat. Probably a light, cloth hat or a peaked golfing-type cap. A straw Western or Mexican hat is ok, too. In cold climates obviously you'll need something warmer—one that pulls down over the ears, perhaps, or you may want to pack a pair of ear muffs. If you burn easily and you're hitchen in hot, sunny weather, take along some ointment for your nose.

THE BACK PACK—Get a good-quality back pack. Tossing a pack in and out of pickup trucks and cramming it into small car trunks is very hard on a back pack. The frame should be welded, not riveted, bolted, pinned, etc. Good frames are made of magnesium-aluminum alloy, and the pack is made of nylon, rayon, canvas tent cloth, etc. It must have heavy duty zippers and a number of small compartments. It must be lightweight and comfortable. Padded straps and hip belt help with the comfort angle. Remember, you may have to walk a long way with this pack. If it seems to drag on you the second hour you wear it, then you have probably bought the wrong pack. Costs of packs vary considerably, depending on type, where you buy one, etc. Normally, you must pay around $50 for a good pack. Perhaps even as high as $80 or, if you're lucky, as little as $35. Shop carefully—don't grab the first one you like. Examine it—the seams, the frame, the style, the material, the zippers, straps, everything. Don't let the sales person rush you. You're the one who is paying for it and who is going to wear it.

THE SLEEPING BAG—If you don't like shivering at night, get a good sleeping bag—lightweight, two to five pounds. Mine is a two-pounder and has so far proved itself to be fully adequate for my needs. Don't carry a single unnecessary pound of anything. Carefully read the manufacturer's performance information. I personally recommend a bag with a comfort range of twenty to thirty-degrees below zero—such a bag is good under any conditions you are likely to encounter. A cheap sleeping bag is only satisfactory in the summer at low altitudes. The bag should be made of rip-stop nylon. For a filling, goose down is the warmest for the weight. Polyester fiber fill is not as warm as the same amount of weight in goose down although polyester does have one advantage—it's easier to dry out if you get it wet. The bag is waterproof when you buy it, but no matter what claims the manufacturer may make, or the salesman, the bag will not stay waterproof. Scotch-Gard it after a few uses and always try to sleep under shelter if rain is likely. Good sleeping bags are really expensive; however, you're probably not going to climb Mount Everest, so an adequate sleeping bag will cost about $60 at Sears, or you can get a better one for $75 to $80. Really dynamite bags cost $150 to $200, but don't spend that much unless you camp a lot.

INSIDE YOUR PACK—Following is a list of items that in my opinion you should take along on your hiking / hitchen / camping trips. Those asterisked would normally be needed only on long trips.

Pocket knife (cheap penknife is OK)

Wooden matches in waterproof container

*Sheath Knife

*One-quart military-type canteen. This type fits in the top side pockets of most back packs, which is a good place to carry water.

Roach dip

*Spare clean socks, spare clean shirt (at least one), spare clean jeans (if you're going on a *long* trip).

A good map on trips of fifty miles or more.

Identification.

Money—the longer your trip, the more money you will need. For coast-to-coast trips, $50 will see you through nicely, although I have managed on less.

Psychology—Key to Successful Hitchen

The key to successful hitchhiking is psychology—your own and that of the people who give you rides. To get rides, you must have the right attitude. When I am hitchen, I think and believe every car approaching me is my ride. When a car passes without stopping I think, well, it will be the next one . . . and so on. Put out good vibes, strong energy forces. Look happy. Don't cringe and look ashamed, with your hitchen hand held close to your thigh. Keep one foot on the curb, a smile on your face (or at least a pleasant expression), arm almost straight out or slightly bent at the elbow, thumb held about shoulder level or a little higher, thumb extended as far as possible. This is the best attitude and style for successful hitchen. Approaching drivers see you well in advance or reaching you. They know you want a ride. You look like a pleasant kind of dude, you are not hiding or looking shifty, you are looking confident as though you just know this driver has enough of the milk of human kindness to give you the ride you need. The driver, believe it or not, actually feels these good vibes you are putting out, and he's a little flattered that you should think so well of him.

Contrary to popular belief, the man with long hair and a beard is more likely to get a ride than is Pretty Bobby Cleancut with short hair and no facial fuzz. The reason is the "freaks" (this is the proper and non-offensive name for what used to be called "hippies") will almost always help other freaks—power to the people and all that. Middle Americans also will give you rides because although freaks have now been around a long time, they are still "different," and businessmen, old ladies, cowboys, truck drivers, etc., are interested in seeing where you're at.

The guy who says he can't get rides because of his long hair actually should blame his attitude. He *thinks* he can't get a ride because he has long hair. He has convinced himself and has subliminally convinced most approaching drivers. But if you have short hair and no whiskers, do not despair—there are rides for you, too—if you maintain the right attitude and believe you are going to get a ride.

Don't feel humble because you are hitchen a free ride—look as though you belong there on the roadside—you've nothing to be ashamed of.

On the other hand, even the best "roadies" have their bad days. As with other occupations and pastimes, sometimes you are in good form, sometimes you are not, no matter how hard you try to cultivate the proper attitude and exude the right vibes. Sometimes there are lots of cars going your way, sometimes few. Sometimes there are lots of cars but no rides. You must have patience for successful and enjoyable hitchen. If you don't have it, keep on hitchen . . . you'll learn patience, believe me!

Rules of Thumb

The following "rules" are really tips to help you hitchhike successfully and to give you a little insight into the gentle art of hitchen. *Drivers generally will not stop where they cannot do so with absolute safety.* They are not going to risk an accident to give you a ride. Make sure you are hitchen at a place where there is room for the car to pull off the busy road—otherwise you are not too likely to get a ride. In addition to pulling safely off the road, remember, your driver has to drop out of the flow of traffic, too. If the traffic is extra heavy and tight (cars close together) you are unlikely to get a ride. Don't pick rush hour.

Drivers will not stop if the traffic is moving very fast for two reasons: First, because they realize it is unsafe to pull out of the traffic flow and stop while in a fast-moving stream. Second, by the time the driver sees you when traveling at sixty mph or faster, there isn't time for him to stop without creating a traffic hazard by suddenly applying his brakes.

Do not hitchhike on the freeway in any state. In most it is illegal to hitchhike on the freeway (although it may not be illegal to hitchhike on other roads). Another negative factor with freeway hitchen is that in many states it is illegal for a motorist to pick up a hitchhiker on the freeway. It is dangerous to yourself to hitchhike on the freeway.

Use the entrance ramp—this is legal in most states. In states where hitchen per se is legal but illegal on the freeway, you may proceed up the entrance ramp on foot but no farther than the sign that says stay off the freeway. In California and certain other states some of the freeways have land dividers consisting of raised dots (known at Bott's Dots, after the inventor). These are there not only to help separate the lanes in fog and other poor-visibility conditions, but also to serve as a warning to drivers who allow their cars to cross into the next lane unnecessarily. They vibrate the car and supposedly shake the driver into alertness. These dots sometimes start on the ramp, below the sign—you are not allowed to stand forward of the point where the dots begin on the ramp. Most hitchhikers realize this unwritten law is merely a sneaky way for the cops to bust you and to squeeze what fine money they can out of you. No signs announce this wierd rule. You are supposed to know it by extra-sensory perception, or something.

Oregon is one state where you may legally hitchhike on the freeway. I know of no others, but I have not yet hitchhiked in every state—only about thirty of them so far. Some states have modified their laws regarding hitchhiking. About four years ago I spent a night in jail in the state of Washington, where hitchhiking was illegal. Now hitchen is legal there although not, of couse, on the freeways. In Colorado a state trooper told me to get off the freeway (I-80) but did not bust me. In most states the legal fines run from $5 to $25 and from a night in jail to thirty days in extreme cases. According to responsible hitchhiking sources, there are states in the southern part of the country where thirty days is more or less mandatory, and you spend it on the chain gang. These states are expected to join the twentieth century and the United States of America almost any time now.

Hitchen in town. Keep one foot on the curb at all times while waiting for a ride. Technically, you must stand off the road but if you have one foot on the curb you can generally get away with it. Remember again that a driver must be able to stop safely or you're going to be out of luck. Don't hitchhike between parked cars because drivers can't see you and aren't likely to stop if they do.

When possible, try to hitchhike near a college or high school or wherever young people are likely to be driving. They are more likely to pick you up than older drivers.

When hitchen at an intersection governed by traffic lights, always stand on the "Through" side, not on the "approach" side.

When hitchen after dark, head for a well-lighted area—under a street lamp is usually best. Wear light-colored clothing so that you can be easily seen by approaching motorists. If you haven't got a ride by 1:00 am, hang it up for the day. That is why you have your sleeping bag along. In town "feel" the traffic before quitting—sometimes on Friday and Saturday nights traffic is plentiful as late as 3:00 am. Stay clear of the driver who is weaving or driving in an unsteady manner—he could be drunk.

When you bed down for the night, try to get off into the bushes if you are in a busy area so that you don't get ripped off, busted or run over by a vehicle. It is best not to advertise your campsite.

Show courtesy at all times. Never curse drivers who fail to stop for you—it's your Kharma, and theirs. Always say "thank you." When there are more than one hitchhiker on a freeway ramp (leading on to the freeway), common courtesy requires that you go up-ramp, giving the first ones there first chance at the rides. You'll get your chance. If there is just one other person there when you arrive, feel free to join him.

Advice to Lady HitchHikers

I do not encourage girls to hitchhike—there are just too many wierdos around and I have talked to many fine girls who have been hassled, beat up, raped, robbed, etc. For those who feel they must hitchhike, the following suggestions may be of some value:

Don't hitchhike alone if you can possibly avoid it.

If you see a car has more than one man in it, let it pass. Generally, you are safer in a car with one man—or even better, with a man and woman and best of all with women travelers.

As the car pulls up, if there's just one man in it, try to make a quick psychological assessment. If you get the impression he's a creep or a wierdo, wave him on. If he insists on stopping, say "I'm sorry I stopped you—I am waiting for my brother and he has a car like yours. Thanks, anyway".

When you open the door to get in, or when the driver opens it for you, make sure there's a handle on the inside. Take hold of it and make sure it works.

If you want to hold up a sign showing your destination, make sure the words are legible from a distance. Use a thick, black felt-tip and space out the letters. (this applies to both male and female hitchhikers.)

In "The Great Escape," Sondi Field sets out a few rules for women hitchhikers. Sondi should know; she's done plenty of it. One of her rules is that in the first few minutes establish a rapport with your driver (I call it psyching him out). If the man starts off saying something like: "Why aren't you wearing a bra?" or "How come a sexy babe like you travels alone?," come on strong immediately. Be offended, tell him to treat you the same as he would a male hitchhiker or let you out of the car. Stay alert at all times. If you fall asleep you may wake up on some lonely dirt road with a forcible invitation to fun and games in the bushes.

"I'll Blow You Sky High!"

My hitchhiking experiences would fill a book, as would those of other thumb riders on the open road. Here's one which made me highly nervous at the time but had no unpleasant outcome. This dude gave me a badly needed ride, but seemed to be afraid that I was bent on doing him harm. For 180 miles he told me over and over that he was a demolition expert for Twentieth Century Fox Studios and that my seat was wired with enough explosives to blow me to bits. His seat was specially shielded so he would not get hurt. He kept repeating this story, with additional embellishments, over and over. Only a paranoid person would behave in this way and if he's paranoid enough to keep saying it, he's probably paranoid enough to do it—or something else harmful to your health and bodily comfort.

One thing about wierdos; they're all different. Some are wierd one way, some another. Observe them carefully and react accordingly, always using psychology. It is always best to keep your pack and bag inside the car with you rather than in the trunk, if possible. Ask if you can just put them on the floor in the back seat—don't put them on the seat itself. If you are not going far, keep them in the front with you. Your bag can go end down between your legs and your pack can stay on your lap. The reason for this is that if you have to make a rapid escape you can do so fairly easily.

You meet wierdos wherever you go in life, not only hitchhiking. Fortunately, even though it sometimes seems every other person you meet is one, these creeps are very much in the minority, and while hitchhiking you are really not likely to meet all that many. For hitchhikers these characters are one of the hazards of the game, like belligerent cops, pouring rain, long waits for rides, etc.

Hitching Rides on Trains

Don't. It is illegal and extremely dangerous. Freight train riders have had legs cut off through mistiming, many have been killed; then you have to worry about the hardened characters who ride the rails—you may be beaten half to death or even killed for the few dollars in your pocket. Just like on the streets of New York, Detroit, Chicago and many other major cities! Then there are strong possibilities of getting yourself busted, especially if you don't know the ropes. I have personally done very little of this type of hitchen, but enough to realize that it is an extremely dangerous business and to stay away from it from now on.

Publications

Needless to say, there is very little printed information on the gentle art of hitchen. One book that lightly touches on it in addition to many other adventure subjects is "The Great Escape," available in bookshops and newsstands. In addition to Sondl Field's advice to women hitchhikers, there is an excellent article by Marion Knox on hitching rides on airplanes. This subject so fascinated me, after reading the article, that I plan to try it in the near future. Magazines of various types from time to time publish articles on hitchen—you might want to check the Periodical Index at the local library.

Snowmobiling

If God had intended people to skim across snow and ice at speeds as high as 80 mph or more He'd have given us powered tracks. Well, he didn't. But fortunately some fun-minded, far-seeing men did, including French-Canadian inventor J. Armand Bombardier whose company makes Ski-Doo and Moto-Ski snowmobiles among other products, and imaginative outdoors enthusiasts Allan Hetteen and David Johnson who designed and built a two-man snowmobile in 1954. Later their products bore the Polaris nameplate.

Monsieur Bombardier's work on snow vehicles started in 1928 and after about ten years of experimentation he patented a drive system that formed the basis for most used today. Bombardier units transported guns and other equipment over snow-covered passes and frozen lakes during World War II. He even built sand units for desert use. Bombardier is generally credited with making the snowmobile financially feasible. In 1959 his company sold 227 and five years later annual sales exceeded 4,800 units. Now, that's feasible! Meanwhile, work by Allan Heteen and David Johnson bore fruit and Polaris snowmobiles hit the market in the mid-fifties.

Turning point for the industry was 1964 when Outboard Marine Corp. (Evinrude, Johnson), Mercury, Harley Davidson and John Deere all entered the snowmobile business. Sales boomed, and by the winter of '69-'70, 445,000 units per year were moving out of dealers' showrooms.

As many as eighty companies entered the industry, but too many of them put too many of their eggs in one basket and only the larger, more diversified companies have survived. By 1975, attrition and economic conditions had reduced the number of snowmobile manufacturers in the USA and Canada to twenty or less.

Production and sales are expected to peak about 1979 with around 480,000 units that year.

Meanwhile, some seven million people in North America are currently enjoying snowmobiling activities. And you can, too, for a relatively modest cash outlay. These fun vehicles start at a few hundred dollars for basic units and go as high as $2,500 or more for the larger, higher-powered competition models. The average snowmobiler spends around $1,400 on his machine, accessories, trailer and clothing. Here's what you get for your money: front steering skis, gasoline tank, engine (size and horsepower vary), engine cowl, a long, padded seat, storage box for tools and spares, running boards, plexiglass windshield, suspension system, tracks with cleats to "dig" you along, handlebars (steering wheel in a few units), and various accessories such as instruments, lights, compass, rear-view mirrors, electric starting kit and more.

What To Wear

You are also going to need good, warm clothing. Earlier snowmobile enthusiasts, pursuing their sport in sub-freezing temperatures, had to don flannel or woollen long johns, two or three pairs of socks, gloves, sweater, scarf, heavy topcoat, earmuffs and stocking cap which usually covered the head and face except for eye holes.

Today's modern fabrics have done away with most of that. You wear your normal underwear, light sweater or shirt, pair of everyday pants, pair of socks, snowmobile boots and a one-piece snowmobile suit. (Two-piece suits also are available.) Your snowmobile suit is not only warm and light-weight, it is also the height of winter fashion. Insulative polyester fill—up to six ounces of it per square yard—is covered with an exterior shell made of closely woven nylon or other modern fabric which screens out the cold winds and keeps you dry.

Every snowmobile suit is supposed to have a tag telling you how much fill it contains and what material is used for the fill. Look for this tag when buying a snowmobile suit; it carries important information. Check the zippers and make sure each zipper has an extra flap of material to protect you from cold air and snow that can enter; examine seams.

Snowmobile boots have felt or similar material inside as liner, and plastic nylon or synthetic rubber uppers and rubber soles. Gauntlet-type snowmobile gloves offer your hands the best protection, either glove style or mittens. Gauntlets keep your hands warm, your fingers active, and they stop cold air and snow from seeping up inside the sleeves of your suit. Snowmobile goggles are a must. The colored lenses protect you from snow blindness and the sun, and the goggles help cut down the driving snow that stings your face and eyes as you drive into it. Clear lenses are used when dull conditions prevail or when driving at night.

Helmets are vitally important, and no serious, responsible snowmobiler is seen on the trail without one. These come in various qualities. Anything but the best is false economy and flirts with injury. Not only does a helmet help protect your cranium from low tree branches and from injury in case of a spill, but it also helps keep your head and ears warm and helps reduce the volume of engine noise in your ears. They are light weight and you soon get used to wearing one. They also add a racy, high-performance look that just seems to go with a good-looking snowmobile suit and a fine machine. A stocking cap beneath your helmet gives added protection against the cold and on occasions you will want to wear a face stocking-mask.

Your First Snowmobile

Most beginners start with one of the more modestly priced, modestly performing units. Then, when proficiency sets in, they trade it or sell it and get themselves something more powerful for really tough riding and competition use.

You will also need means of transporting your powered sled to and from snowmobiling areas. Many snowmobiles have such low profiles they can fit into the back of a station wagon. Some have fold-down handlebars and windshield for this purpose. Pickup trucks are often used to carry snowmobiles. Most owners, however, use trailers, which come in one, two or four snowmobile size. There are also six-sled trailers available, used mostly by teams. A weatherproof cover is a good idea, especially when the unit is not being used and is stored outdoors in all kinds of weather.

Because of the fuel situation, snowmobiles have come under heavy criticism from often uninformed and misguided officials, various pressure groups including some of the media, consumer advocate Ralph Nader and private citizens. Let's review the facts concerning gasoline use by snowmobilers. In the first place, the family that spends weekends snowmobiling is not spending those two or three days using their cars. Secondly, most snowmobiles will run for hours on one tank of gas—four or five gallons or so. The most the average snowmobile is likely to use over a weekend is maybe eight or nine gallons. And that's running the machine just about the whole time.

How To Buy a Snowmobile

The Popular Science Annual Snowmobile Handbook ($1.50) contains performance comparisons on various units, plus much additional information of interest and value to both beginner snowmobilers and those who are experienced. If there's a snowmobile show anywhere near you, go and look at the various models and accessories on display. Talk with the salespeople—they are usually quite knowledgeable about their products. Collect brochures and folders for later study. The shows almost always present snowmobiling films, which give you good insight into the sport. Once you have narrowed your search down to a few models, start visiting snowmobile dealerships in your area and spending time to examine the various units close up. Again, discuss your needs with the dealer. Tell him how much you feel you can pay for your first unit and how you plan to use it.

How to Operate Your Snowmobile

Finally you have your snowmobile (or perhaps you bought two) on a trailer behind your car and you head for the nearest snowmobile area. When you get there, if you were too short-sighted to buy ramps to drive your snowmobile off the trailer, borrow a pair—almost any other snowmobiler will be glad to help you. Some trailers can be tipped for on and off driving. If you arrive when everyone is out on the trail, you can back your trailer up tight against a snowbank and drive off the trailer onto the snow. Make sure it is a well-packed bank, not a snowdrift.

Now let's take a look at the controls. Steering is accomplished by means of handlebars (on most units, a steering wheel on a few) similar to those on a motorcycle. In addition to using the handlebars to steer your snowmobile, you also shift your weight for additional friction on the snow or ice. Head and tail lights are now standard equipment on snowmobiles—they are operated by a toggle switch on the dashboard or console or by an extra position on the ignition switch. The ignition switch is similar to that on a car or motorcycle. Some units have a key starter like a car; most are easily started by a pull-cord.

Before switching on and starting your snowmobile, you should always first check the throttle to make sure it works freely and does not stick open. Moisture can collect in cable housing and freeze there. Don't start up while holding the throttle open or your sled may suddenly burst into life and take off without you. It may then hit someone or another snowmobile and you are legally liable. Your snowmobile should start without having throttle open. If it does not, it needs adjusting by your dealer—unless you know enough about the machine to do it yourself. Always work the throttle a few times before starting up to make sure it moves freely open and closed. The ignition switch acts as an emergency OFF switch—flick it to the OFF position and your machine comes to a safe stop. In addition, many units feature an additional emergency OFF switch. Your throttle is mounted on the right-hand handlebar, the brake control on the left handlebar—on all snowmobiles that have handlebars, that is. Some snowmobiles in the lower price ranges carry no instruments; others have speedometer, odometer, and tachometer, while some include compass, fuel gauge, headlight dimmer, map light, etc.

Some snowmobiles have a dash-mounted choke lever to enrich fuel/air mixture for extra cold-weather starts.

Riding Your Snowmobile

You do not normally expect to have to learn how to sit down, but on a snowmobile there's a right way and there are several wrong ways. Actually there are three basic snowmobile riding positions—sitting astride the seat, kneeling on the seat, and standing (which includes half-standing or crouching). The easiest, most relaxed of these is, of course, the sitting position, generally used when riding a fairly straight course on fairly level ground (or ice).

The correct sitting position is with your weight centered over the tracks so that you can extend your arms and place your hands comfortably on the handlebars with your elbows slightly bent. You should not have to reach or stretch. Some snowmobiles have built-in "stirrups". You sit with your knees forward and legs from the knees down sloping toward the rear. If there are no toe-stirrups, the balls of your feet should be resting on the running board directly beneath your rear end, in a straight line with the body and shoulders. Sitting with legs and feet tucked under the cowling is not a safe riding position. Your feet and legs help serve as shock-absorbers—you are likely to take quite a few bumps. However, you may want to vary the position of the feet and the feet-knees-hips "shock absorber system" according to the terrain.

There are occasions when you will prefer to drive from a kneeling position, which offers several advantages: you have better forward vision; your thighs and hips provide an improved shock-absorbing effect, and it is easier for you to transfer your weight from side to side quickly in turns—such as on a slalom course. A variation of the kneeling position is to kneel on one knee; the other leg is extended with knee bent and foot on the running board.

Generally, the standing position is not recommended although you see it often used, particularly in rough terrain. This position enables you to transfer your weight forward or aft and from side to side very rapidly. Again, you have more forward vision from the standing or half-standing position. It is not an easy position to maintain for very long and, since some of your weight is necessarily taken by the handlebars, there is some diminishing of control. With the kneeling and standing or crouching positions, you lose the protection of the wind shield, and when moving fairly fast into an extremely cold wind, it is not difficult to get a slight case of frost bite on exposed areas of the face . . . a face mask helps prevent this. For safest control of your snowmobile, for comfort and for your own protection, you will find the sitting position best.

For Your Snowmobile Library

SNOWMOBILE TRAILS, by Mike Michaelson, published by Great-lakes Living Press, Ltd., Chicago, Illinois. Covers hundreds of marked and groomed trails throughout the USA and Canada and a great many areas where snowmobiling activities are held, though not necessarily on marked trails. Book also lists accommodations and presents a great deal of additional information of value to snowmobilers. Available in book shops and on newsstands.

SNOWMOBILE TRAVEL GUIDE, published by Hertzberg & Kramer, Inc., Niles, Illinois. Lists snowmobiling campgrounds in twenty-five states including Quebec and Ontario, Canada. Also covers hundreds of resorts, trails, and other information. Available in bookshops and newsstands or from the publishers.

SAFE SNOWMOBILING, by James L. Thomas, Sterling Publishing Co., Inc., New York. Covers snowmobile operation, uses, accessories, clothing, competition, and safety. Available in bookshops.

SNOWMOBILE HANDBOOK, published annually by *Popular Science Magazine*, Times Mirror Magazines, Inc., New York. Contains a rich fund of information of interest to snowmobilers, discusses various types of equipment, covers techniques, competition driving, safety, comparisons of machines, lists of snowmobile trails with detailed state-by-state atlas, etc. Available on newsstands.

THE COMPLETE SNOWMOBILE REPAIR HANDBOOK, by Paul Dempsey, TAB Books Inc., Blue Ridge Summit, Pennsylvania. This 347-page manual is designed to save snowmobile owners repair bills by presenting maintenance information and repair instructions in a simple, illustrated manner. Available in bookshops.

THE SNOWMOBILER'S COMPANION, by Sally Wimer, Scribner & Co. Inc., New York. Presents a wide range of information of interest and value to snowmobiling families. Available in most book stores.

CHICAGOLAND SNOWMOBILER, published monthly September through March by Hertzberg & Kramer Inc., Niles, Illinois. Covers the snowmobiling scene in the seven-state midwest area with articles on winter camping, resorts, trails, ice fishing, latest snowmobile machine and accessories, competitions, etc. Available during the season on most newsstands in the midwest.

SNOW SPORTS, published by Snow Sports Inc., Minneapolis, Minnesota. Covers various aspects of snowmobiling and other winter sports. Available on newsstands throughout the snowmobiling season.

SNOW GOER, published by Webb Publishing Corp., Minneapolis, Minnesota. Usually available on newsstands throughout the midwest.

SNO TRACK, published by Market Communications, Milwaukee, Wisconsin and usually available on newsstands throughout the season.

Walk Before Running

Some new snowmobile owners, with more enthusiasm than common sense, take their new machines out to the nearest trail and at once attempt to establish new speed records. Some of them do establish new speed records—in getting themselves hurt. Don't try to tackle a hill unless other snowmobiles have already successfully climbed it. Don't test out your steering ability by making fast, tight turns, or you will surely tip over. A snowmobile is not built to make ninety-degree turns at high speed, and it just won't do it. The slower you drive, the tighter the turns you can make; the faster you drive the more time and distance you will need for your turns.

As with learning to ride almost everything (including a horse) there is absolutely no substitute for knowledgeable instruction. Join a club where there are experienced snowmobilers who will gladly coach you. In any case, you bought your sled for fun, so relax and take it easy; gradually accustom yourself to this new type of locomotion. Enjoy it; don't make hard work out of it. If you approach snowmobiling aggressively you will reduce your enjoyment considerably.

Be A Nice-Guy Snowmobiler

Much has been written about snowmobile courtesy and consideration for others. The following ten-point "Snowmobiler's Code of Ethics" was compiled by a committee of representatives from the US Forest Service, Bureau of Outdoor Recreation, Michigan Department of Natural Resources, Minnesota Department of Natural Resources, Department of Lands and Forests, Ontario, Canada, the US National Park Service, and snowmobile manufacturers.

1. I will be a good sportsman. I recognize that people judge all snowmobilers by my actions. I will use my influence with other snowmobile owners to promote sportsman-like conduct.

2. I will not litter trails or camping areas, nor pollute streams or lakes.

3. I will not damage living trees, shrubs, or other natural features.

4. I will respect other people's property and rights.

5. I will lend a helping hand when I see someone in distress.

6. I will make myself and vehicle available to assist search-and-rescue parties.

7. I will not interfere with nor harass hikers, skiers, snowshoers, ice fishermen, or other winter sportsmen; I will respect their rights to enjoy our recreation facilities.

8. I will know and obey all federal, state and local rules regulating the operation of snowmobiles in areas where I use my vehicle. I will inform public officials when using public lands.

9. I will not harrass wildlife; I will avoid areas posted for the protection or feeding wildlife.

10. I will stay on marked trails or marked back roads open to snowmobiles. I will avoid cross-country travel unless specifically authorized.

Be A Safe Snowmobiler

The International Snowmobile Industry Association, with national headquarters near Washington, DC, is one of a number of organizations actively promoting snowmobile safety. The ISIA issues these safety tips, among others and additional information of value to snowmobilers:

NEVER CHECK FUEL LEVER OR BATTERY BY LIGHT OF A MATCH— Sounds silly, but it has been done by snowmobilers without flashlights on a dark night. But it has rarely been done with pleasant results.

*KEEP AWAY FROM ALL IDLING OR RUNNING MACHINES WHEN MIXING GAS AND OIL—*Follow manufacturer's recommendations for perfect mixture.

*NEVER ADD FUEL WHILE YOUR SNOWMOBILE IS RUNNING—*This is another of those "elementary, my dear Watson" tips, but accidents have been caused by people doing this.

*KEEP YOUR MACHINE IN TOP OPERATING CONDITION—*Never ride a snowmobile with mechanical problems. They may "work out" as you drive; then again they may not, and you could have an accident, break down far from help, or incur major repair expenses.

*MAKE SURE LIGHTS ARE WORKING PROPERLY, AND ARE CLEAN—*Don't depend on moonlight—ever hear of clouds? Also, moonlight does funny things with shadows, so keep your lights on and don't over-drive them. Carry a flashlight in working order.

*DON'T BREAK NEW TRAILS OR VENTURE OFF ON YOUR OWN IN COUNTRY YOU DO NOT KNOW WELL—*Follow established trails, where you can be found if you break down and where you are not likely to suddenly run into a fence, guy wires, surveyor's stakes, snow-covered rock outcroppings, etc.

*KNOW YOUR CRUISING RANGE—*Snow and terrain conditions vary day to day so never depend on a miles-per-gallon guess. Know your limits, you machine's limitations, the countryside, map reading and compass directions.

*CARRY AT LEAST MINIMUM SAFETY EQUIPMENT—*tool kit, knife, spare spark plugs, spare drive belt, first aid kit, rope, waterproof matches, flashlight and spare batteries, extra ignition key, a sheet of plastic to curl up in if you get stuck overnight and a trail map or geological survey map.

*DO NOT OPERATE YOUR MACHINE AT EXCESSIVE SPEEDS—*always consider terrain, weather conditions, other snowmobilers and other people using the area, and know your machine thoroughly.

*DON'T OVERLOAD YOUR MACHINE—*If you have a one-person snowmobile, never carry a passenger (except in emergency). Don't carry more freight than the machine is designed to safely carry.

*NEVER LOAN YOUR MACHINE TO A STRANGER—*You may be held responsible for his carelessness or damage he may cause.

*NEVER LEAVE YOUR MACHINE IDLING—*Always turn it off, and take the key with you even for a moment or two.

NEVER ATTEMPT TO CLEAR TRACK BY LIFTING REAR OF MACHINE WHILE ENGINE IS RUNNING—This is extremely dangerous—rocks and twigs and other debris may be hurled at you at high velocities.

DON'T TAIL-GATE OTHER MACHINES—This may seem like fun, but if the machine ahead suddenly slows down or hits a bump or obstacle you could cause injury to one or both drivers by colliding with the front machine or by over-riding it.

IF STUCK IN DEEP SNOW, turn the engine off and free the skis by pulling them out and downhill. Place rear of machine uphill or on undisturbed snow and ease out with slow, even throttle pressure.

MAKE TURNS CAREFULLY ON ICE OR HARD-PACKED SNOW— These slick surfaces make it difficult for you to turn your machine. You must allow a greater distance for turning and for stopping. Speed must be reduced when driving on this type of surface.

DRIVING UPHILL can be tricky, depending on the steepness of the grade. On a steep hill, accelerate *before* you start the climb and reduce throttle pressure as necessary to prevent track slippage.

DRIVING DOWNHILL requires that you have full control of your machine. Maintain slight throttle pressure and allow the machine to run down on the engine compression. If you pick up too much speed, use the brake to slow down, but with a light touch. Don't jam it down or you'll lock the tracks and slide down out of control.

CROSSING A SIDEHILL, driver (and passenger, if any) must lean out against the hill—never lean toward the downhill side or you may tip over.

RAILROAD TRACKS are private property and may be crossed when necessary after making absolutely sure there is no train approaching from either direction. Never drive along tracks—it is illegal and dangerous. Your engine will often drown out the sound of an approaching train.

CROSSING A ROAD requires special care—again, your engine may make it difficult for you to hear traffic, and snow banks or hills may restrict your view, so extra caution is advised.

NEVER TOW ANOTHER SNOWMOBILE, SLED, TOBOGGAN, ETC. WITH A ROPE—Always use a rigid tow bar. Ropes can go slack and get caught in tracks or drive mechanism. And never tow a skier.

LEARN AND OBEY ALL THE RULES—Know the laws. They protect you and all of us who use snow and ice for winter recreation.

MAKE SURE YOUR PASSENGER KNOWS how to sit with feet firmly on running boards and hands gripping the safety handles. This is especially important with children. A bump can throw a child off and into the path of another snowmobile.

USE COMMON SENSE always, when driving a snowmobile or trailering. This applies also to clothing; a long scarf can get caught in bogies or engine. There are cases on record of snowmobilers being strangled in this manner. Loose clothing can also be a hazard. Don't ride alone at nights, no matter how good your lights. Don't ride alone by day, either, except on well-used trails.

Beware of Frost Bite

If the temperature is ten-degrees F and you are traveling at thirty mph, the wind chill factor is thirty-three-degrees *below* zero. You can be your own wind-chill expert with the following US Army Wind Chill Index:

U.S. ARMY WIND CHILL INDEX
(EQUIVALENT TEMP. in cooling power on
exposed flesh under calm conditions)

TEMP WIND MPH	30	20	10	0	-10	-20	-30
10	16	2	- 9	-22	-31	-45	-58
15	11	- 6	-18	-33	45	-60	-70
20	3	- 9	-24	-40	-52	-68	-81
25	0	-15	-29	-45	-58	-75	-89
30	- 2	-18	-33	-49	-63	-78	-94
35	- 4	-20	-35	-52	-67	-83	-98
40	- 4	-22	-36	-54	-69	-87	-101

(Wind speeds above 40 mph have little additional chilling effect)

The necessity for wearing warm clothing cannot be over-stressed.

Learn Survival

There are many excellent publications on the market that cover winter wilderness survival. Read one or more of these books to learn the rudiments of survival. The following are nationally accepted distress signals. If you should get lost or break down or need assistance of any kind, tramp the appropriate letters deep in the snow, about 100 feet long. you can also use heavy tree branches, which have the additional advantage of casting shadows when the sun is shining and are easily seen from a search plane:

I — Require a doctor; serious injury.

II — Need medical supplies.

X — Unable to proceed.

O — Need map and compass.

F — Need food and water.

V — Indicate direction to proceed.

LL — All is well, do not require assistance.

One of the best and simplest survival techniques is to make sure others know your approximate route before you depart and the time you expect to return. Then if you do not show up within a reasonable time of your expected arrival, a search can be initiated along the route you took. However, if, when you return, your friends do not happen to notice you are back, seek them out and tell them so that searchers do not go out needlessly.

Where to Snowmobile

A great many properties of the National Forest System, US Department of Agriculture, provide snowmobile trails and rally areas, sometimes with winter campgrounds. For a list of those in your geographical area, contact your nearest Forest Service Regional Office. Other governmental organizations from which snowmobiling information may be obtained include the Bureau of Outdoor Recreation; the National Park Service; the Department of Lands and Forest in Ontario, Canada; your state's Department of Natural Resources, Department of Economic Development, Department of Fisheries; local Chambers of Commerce, your local snowmobile dealers, snowmobile clubs, etc.

Snowmobiling on Water?

At Webster, Wisconsin, some of the more experienced snowmobilers have discovered a new sport that is rapidly spreading to other snowmobile resorts across the country. These guys have chopped away about 200 feet of ice from the surface of a thickly frozen lake at one end. They then start several hundred yards back on the ice, open up their throttles achieving seventy mph and better and *hydroplane*

Hydroplaning a snowmobile across an ice-less portion of a lake near Webster, Wisconsin. Speeds in excess of 80 mph are necessary for this new, fun sport. (Photo courtesy Peter Dupre.)

their machines across the water! This is usually done on Sundays, around mid-day and attracts a large crowd of spectators.

Occasionally one of the machines doesn't make it across the water, which results in a very wet, very cold snowmobiler and a machine a few feet under the water. No big deal—the young men get a hook on the sunken machine and all hands man a rope to pull it out. Quite often, a machine that has been immersed in this manner will start with little trouble, and after a change of snowsuits, the driver takes off across the ice for another try.

The technique here is to get up as much speed as possible and hold the handlebars steady to keep the front skis straight. Just as the machine has almost crossed the water, the driver lets up a little on the throttle so that his snowmobile does not hit the ground beyond the water too hard.

This is not a trick that a beginner should try, and it should never be attempted by a lone snowmobiler—you may need help to get your machine and yourself out of that ice-cold water. Have a change of clothing and a fresh snowsuit snowmobile suit handy, too. For safety's sake, some of these hydroplaners wear life jackets, and as this sport grows in popularity we should see life jackets on all participants.

Watch Out For Low Branches

The people who build vehicles intended to provide family shelter for traveling or camping decided years ago to call their products "recreational vehicles." At that time there were no all-terrain vehicles, snowmobiles, trail bikes, etc., so the industry felt safe selecting that designation. However, considerable confusion has since arisen because manufacturers and owners of all-terrain vehicles (ATVs), snowmobiles, four-wheel drive units and others, have applied the term "recreational vehicles" to their products. And quite rightly so. In fact, virtually any vehicle used for leisure or recreation can be termed a recreational vehicle, including (but not limited to) snowmobiles, dirt and trail bikes, off-road vehicles such as dune buggies, four-wheel drive units, light pickup trucks, sports cars, ground-effect vehicles, boats, swamp buggies (or air boats) and many more.

At one time, units now called travel trailers by the industry were known as "house trailers," since they provided living quarters of a sort. Earlier motor homes were called "house cares" and still officially are called by that name in a number of states. Fold-down trailers known by the industry as "camping trailers" are often referred to as "tent trailers," "fold-downs," "trailer tents," "pop-ups," and others. The box-style shelter carried in the bed of a pick-up truck is designated a "truck camper" by the industry. Many governmental departments, however, call these units "pickup coaches," "pickup campers," and just plain "campers."

If this terminological mish-mash has got you thoroughly confused, join the crowd. It has also confounded various legislative bodies, trade associations, suppliers of all kinds, unit manufacturers, dealers, salesmen, insurance companies, financing institutions and, finally, the poor, bewildered consumer.

Well, let's add one more name to the plethora of designations already in use—but a name that in itself, clears up the whole jumble: *"camping vehicles."* This adequately describes the four basic categories of shelter units—motor homes, travel trailers, camping trailers, and truck campers. All of which provide shelter for camping or for use when touring or traveling (which is really modern camping). Let us

188

consider these four basic categories which (in line with what appears to be an industry-wide attempt to compound the confusion), have a number of sub-categories.

Meet The Motor Home

A motor home is self-powered—engine, wheels, body with living quarters, everything, all in one hunk. The camping/motoring public has long demanded units that provide "self-containment." The motor home does just that. But to really understand the motor home, we must consider each of its three sub-categories individually. In a masterly attempt to reduce some of the nomenclature confusion the various terminologies have created, the industry has given the three sub-categories of motor homes the designations A, B and C. That's fairly simple until you discover that in appearance they vary widely and again, often resemble each other quite closely.

Let's take a look at Type A motor homes, sometimes called "conventional" motor homes, although there is little about most of them that can be considered "conventional." Unless you call a motor vehicle with hot and cold shower, ice-cube maker, built-in color TV, vacuum cleaning system, and similar home comforts, "conventional."

Most Type A motor homes are built on truck chassis. And Dodge makes most of the chassis used in the motor-home industry. However, Chevrolet, GMC, Ford and International have entered this market and are expected to increase their shares in the future. Automobile or truck manufacturers furnish motor-home builders with chassis containing all drive components; the motor-home company builds a body right on the truck chassis, enclosing the engine in the process. Camping equipment such as stove and bed are installed, and a few conveniences and luxuries are added such as water heater, hot air furnace, air conditioning, flush toilet with holding tank, kitchen and bathroom sinks, shower (and often a tub), additional microwave oven, stereophonic sound system, dinette (which usually converts into another bed), comfortable seats (which also convert into beds), refrigerator with freezer, ice cube maker, built-in vacuum cleaning system, bar, clothes closet, cabinets, clocks, wall thermostat, retractable exterior awning, sun roof, bottles for liquid petroleum gas, and a converter and electric cord so that the entire unit may be plugged into a 220-volt (sometimes 110-volt) outlet in a campground like some giant electric appliance.

Type A motor homes vary considerably in appearance. For years they were essentially boxy-looking units, but in line with more modern design styling and the need to reduce air friction in an effort to conserve gasoline, there has been a growing trend toward streamlining. It has not been satisfactorily proven, however, that a little streamlining at the front does very much to increase gasoline mileage since a big culprit in the relatively high consumption of fuel by high-profile units is what is known as vacuum drag—an effect that takes place at the rear of the unit which increases as the speed of the motor home increases. Weight also is an important factor in gasoline use.

Type A motor home, also called a "conventional" motor home. (Photo courtesy Champion.)

Are They Gas Gobblers?

Gasoline consumption is actually affected by several factors: weight, size and shape, engine type, speed and the way it is driven, type of terrain and altitude, temperature conditions, and vacuum drag.

Gasoline mileage in motor homes, under average conditions, with normally careful driving, can be as low as four or five miles per gallon and as high as twelve mpg or more, depending on some or all of the above factors.

Since aerodynamic drag does not become a really significant factor (except in strong head winds) at speeds below about fifty mph, the fuel-conscious owner tries to maintain fifty or a bit less, which is in line with fuel-saving regulations now in force.

Generally speaking, with most motor homes, forty to forty-five mph seems to be about the most economical speed.

At the lower speeds, with a rig this size, you considerably lessen engine and transmission wear, lengthen tire and brake life (and probably your own), and you are likely to enjoy the drive more. After all, this is a leisure vehicle, so why rush along like a late commuter?

Largest manufacturer of Type A motor homes is Winnebago Industries, generally credited with starting the motor-home business on a meaningful production basis. Others include Alco Standard, AMF, AVCO, Barth, Bendix Home Systems, Brougham, Blazon, Champion, Chinook, Coachman, Executive, Explorer, Ferien, FMC, Xplorer, GMC, Grumman, King's Highway, Mobile Traveler, Rectrans, Starcraft, Superior, Travel Equipment Corp., Ute Liner, Vogue, and Wickes.

Driving to Conserve Fuel

In the meantime, purchasers of motor homes must consider other means by which to reduce gasoline consumption so they may enjoy their units and get where they want to go and home again with minimal fuel consumption. The following may help motor home owners toward these goals.

- Do not buy a motor home larger than you need. Shop around carefully. Some twenty-four-foot units appear roomier inside than some twenty-eight-foot units, yet contain the same basic equipment and storage space. The reason is usually to be found in the floor plan—one manufacturer's plans show better space utilization than another's. Also, one motor-home manufacturer may obtain appliances and other items from a supplier who makes them an inch or two smaller than does the supplier for another builder. In a motor home, inches count. By buying the right size unit—in other words, the smallest one that adequately fits your needs—you will probably save fuel over buying a larger model.
- A unit that has some aerodynamic shaping may use a little less gasoline than the squared-off box-shaped unit. If it is only two percent it will help.
- Don't buy a unit with more engine than you need. Consider: Are you really going to spend most of your motor-home vacations

climbing the Rockies or ascending Pike's Peak? Do you *really need* those extra horses at the moderate speeds you will be driving?
- Use the grade of gasoline recommended by the chassis manufacturer.
- Don't keep engine running unnecessarily for warm-up purposes or while you are loading for a trip. Shut the engine off even when you run into the store for a paper, or dash back into the house for something you've forgotten. Every minute the engine is running it is using up precious—and expensive—gasoline.
- Maintain proper tire pressures, as suggested by the manufacturer. (Steel-belted radials give slightly better mileage, generally).
- Keep your front end properly aligned.
- Avoid rapid acceleration and higher speeds. If you can keep your motor home down to about forty mph you will certainly increase gas mileage (not always possible on high-speed expressways).
- Do not load more items into your motor home than you really need. Just because you have plenty of room, there's no need to take along things you will not use. Why put several pounds of food in your unit if you are passing through towns or visiting an area where there are plenty of food markets? For every 100 pounds of load, you lose about one mile per gallon, according to the AAA.
- Try to maintain constant, even speeds, avoiding acceleration and deceleration as much as possible.
- Decelerate as far in advance of a stop as possible. Avoid unnecessary braking.
- Don't use your air conditioner, heater, defroster, or gas-driven one hundred ten-volt generator more than necessary.
- Don't drive your motor home unnecessarily.
- Avoid driving up steep grades and hills if possible. Stay on the hardtop; driving on mud and gravel can increase gasoline consumption.

General Driving Tips

Let us consider handling a large motor home. If you can drive a car you can drive a motor home.—Today's units have power steering, power brakes, automatic transmissions and all the comforts of home. However, this is a large-profile unit, a big object. It is not a sports car, so don't try whipping around corners at fifty mph or you'll find yourself wishing you hadn't while trying to climb out of your over-turned rig.

When you buy your new motor home, familiarize yourself thoroughly with its dimensions. How long is it? One and a half car lengths? Two car lengths? How wide? How much wider than the car you normally drive? How high? How many feet of motor home are there above your head when you're sitting in the driving seat? Hitting a low overhand in a gas station can be expensive and adds nothing to the appearance of the top of your unit. Also, you may damage a roof-mounted air conditioner or roof vent, you may cause a rain leak, and if your insurance doesn't cover you, you may find the repairs to the gas station structure and to your motor home quite expensive. Make sure your beautiful unit will fit between those trees or posts before you try it. Know how much overhang you have behind the rear wheels so you can back up safely. Look underneath to see how much ground clearance you have. Because of holding tank plumbing you usually find that there isn't much clearance considering the size of the unit. Practice driving it in parking lots and quiet streets.

Until you are thoroughly used to driving your motor home, have someone guide you back into camping or parking spaces. If you are alone, get out, walk around, and review the situation before attempting any tight maneuvers or backing up unless you have a clear open course behind you. Learn to rely on your large side mirrors. Most motor homes provide little, if any, rear view vision from the inside mirror. Adjust both outside mirrors properly before driving anywhere. You should have clear vision to the rear while sitting comfortably in a normal driving position. You should not have to crane your neck or move your position to be able to see into both side mirrors.

It is important to be comfortable when driving a motor home, particularly if you are going on a lengthy trip. If the seat is not entirely comfortable for your body configuration, experiment with seat adjustments, additional cushions, pads, etc., until your back is firmly supported and you sit comfortably at the wheel with your seat belt fastened.

Be A Safe Motor Home Driver

There are a lot of controls in a motor home—knobs, switches, buttons, etc. Some of these are for driving, some control equipment in the coach portion—the generator, for instance—and sometimes there are gauges with push buttons that give instant indication of the amount of water in your water tank or waste in the holding tank. These controls are sometimes located in the driving area. Make sure you understand exactly what each control does. You do not want to be fiddling with them while you are driving.

Because of the size of your unit (compared to most cars) and the fact that you probably have your family with you, it is vitally important to follow good, safe driving practices. Don't let the children run around inside the motor home while you're driving. A sudden touch on the brake or turn of the wheel, and a youngster has banged a tender head against a cabinet, the stove, etc. Have them properly seated with their seat belts fastened.

Avoid having loose objects on floor, seats, counter tops, etc. Nothing worse than having a cast iron frying pan on the rampage inside a motor home. Avoid letting the children get too bored. Give them reading materials, or any of many games on the market to keep them occupied. Don't play your radio or tape deck too loud. You may not hear a significant siren or you may not hear junior say: "I've got to go to the bathroom!"

In spite of the convenience, avoid eating and drinking while you are driving except for perhaps a mouthful of water or soda if you are really thirsty. Make frequent stops—at least one an hour—this will give you plenty of opportunities for refreshments so that your driving does ot suffer while you try to avoid spilling hot coffee on your lap or wrestle with a slice of pizza. Never, ever allow anyone to cook while the vehicle is in motion. Always turn off all L-P gas appliances and pilot lights when your tanks are being filled with gasoline.

The Busy B

The Type B motor home, also called a "van conversion" is a very practical unit for the small family that likes a little more convenience than a tent but does not want to go overboard with luxuries. This unit is also considerably less expensive than Type A or Type C motor homes. Average price for a Type B in 1974 was around $6,500.,

Type B motor home or van conversion. (Photo courtesy Turtle Top.)

Type C motor home or chopped van. (Photo courtesy El Dorado.)

although many models are available for $5,500 and the larger, better-equipped ones can run as high as $10,000 or more for special units.

Many families purchase these units in lieu of a station wagon or second car. They are easy to drive, handle, park, use less gasoline than the larger units and are ideal for shopping trips, taking the kids to a ballgame, for family camping weekends, for hunting and fishing trips, and for business purposes.

They are called van conversions because that's what they are. The motor-home builder buys light delivery vans from auto manufacturers and converts them into small motor homes by adding a roof extension (either fixed or pop-up type), and installing cooking and sleeping facilities and in some cases bathrooms with chemical or flush toilets. The roof extension enables people to stand erect in the living area.

Some manufacturers of van conversion motor homes are: Volkswagen, Travco, Recreational Vans, Travel Equipment, Turtle Top, Crusaire, Coachmen, Fleetwood, and others.

The Chopped Van

Until the last few years, Type C motor homes—known as "chopped vans"—were made from light delivery vans which the motor home builder bought from Detroit. He cut away the entire van body from behind the driving area, leaving a chassis with engine and two seats in the forward part and partial cab. A motor-home coach body was then built on the chassis, butted up to the open end of the cab. A forward extension over the cab roof provides additional sleeping area.

Type C motor homes are designated "mini-motor homes" by some manufacturers. But whatever you call them they are extremely popular, practical, comfortable, attractive and economical to buy and operate (compared to most larger Type A units). As with Type B, these motor homes are often purchased as second cars or in lieu of station wagons. Although generally smaller than Type A motor homes, they contain all the basic living conveniences—bathroom with shower (sometimes a small tub), stove with oven, refrigerator with freezer, kitchen sink, cabinets, clothes closet, flush toilet, dinette and sleeping accommodation for up to eight people. Prices start at about $8,000 and go up to $14,000 or more in some cases. As Winnebago is the country's largest manufacturer of Type A motor homes, El Dorado Industries is the principal manufacturer of Type C chopped van units. Other principal manufacturers include Coachmen, Argosy, Champion, Bendix Home Systems, Blazon, Brougham, Chinook, Cobra, Coons, Midas International, Mobile Traveler, Red Dale, Starcraft, Wickes and Winnebago.

Towing A Travel Trailer

No one but a proficient automobile driver should attempt to tow a trailer of any kind. Student drivers should master the auto first before attempting to tow a trailer. Not that trailer towing is all that difficult; it's just that when learning to drive a car you need all your concentration on that without the additional concern. High school driving programs should include trailer towing instruction for students who have passed the basic driving course and earned their licenses.

Getting Hitched

The first thing you must consider is the hitch. Without a proper hitch, correctly fastened to both tow vehicle and trailer, you will not have the degree of control necessary to learn to operate the two-vehicle rig. Furthermore, you will be in constant danger of having the trailer come loose, which can be embarrassing and dangerous. Especially on a busy highway.

The best thing is to have a frame hitch receiver mounted underneath your vehicle, making sure, first, that your car or truck is suitable for towing this particular trailer. There are two basic types of trailer hitches—the safe kind and the unsafe kind. The safe kind is not the type that clamps onto your rear bumper and jumps off when you hit a bump. The frame hitch is the best by all counts. Here you have the receiver portion bolted or welded to the frame of your car with an open square-ended steel bar in the center facing to the rear. Into this opening fits a square that has the hitch ball fastened to it. The travel trailer comes with its portion of the hitch welded securely to the front of the trailer—an A-frame arrangement with the mechanism and female portion of the ball hitch, safety chains, weather-tight light plug and all necessary fastening devices, sway control mechanism, etc. A sway control limits side-to-side movement of the trailer and helps stabilize it behind the tow car.

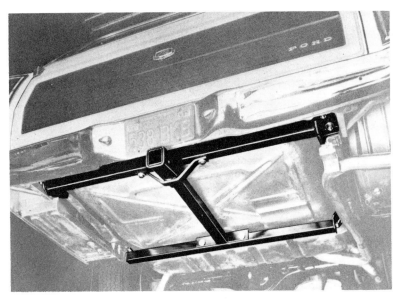

Under-car trailer hitch receiver securely bolted in place. Square-ended steel shaft of Class 3 frame or load-equalizing hitch fits into square opening of receiver beneath license plate. (Photo courtesy Valley Tow-Rite.)

The reason we must understand the hitching arrangement is that this knowledge helps us understand the forces that come into play when towing a trailer and helps us learn to control the entire rig. Load-leveling springs on your car are also a necessary part of your tow package if you are buying a large trailer.

Complete information about hitches may be obtained from Valley Tow-Rite, P.O. Box 850, 1313 S. Stockton St., Lodi, CA 95240, and from Reese Products, Inc., P.O. Box 940, 4013 Cassopolis Rd., Elkhart, IN 46514.

Another important factor that can affect your ability to drive while towing a trailer, as well as contribute to the safety or lack thereof of the entire rig, is the weight of your trailer in relation to the weight of your towing car and the type of hitch. Trailer weight must be considered when fully loaded with all appliances, beds, bedding, pots, dishes, and all the paraphernalia you normally pack inside your trailer. Engineers classify trailer weight in three categories:
- small, lightweight trailers which weigh less than the towing vehicle.
- larger, heavier trailers which weigh about the same amount as the towing vehicle.
- trailers that weigh more than the towing vehicle.

These categories are known in trailerese as Class I, Class II and Class III trailers. For Class II and III trailers you should have power brakes or surge or "police" type brakes put on your towing car; high-pressure radiator cap and a multi-bladed or larger cooling fan installed to permit the engine to operate at the higher temperatures generated by towing. Power steering is also a must when towing a heavy trailer. Automatic transmission is generally considered best, but if you have manual transmission on your towing car or truck, have a heavy-duty clutch installed.

You also need large, truck-type sideview mirrors on both sides and larger tires on your tow vehicle will provide an extra margin of safety. If you plan to do much off-road driving with your trailer, consider having an anti-slip differential installed (about $150.).

Once you have modified your tow car, installed the proper hitch, and made sure everything is properly connected, the next thing you do is not to start driving. What you do is you walk up and down the entire length of the two-unit rig; walk all around it several times. Fix firmly in your mind its total length. Is it twice as long as the car alone? Two and half times? How much parking space will it take up? Two spaces? Three? Now check width—eight feet is the maximum permitted on the highways and you probably will not find a trailer wider than that. Nevertheless, it is wider than your car; understand how much wider it is.

How much higher is your trailer than your car? You may meet low overhangs in gasoline stations, low tree branches, etc., and you don't want to slice the top off that expensive new travel trailer.

Now we have learned all about the dimensions, let's drive. The additional weight will obviously require more acceleration to get you moving, and it is important to accelerate evenly and slowly. Likewise the added weight adds momentum and the rig will take longer to stop. Allow twice the distance for stopping as you normally need for the tow vehicle alone. In fact, be safe; allow more than twice that distance, which means a much greater interval between your rig and the vehicle ahead of you.

When passing, you must again remember your extra length and allow twice or more the distance you would allow for the tow car alone. Remember that when turning, trailer wheels do not follow the same path as the car wheels so you must turn wide enough to prevent the trailer cutting across the towing vehicle's tracks and mounting the curb or hitting something. You also need a wider turning radius when towing a trailer if you make a U-turn. Before getting out there on the highway, do a little practice driving on an empty section of the local supermarket's parking lot or around your quiet, suburban streets.

A great many travel trailers are about as aerodynamic as an old-fashioned bath tub, and air currents and wind greatly affect your driving. If wind or the trememdous draft created by a fast-moving big truck cause your trailer to weave or sway or slip off the pavement onto the shoulder, do not over-react. Remove your foot from the gas pedal and steer as straight a course as possible graudally easing your rig back into its lane. If your trailer has electric surge brakes (and if it's a large trailer it should have), apply these very gently. Do not exceed the speed limit established for trailers, not even to pass, until you have become really skilled at driving your vehicle with a trailer in tow.

Backing up with a trailer is like backing up a car. Only different. Completely opposite, in fact. Before taking off on a trip with your trailer, get into a vacant or near-vacant parking lot and practice trailer driving and handling in general and backing up in particular. When backing a trailer you turn your steering wheel in the opposite direction than when backing a car alone. This takes a little getting used to, but it must be learned. An old hand at trailer towing showed me a method I now always use when backing up a trailer. Hold the steering wheel at the bottom with both hands together, then, keeping your hands in that position turn the wheel in the same direction you wish the rear end of the trailer to go. In other words, if you want the back of the trailer to cut to your right as you face the front from the driving seat, move your hands on the wheel to the right; if the rear end of the trailer has to go left, move your hands to the left.

Parallel parking and other maneuvers soon become routine if you follow these basic tips and get lots or practice.

One of the larger manufacturers of conventional travel trailers is Jayco, Inc. Others prominent in this field are El Dorado, Blazon, Boles-Aero, Carriage, Brougham, Champion, Coachmen, Coons Manufacturing, Farenwald, Holiday Rambler, Kayot, Mallard, Midas-International, Serro, Starcraft, Travel Equipment, Trotwood, Vega, Wickes, Winnebago, and Yellowstone.

Airstream, its subsidiary Argosy, Streamline, and a few other manufacturers of conventional travel trailers are worthy of special note

Streamline design of Airstream and some other travel trailers reduces air drag, saves gasoline. (Photo courtesy Airstream.)

since these companies build units with aerodynamic styling, stream-lining them to present less surface area to the approaching air and wind, with consequently better gasoline mileage. This type of design was pioneered by Airstream, whose sleek aluminum, aircraft-body styled travel trailers are seen in virtually every country in the world as members of the huge Airstream owners' clubs spread goodwill and American dollars wherever they go.

The Fifth Wheel

Designed along the baic lines of the freight-hauling tractor-trailers or semis, is the fast-growing fifth-wheel travel trailer. It gets its name from the special circular hitch arrangement situated in the bed of the towing truck, immediately above the truck's rear axle. The trailers have tandem axles at the rear and, because of the "fifth-wheel" or swivel-type hitch underneath the front overhang which attaches the unit to the towing truck, this type unit is easier to tow than a conventional travel trailer hitched behind a car. The forward portion, which extends out over the truck bed, provides a large sleeping area which makes these trailers roomier than the conventional kind. Many modern fifth-wheel trailers are virtually luxurious homes on wheels, and a great number of retired people live in them, spending their Autumn years traveling, seeing the country and stopping in campgrounds and resorts. In addition to truck towing, a fifth-wheel trailer may be towed by a full-sized family car using a special two-wheeled Ace fifth-wheel adapter (Winter Welding & Machine Corp., 2580 W. Philadelphis, York, PA 17404). Perhaps the largest manufacturers of top quality

Fifth-wheel travel trailer. (Photo courtesy El Dorado.)

fifth-wheel trailers are El Dorado and Jayco. Other major manufactur-
ers include: Bendix Home Systems, Blazon, Bonanza Travelers,
Chinook, Cobra, Fan Coach, Globestar, Kayot, Midas-International,
Red Dale, Skippy, Swisslander, Travel Equipment, Vega, Wickes, and
Winnebago.

Camping Trailers

Tents on wheels, collapsible trailers, fold-downs, pop-ups . . .
these are some of the names by which camping trailers are identified.
And from a descriptive standpoint they are all accurate; however,
camping trailers are more than mere tents on wheels. Most open up to
provide more interior space than large family-sized tents, and they
contain two mattresses—one in each wing—which form large,
double-sized beds. In addition, some models have dinettes which
open up to form an additional bed. Virtually all camping trailers sleep
four comfortably, and many can accommodate an extra child or two.

Typical camping trailer. (Photo courtesy Valley Forge.)

Though not as well equipped as travel trailers or motor homes, they
usually offer a three-burner stove, an ice-box (or refrigerator at additional cost), a hot-air furnace, a water supply and sink with hand pump
and some have add-on screened rooms or awnings.

For the family with fairly small children that likes to experience the
"feel" of camping without roughing it too much, the camping trailer is
the answer. Starting at about $450, they cost considerably less to pur-

chase than other units, and when folded down for travel they provide a low profile for easy towing and storing in the family garage. Effects of towing most camping trailers with average cars, on gasoline mileage, are very slight since they offer little wind and air resistance and, because of their light weight, not much rolling resistance. They present no special driving problems. Backing up instructions for travel trailers apply.

Coleman, Jayco, Apache, Coachmen, Camel, Krown, Valley Forge, are a few of the many manufacturers of camping trailers.

Truck camper. (Photo courtesy El Dorado.)

The Truck Bed Apartment

Families who normally own a pickup truck for farming or trade purposes are missing a lot if they do not have a truck camper unit which slides into the bed of the pickup, allowing the truck to serve a double purpose—work and pleasure. Pickup coaches range from six feet to about eleven and one-half feet long and, depending on size and price, offer comfortable sleeping accommodations for four or more, a cooking range, kitchen sink, toilet and shower, dinette, refrigerator and storage cabinets. The over-cab bed is usually large enough to serve as a double bed for two adults or up to four small children. The dinette usually forms a bed, and in some models there is an additional seat which makes a single bed. The camper module can be removed from the truck bed and, using built-in jacks, can serve as a lakeside cabin or base camp, while the truck is used to get the fishermen in the family back to the hidden ponds and streams where the big ones are.

Truck campers range from about $1,500 to as high as $5,000 or more (without the truck, or course). A great many truck camper manufacturers market their products throughout the United States and Canada, but there are probably more truck campers on the roads bearing the El Dorado brand than any other make. Also big in truck campers are Coachmen Industries, Amerigo-Gardner, Bendix Home Systems, Coons Manufacturing, Huntsman, Midas-International, Starcraft, Travel Equipment Corp., Trotwood, Vega, Wickes RV and Winnebago.

It is important to obtain the proper match of camper to truck. Some campers will fit fine into the bed of a one-quarter-ton pickup truck, but when fully loaded, weight may exceed the gross vehicle weight rating for the truck. A one-half-ton truck may be needed, and for some campers you are safer with a three-quarter-ton or one-ton pickup. Check this out carefully with your dealer when purchasing a camper for a truck you already own, a truck-camper combination, or a new truck when you already own a camper. There is a certain "top-heavy" feeling when driving a truck with a camper in the bed, particularly on corners. It is wise to take corners easy and not to speed at any time. Like a motor home, a truck with a camper mounted in the bed and extending over the cab is a high-profile unit and displaces a lot of air. If you drive too fast or take bends too fast, you will experience various handling difficulties. These can go as far as over-turning. The same gasoline-conserving driving methods should be observed as with a motor home.

A small camper-type unit on the market is what the industry calls a pickup cover, usually aluminum or fiberglass, used to enclose the bed of the truck. These units sell for as little as about $350, and, since they are basically shells with windows, rear door and perhaps insulation and electric wiring, they do not normally come with the built-in amenities associated with truck campers or other units. Such covers are popular with hunters and fishermen who like to get back off the beaten track and have a modicum of shelter both for their sporting equipment, ice chest, and supplies, and for protection on cold nights. Because of their low-profile and light-weight, pickup covers do not

Pickup cover (also called cap or shell).

add any particular driving problems. Many companies make pickup covers; the largest are Gem Top, Ford, Leer, Hop Cap, and Winnebago.

How To Use Your Camping Vehicle

"The world is a vast book, and he who never leaves home reads but a single page" (Chinese proverb).

Many families purchase a camping vehicle and in the beginning, make frequent trips. When the novelty wears off the unit spends almost all its time in storage or in the owner's driveway. Such a family has not only wasted a good deal of money but is continually wasting a golden opportunity to enjoy the pleasure that owning a camping vehicle can give. Camping trips with one of these units are inexpensive yet supremely rewarding. For promoting family togetherness, it is hard to beat camping—especially within the close confines of a camping vehicles. Your unit will take you to the woods, the lakes and streams, the mountains, the ski slopes and snowmobile trails, the ocean shores, the deserts. It will take you up into Canada, down into Mexico

and to every corner of this huge, beautiful country. Visit with the
Amish and enjoy their magnificent, wholesome cooking and friendly
smiles. Camp out with the Indians on one of many reservations that
welcome campers. Try out your French in Quebec and your Spanish
south of the border. Before you fall asleep listen to coyotes calling,
ocean waves breaking, the wind in the pine trees, the distant call of a
lonely whipoorwill. Take the kids to Disneyland in California, to Dis-
neyworld in Florida, to one of the fun-filled Six Flags amusement
parks. Visit your country's capital, ponder awhile at Gettysburg,
breathe a quite prayer at Plymouth Rock, see what's left of the Alamo
and remember the brave men who died there.

Listen to the crashing of the waves at Big Sur, and watch the daring
young. Visit the great northwest and watch men planting young trees
to replace those they must harvest.

Wait with anxious wives for returning shrimp boats at the Gulf;
watch great racing drivers hurl their machines around the track at
Indianapolis; hold your breath at an important golf tournament.

Make friends with other campers, compare units with other camping vehicle owners, send postcards to relatives and friends from all
kinds of wonderful places.

Listen to and watch your steaks sizzling on a grill over charcoal;
drink a cold beer under the hot desert sun, toast marshmallows on a
wire coathanger around a roaring campfire, and as the evening grows
late and perhaps chilly, retire to your camping vehicle's warm beds.

And you will never have to ask the question: "What on earth would I
do with one of those?"

Publications

Recreational Vehicle Handbook by Connie B. Howes, published by
Rand McNally & Company, Chicago, Illinois, is a well-written book
full of valuable tips for both potential purchaser and owner of a camping vehicle. Discusses types available, presents instructional information on driving, towing, loading, financing, insurance, and the various systems that make a camping vehicle work. Well-illustrated with
explicit photographs. At $1.95, this handbook belongs in every camp-
ing vehicle owner's rig and in the library of those still considering a
first purchase. On newsstands and in bookshops.

Camping On Wheels, published by *Field & Stream Magazine*. Buyer's
Guide to camping vehicles with specifications, accessories, how-to-
do-it articles, etc. Available on newsstands.

Woodall's/NLPGA L-P Gas Refueling Directory, published by Woodall Publishing Company, Highland Park, Illinois, in conjunction with
the National Liquefied Petroleum Gas Association. Lists over 10,000
L-P gas supply stations in the USA, Canada and Mexico. Also contains safety information and lists tunnels and bridges that have spe-

cial regulations governing transportation of L-P gas. Available in bookstores.

Directory of RV Sanitary Stations, Rajo Publications, Inc., Mill Valley, California. Lists national, state and private campgrounds, camping vehicle dealerships, service stations, etc., where holding tank dumping facilities exist. Covers USA and Canada. Available from publisher.

Hiking Trails In The Midwest, by Jerry Sullivan and Glenda Daniel, published by Greatlakes Living Press, Ltd., Chicago, Illinois. Available in book stores, and at some sporting goods stores. Lists well-known and little-known trails in the Midwest accessible by camping vehicle. Includes maps showing trails in the seven-state Midwest area and in neighboring Ontario, Canada.

Ontario Campsites and *Ontario, Canada, Camping*, two publications available free from Ministry of Industry and Tourism, Parliament Building, Toronto, Ontario, Canada.

The Sportsman On Wheels, by Erwin Bauer, published by Outdoor Life/E. P. Dutton & Co., New York. In scarce supply; may be found in libraries and in some bookshops or may be obtained from the publisher. Covers camping vehicles and other types of recreational vehicles.

Vacation Guide to Lower Rio Grande Valley is especially oriented toward travelers in camping vehicles. The various communities in the area have made tremendous efforts to attract camping vehicle families and have provided some of the best facilities in the country. Area covered is at the southern tip of Texas, on main route into Mexico. Available from Harlingen Chamber of Commerce, Harlingen, Texas.

Camping & Trailering, series published by American Automobile Association, Washington, DC. Covers geographical areas across the country listing campgrounds by state and presents additional information.

Ten-Gallon RV Weekends, published by Woodall Publishing Company, Highland Park, Illinois. Series of $1 books, covering various areas of the country that can be reached from major metropolitan areas with minimal expenditure of gasoline.

Trailering Parks & Campgrounds, published by Woodall Publishing Co., Inc., Highland Park, Illinois. Takes guesswork out of camping in the USA, Canada and Mexico by listing close to 20,000 public and private campgrounds regularly inspected by publisher's representatives. Also contains interesting and helpful articles on various aspects of vehicle camping.

Campground & Trailer Park Guide, published by Rand McNally & Co., available in bookshops, on most newsstands and in many RV dealerships. Presents the kind of detailed maps for which the company is well-known and locates campgrounds by state and in Mexico and

Canada.

Chilton's RV Guides cover, among other types of vehicles, various camping vehicles. Books are maintenance and repair guides, contain diagnostic information, trouble-shooting and repair procedures, etc. Fully illustrated. Available from Chilton Book Co., Inc., Radnor, Pennsylvania.

KOA Handbook and Directory for Campers lists around a thousand places to enjoy camping. All campgrounds listed are Kampgrounds of America ownerships and must meet the parent company's rigid standards. Includes maps and many discount coupons for museums and other places of interest. Also contains articles on RV camping, outdoor recipes, etc. Available at RV dealerships, camping supply stores, KOA campgrounds, or from KOA Handbook for Campers, St. Paul, Minnesota.

Directory of Recreational Vehicle Manufacturers, published annually by Trailer-Dealer Publishing Company, Chicago, Illinois. Gives complete nationwide listing of camping vehicle manufacturers, suppliers of parts and accessories, and various allied services.

Motor Home Rental Directory, Hollywood, California. $1.00 per copy.

The Trailerist Cookbook, by Charlotte Dawson, $2.50 from Trail-R-Clubs of America, Beverly Hills, California.

Periodicals

Arizona Mobile Citizen, 4110 E. Van Buren St., Phoenix, AZ. 85008.

Camper Coachman, Trailer Life Publishing Co. Inc., 23945 Craftsman Road, Calabasas, CA 91302.

Family Motor Coaching, official monthly publication of the Family Motor Coach Association, PO Box 44144, Cincinnati, OH 45244.

Four Seasons Trails, 29563 Northwestern Hwy., Southfield, MI 48079.

Great Lakes Sportsman, 30555 Southfield Rd., Southfield, MI 48075.

Holiday Magazine, Aventour Marketing Ltd., 222 S. Prospect Ave., Park Ridge, IL 60068.

Michigan Out-of-Doors, Box 2235, Lansing, MI 48911.

Midwest Outdoors, PO Box 426, Downers Grove, IL 60515.

Midwest Sportsman, Hertzberg & Kramer, Inc., 7400 N. Waukegan Ave., Nile IL 60648.

Mobile Home Trailer News, PO Box 967, Kendall Branch, Miami, FL 33156.

Mobile Living, 1359 Main St., Sarasota, FL 33578.

Mobile Messenger, PO Box 809, Apache Junction, AZ 85220.

Northeast Outdoors, 95 North Main St., Waterbury, CN 06702.

Northwest Trailer & Mobile Home News, 527 Pittock Block, Portland, OR 97205.

RV World, 16200 Ventura Blve., Encino, CA 91316.

Trailer Life, Trailer Life Publishing Co., Inc., 23945 Craftsman Rd., Calabasas, CA 91302.

Trailer Times, PO Box 07, College Grove Center, San Diego, CA 92115.

Trailer Travel, Clark-Woodall Publishing Co., Inc. 3500 Western Ave., Highland Park, IL 60035.

Trails-A-Way, 109 N. Lafayette St., Greenville, MI 48838.

Western Mobile News, 4043 Irving Place, Culver City, CA 90230.

Western Outdoors, 3939 Birch Street, Newport Beach, CA 92660.

Who Needs Roads?

Off-road vehicles of one kind or another have been with us for a good many years although only fairly recently have they come into their own as fun vehicles. Tractors are ORVs and in the automobile's infancy, when there were no super highways and relatively few paved roads, early cars and trucks were used in off-road situations of necessity. Small rural communities and isolated farms were often reached only by mud trails and tracks made by horses and horse or oxen-drawn wagons. Since these approaches were frequently deep-rutted and filled with water and mud, it was often more expedient for automotive vehicles to avoid them and make their approaches as best they could over fields, open ground, through woods, etc. Although they were not built as ORVs, earlier cars and trucks by their very design, light-weight and large wheels, lent themselves better to off-road travel than do today's heavier, low-clearance, small-wheeled automobiles.

Several books on early motoring and the history of the American automobile contain amusing photographs of groups of carefree motorists, the ladies wearing huge-brimmed hats, tied prettily around their faces, the men sporting peaked caps, riding breeches, boots or leggings and with long, hand-knitted woollen scarves flying in the breeze—heading across a field to a picnic or just having fun driving where no others had driven before.

Aside from the farm tractor and varous items of excavation and construction equipment, the first vehicle manufactured in this country on a production basis with built-in off-road capability was the World War II Jeep built by several companies to strict military specifications. When these sturdy little workhorses were first shipped to the British Army in North Africa during the interminable desert campaigns that ranged over thousands of miles of desolate terrain for close to four years, they gave the British a mobility far superior to anything they had previously known and to that enjoyed by their adversaries.

All movies to the contrary, the spunky little Jeeps were never truly equipped as fighting vehicles. Although they frequently carried light machine guns and their crews were well-armed, Jeeps served the British (and later, or course, their American allies) as fast reconnaisance units, command vehicles, dispatch units and other uses where off-road capability combined with rugged construction and speed were needed.

After the war, Jeeps became available to the general public and were quickly purchased by oil companies, miners, surveyors, farmers, hunters, various federal, state and civilian agencies and departments, construction companies, and by sports who just liked to take off across the wilderness on their own.

Toady, vehicles with four-wheel drive and off-road capability are manufactured by Ford, Chevrolet, GMC, Plymouth, Dodge, American Motors (which builds today's Jeeps), and International Harvester. Imports include the famed British Land Rover, the Datsun Patrol, the Rumanian Aro, Toyota and Suzuki, and others.

The rugged off-road capability of the World War II Jeep is less evident in some of its successors which seem to have gone the way of all American automobiles—flashy design, chrome trim, two-tone paint jobs, air conditioning, carpeting, stereophonic sound systems, imitation wood paneling, monstrously over-powered engines, automatic transmissions, power steering, and glitter galore. The person or family wanting all that expensive rubbish can purchase the standard American sedan. Today's true off-road enthusiast has trouble obtaining the vehicle he needs at a realistic price since all these fancy accessories add considerably to the cost. Instead of purchasing $2,500-worth of tough, off-road vehicle, you must often purchase an additional $2,000 or $3,000-worth of gadgetry and ostentatiousness you probably don't want and definitely don't need. Detroit has tried to marry the rugged four-wheel drive utility vehicle to the flashy, overdone American automobile.

Modifying the 4 x 4

In self-defense therefore, true off-road enthusiasts either buy foreign-made units or take old Jeeps, Broncos, Scouts, etc., and virtually rebuild them. If Detroit experts were to spend a few weeks attending off-road rallies, races, endurance drives, club meets, trail rides, etc., held in most parts of the country throughout the year, they might begin to understand what the off-road driver wants. And it isn't chrome trim, crushed velvet seat covers and automatic drive systems. The basic, military-type Jeep, the CJ-5 and its kid brother, the Jeep Renegade are the exceptions. In view of the fact that off-road vehicle enthusiasts now number close to three quarters of a million, plus many thousands of farmers, oil company personnel, etc., it would seem that Detroit is missing a good bet by not building and marketing basic vehicles with rugged off-road capabilities at realistic prices.

However, Detroit's failure to understand what its customers want in the way of trucks, 4 x 4's and even family cars is good for the imported vehicle industry . . . And it has cleared the way for a new type of business—the 4 x 4 modification shops which are growing in number throughout the country. Fortunately, unlike Detroit, the 4 x 4 modification people understand perfectly well what off-road enthusiasts want, providing such modifications as stripping away expensive and useless chunks of chrome, removing vinyl "trim" panels, strengthening the chassis (usually by "boxing"—adding sheet metal to the open side), removing fancy seats and installing serviceable "Baja"-type buckets, adding skid plates underneath to protect against rocks, etc., shortening the wheelbase in some cases, adding roll bars or roll cages, installing additional gas-carrying capacity, installing larger or multi-bladed cooling fans and large radiators, changing wheels and tires to ones more serviceable under off-road mud or sand conditions, adding extra shock absorbers, installing heavy-duty springs with extra leaves, installing larger air cleaners, installing rugged gear levers, adding racing lights for night competitions, carrying out various engine changes, etc. These modifications can be quite costly but at least you wind up with a vehicle with the capabilities you need for rugged off-road driving and for competition use. You wind up, in fact with the kind of vehicle Detroit could very well have built in the first place!

There are two types of four-wheel drive systems—one uses special front wheel hubs which can be engaged and disengaged as needed and the newer "constant" or "full-time" four-wheel drive system whereby all four wheels are engaged all the time. The former results in both front wheels turning at the same rate of speed causing wheel drag on sharp bends. With the "full-time" type, front wheels turn at different speeds depending on the degree of turn.

4 x 4 Driving Techniques

Driving a 4 x 4 in various off-road situations requires a thorough knowledge of the vehicle's capabilities, what it can be expected to do and what cannot be expected of it. It also requires a knowledge of the various types of off-road terrain and how to adapt one's driving techniques to each particular surface. A great many off-road drivers attempt to climb grades too steep for their 4 x 4s forgetting that load tends to shift toward the downhill side to a certain degree, depending upon the steepness of the grade. Then again, a vehicle may climb a rough, rocky hill but will not make it up the same degree of grade with a different surface—shale, for instance, or soft sand—(A lot depends on the type tires you use)—Wet mud soon fills even the deepest tire treads and affects your vehicle's ability to climb a muddy hill. Snow and ice present their own problems on a grade, so do hard surfaces such as blacktop, concrete, etc. Grass can prove to be too slippery, sometimes, for even the toughest 4 x 4s on a steep climb.

The true off-road enthusiast knows instinctively, through trial and error, how steep a grade of any particular surface his unit will successfully negotiate. Ascending a steep hill by traversing it slalom-style can often be a useful technique. In some cases, you will want to get well away from the steepest part of the grade and virtually make a run for it—sometimes you reach the top before loss of momentum and weight shift defeats you.

Desert Driving

On the desert one frequently sees vehicles of all kinds stuck in soft sand. Sometimes this is due to improper driving and sometimes it is the result of sand that is just too loose for sufficient traction to keep you going. What is difficult to understand is the large number of drivers who, finding that even in four-wheel drive they aren't going anywhere, immediately use a shovel or their hands to dig the soft sand away from under the wheels. This is one of the worst things you can do. It rarely helps at all. What it does, in fact, is lowers your entire vehicle until the differential housing is resting firmly on the ground. Now you not only have the problem of trying to get enough traction to turn your wheels and give you forward or backward movement, you also have the additional problem of trying to drag your vehicle's differential housing and other low-lying sub-assemblies through the sand.

When stuck in soft sand, it takes only a moment or two of trying to move forward and backward for you to know whether or not you are likely to extricate your car from the insidious sand. No sense sitting there revving away like mad for nothing. You merely dig in farther. Here are some steps you can take to remedy the situation:

Switch off and dismount. Many drivers, for some reason, find this step the hardest of all. They just refuse to get off their rear ends, preferring to sit there jamming down the gas pedal and digging farther in all the time.

Make sure your front transfer case is engaged—that you are, in fact, in four-wheel drive (if you have 4 x 4 that is).

Make sure your front wheels are in line with the back wheels and not turned even slightly.

Investigate the ground around your wheels—DON'T DIG IT AWAY! See if perhaps one of your wheels is hung up on a rock or if there's a large, smooth rock right in front of a wheel. If so, you must either excavate the rock or, if it is too large, you must concentrate your efforts on moving in just the one direction. If the rock is in front of a rear wheel and you can't move it, you are only going to be able to drive out of there in reverse. In this case, make sure as you back up slowly, that your front wheel doesn't get hung up on the same rock. Sometimes you can take a hammer and chisel if you have one (or sometimes just the hammer alone) and break up the rock.

Determine what is holding you. In all probability it is plain old soft sand, too loose for your tires to obtain the necessary traction. Find out which wheels are not getting traction. Often it happens that only one rear wheel is in real trouble. In that case, you have only the one to worry about.

Look for large chunks of fairly flat rock, twigs, bits of wood, etc., that you can pack under the wheel or wheels where you are having problems. Avoid disturbing the sand immediately under the wheels as far as possible. If there are no suitable rocks around, no hunks of dried out cholla, yucca, manzanita roots, or other such items around, then you are going to have to use something else. What?

Use your sleeping bag, duffle bag, blankets, floor mats, even clothing. Anything that will give your wheels something to bite on for just a second or so—enough to move you an inch or two, perhaps. Jack the wheels up if necessary to pack the objects underneath.

Use the highest gear and release the clutch very gradually, applying more gas as necessary to prevent stalling. If the vehicle won't move, try the next highest gear. Do not start with the lowest gear and jam down the gas pedal. This will accompllish little but spin your wheels rapidly, throw out the items you have carefully packed underneath, and dig down deeper into the sand. The slower you can get your wheels to turn the better your chances of inching out. Once you start moving, keep going but at the same steady pace. Do increase throttle.

If none of this gets you out you have various alternatives. One is to sit tight until another vehicle comes along. Warn the driver of the soft sand before he hits it and, of course, you should have a tow chain or tow rope or cable with you. Use your engine simultaneously with your rescuer's and you should be able to get out. If you have a winch on front and there's a tree within cable's reach, you will have little trouble winching yourself out. If you are equipped with a winch, a good emergency tool to carry aboard your 4 x 4. If you are going off into the desert alone much, you should carry a couple of metal surveyor's stakes and a good heavy hammer (preferably a sledge hammer). Drive the stake into the ground well within cable length and at an acute angle, with the point of the stake toward your vehicle and the top sloping away. When the arrow-point stake is firmly embedded, put the winch cable hook around the stake as close to the ground as possible. Using your winch and your engine, draw yourself forward. If you still cannot find ground solid enough for wheel traction, excavate the stake and repeat the process until you do. You can also use your winch in conjunction with a towing vehicle.

Most of the preceding information applies also if you get stuck in soft mud, volcanic ash, or snow. However, you usually know how deep snow is and can dig at it until you hit solid ground. If it is frozen too hard, try chopping it or de-freezing it with gasoline if you were too short-sighted to bring rock salt or other de-freezer.

In any event, when driving a 4 x 4 in unfamiliar and untraveled terrain, it is a good idea to stop every so often, even if you are getting along fine, and walk ahead a bit to "feel out" the trail. In the desert, patches of quicksand are not always recognizable and can present real problems.

Much has been written about people, animals and vehicles being trapped in so-called quicksand and sucked down into the bowels of the earth. Hollywood movies have done their share to exaggerate this danger. These tales, although often thrilling, are fortunately without basis in fact. First of all, let us consider what causes "quicksand". This is not a "phenomenon." There's nothing strange or weird about it. Here's how it occurs. To begin with there's got to be a hole in the ground of some kind. It might be a deep gash or a fairly small, more or less round pothole, or a larger depression such as a former creek bed, etc. The desert wind blows very fine sand—dust, almost—into the hole and over a period of time, these fine particles will fill the hole to ground level. These particles of fine sand and dust are not packed down; they are piled in very loosely. Consequently, when you step or drive on this filled-in area, they sometimes do not offer enough resistance to your weight to support you and you sink in. It doesn't "suck you down;" it merely does not hold you up very well. If you are afoot, immediately lie down, spread eagled. In this position, with your body weight distributed widely instead of concentrated on two rather small areas of feet, you are not likely to sink any farther. Now extricate your legs one at a time and roll over until you're on solid ground.

It is rather difficult to duplicate this feat in a 4 x 4, however, and if you have been careless enough to drive all four wheels into a depression full of dust and light sand—"quick" sand—turn off your engine and jump clear of the vehicle. This is a mere precaution, for it is not very likely that your entire car is going to sink rapidly out of sight with you aboard. Still, it could conceivably happen, so get clear and wait for the vehicle to settle. If it gets down to the chassis or lower, you are in real trouble and are probably never going to get it out of there by yourself. Wait for help, or climb the nearest high point and watch for another vehicle or other signs of possible assistance.

Meanwhile walk slowly, one foot at a time back to your vehicle from each direction—front, rear and sides to get an idea of how large the hole is. If you have a winch, there's a slight chance. Lie down in front of your unit after it has finished settling and get the sand away from the winch. Even if you see nothing in sight, pull the cable all the way out in front and look for a rock, tree, anything you can hook onto. If there's nothing, use your surveyor's stakes, making sure to drive them in where the ground is solid. Behind a deeply imbedded rock is a good place. Then carefully make your way back into the cab and start the winch motor. If you are in up to the tops of your wheels or higher, DO NOT TRY TO DRIVE OUT. You haven't a chance. If the winch doesn't help or you have no winch, re-read the last sentence of the preceding paragraph and lots of luck.

When driving in the desert after heavy rains, always be alert for flash floods which mean flooded trails or creek beds and low-lying areas . . . any depression can fill with water. Before slipping into a lower gear and hitting the gas with the idea of charging through the water, stop. Get out and find out how deep it is. You may be surprised—like quicksand, water can sometimes fill a very deep depression out in the desert. And most 4 x 4s float like an over-loaded tractor. Mexican highways and other roads frequently have a depth post at the lowest points in road dips. The posts are marked clearly so that you can see the depth of the water before blundering into it, assuming you take the time to stop and check. Flash floods can cause other driving problems. Water will rush down hillsides carrying tons and tons of sand, which it may dump in the road dips or just along an entire length of road. This is often very soft sand and most difficult to get out of once you are caught in it. Landslides, too, are often the result of flash flooding and should be watched for carefully when driving in desert areas either in the USA or in Mexico.

Other hazards you may encounter when driving off the road in wilderness areas include sand storms (protect your windshield from sandblast), engine overheating (always carry a spare fan belt), tire damage from sharp rocks, damage to wheel rims, ruptured muffler or exhaust pipes, radiator leaks (from scraping on rocks), loss of brake fluid and engine oil, running out of gas, cactus spikes (they can penetrate the toughest tires), rock out-croppings that may cause damage to the sides of your vehicle, landslides—you suddenly round a bend in the trail and there are several tons of rocks in your path—soft edges, and occasionally banditos (both in the USA and Mexico, but mostly in the USA). One other hazard worth bearing in mind is the degree to which the sun can heat the metal body of your vehicle. Many an unknowledgeable driver has received really bad burns in the desert by carelessly placing a bare arm on his car. In Baja California, I have personally fried eggs and cooked other food on a piece of foil on the hood of my Scout.

You're Not The Only 4 x 4 Nut

ORV clubs, sometimes called 4 x 4 clubs, have been formed in almost every state during recent years, offering 4 x 4 enthusiasts opportunities to meet with others who have similar interests, to participate in rallies, trail drives, hill climbs, dirt drags, swap meets, and modifications seminars.

One of the Midwest's oldest and most active clubs is the Flatlanders

Club, headquartered in Rockford, Illinois. This enthusiastic group is responsible for many off-road endurance contests, obstacle races, dirt and hill drags, off-road grand prix racing, and family camp outs for non-competitors. Another very active Midwest group is the Badgerland 4 x 4 Club headquartered in Milwaukee. Club members do not consider they've had a good weekend meet if their vehicles have not jumped a few ten-foot ditches or literally flown off the top of a steep incline or dune. The Flatlanders and Badgerland clubs have set the standard for many clubs of the type throughout the greater Midwest area. Michigan is the home of a number of 4 x 4 clubs and many exciting events are held in various parts of the state throughout the year. It is estimated that there are over 300,000 4 x 4 units in use in Michigan. Iowa and Minnesota have their share of four-wheel clubs and events. One of the big clubs is the Minnesota GO-4 Wheelers, St. Paul, Minnesota.

On the West Coast there is not only considerable activity in this field but there are a number of organized racing programs associated with top names in racing—Parnelli Jones, Mickey Thompson, and others. The sport began on the West Coast around 1960, with a few clubs and loosely organized groups of aficionados who liked to go off into the Arizona and California deserts and down into Mexico's Baja California to get away from the crowds and do their thing. Out of these evolved the National Off-Road Racing Association which for a number of years sponsored and conducted big-money races south of the border. In those days these were rugged races indeed, along dirt roads and sand trails that were frequently non-existent for many miles . . . often closed by land slides, rendered impassable by flash floods and broken bridges, disrupted by Mexican sheep, goats, burros, cattle and people, and made additionally hazardous by careening Mexican trucks and ancient buses and other vehicles that should have been given a decent burial twenty years before. Baja California races are now ably conducted by the Mexicans through the Baja Racing Association.

Texas, New Mexico, Utah, Arizona, Nevada and many more states have regular off-road driving events and off-road activities have spread to New England, the far Northwest and up into Canada.

Yes, Detroit, there is a fast-growing market for basic, rugged, ugly, tough four-wheel drive units without all that cost-boosting imitation wood paneling, vinyl color coordination, chrome and gadgetry.

An ATV Is Also An ORV

All-Terrain Vehicles (ATVs) are units especially built for driving on various off-road surfaces including sand, mud, rocks, shale, hills, snow, ice and water.

There are a number of ATV configurations available; the most popular seems to be the six-wheeled units with fiberglass bodies and roll bars.

Tires for these go-anywhere units are usually 12 x 20.0—the first figure indicates the total width of the tread and the second the diameter of the tire. These tires (largely made by Firestone under various brand names, and by Goodyear) contain no fabric. They are made of a blend of natural and synthetic rubber. They are inflated to only two or three pounds per square inch. Each tire is molded to a metal hub. Instead of a conventional tire tread, ATV tires often have raised V-shaped ridges across the surface. In water the driving wheels are turned by the engine as on land. The raised "tread" causes the wheels to act like miniature paddle wheels to propel the vehicle through the water at low speed (two or three mph, usually). Probably the main supplier of ATV tires is Firestone Tire and Rubber Company. Goodyear is also active in this area as are two or three other tire manufacturers. The biggest share fo the ATV market is enjoyed by ATV Manufacturing Company, producer of the Attex line of these interesting powered "tubs." Their six-wheeled, two-seater 252 Colt has the engine mounted under the fiberglass body immediately behind the two seats.

ATVs are steered by either a steering wheel, a joystick or a pair of "tillers" which lock the wheels on one side turning the vehicle sharply in that direction. ATVs start at around $1,000, and many options are offered.

The National All-Terrain Vehicle Association, sponsors ATV rallies and various competitive events across the country including the "Summernationals" in Ashtabula, Ohio. There are two broad categories for ATV competitions—stock and modified but these are again broken down according to horsepower.

Although perhaps not as popular as 4 x 4 units (ORVs), the ATVs are rapidly achieving economic significance. In 1969 13,000 units were sold. Six years later annual sales exceeded a quarter million.

Dune Buggies

In addition to the type of units we have discussed, desert driving enthusiasts build an amazing variety of vehicles loosely called "dune buggies." Many are stripped Volkswagens with roll bars, special desert tires and other modifications. Many, too, are virtually built from the ground up by their owners. On the sand dunes of Southern California, Arizona, Nevada and other states, enormous meets are held involving sometimes hundreds of these units. The sport here is primarily dune climbing. Drivers approach dunes at high speed and try to get their units over the crest. It is a test of driving skill, of vehicles, tires, timing and tenacity. Many of these dune buggies resemble the kind of "rails" seen in drag races, and more and more of these skeletal units are observed participating in the big off-road races. A number of companies are making dune buggies commercially and selling them to a growing number of customers.

Swamp Buggies and Air Boats

Hovercraft ride on a cushion of air above the surface of the water or ground, swampland, mudflats, etc. A swamp buggie is a different type of vehicle entirely. Whereas the hovercraft keeps clear of the mud and slime of a bog or marsh, the swamp buggie ploughs right through it. These units are not built and sold commercially. There is little market for them. They are almost always home-built jobs, constructed with no thought of aesthetics. They are made to operate in swampy areas too shallow and overgrown with weeds for effective passage of any ordinary boat and too wet and muddy for any ordinary vehicle.

These strange-looking contraptions are used by hunters and fishermen and, it is said, by moonshiners. Their principal habitat is the Everglades and Big Cypress Swamp in southern Florida. Each year, swamp buggie races are held near Naples. The winner gets the purse and is crowned "Swamp Buggie King." Electrical systems are waterproofed, and huge wheels from tractors or earth-moving monsters propel the thing through the water and slush. If you're lucky. More often they get you stuck and churn up an awful amount of slime and mud as you accelerate to get free. An automobile or truck chassis with engine, transmission, roll bars and a few other additions complete the strange rig. It is advisable to go down there and see these units and what their owners do with them before starting to build your own. You'll probably chicken out of the deal!

Air boats are no laughing matter. These are commercially available and—although they have their leisure uses—are much in evidence in swampy areas such as the Everglades, the Okefenokee and others as transportation for game wardens, power and phone company technicians, fishermen, hunters, ornithologists, surveyors, pest control officials, wild game protection agents, search and rescue squads, etc.

Air boats receive propulsion from a large pusher-prop mounted above the boat at the rear. A safety screen protects the occupants. This prop, driven by an engine, takes air into the big "fan" housing and blows it out behind the boat. This causes the boat to move forward quite rapidly, achieving a hydroplaning effect. There is no propeller to get caught in weeds or to become damaged by striking logs, crocodiles or other obstacles. The driver and passenger usually occupy a seat elevated above the boat's deck for improved visibility. The boat itself is almost flat-bottomed, with a shallow keel. Speeds up to thirty mph are possible with some units on unobstructed, calm water.

It is advisable to wear a safety helmet, because boats of this type find their best usage in bodies of water that are frequently overgrown with weeds and have low-hanging tree branches. And, of course, life jackets should be worn in any type of boat.

Manufacturers of 4 x 4 Vehicles

Chevrolet Motor Division, General Motors Building, Detroit, MI 48202.
Dodge Truck Division, Chrysler Corporation, PO Box 1919, Detroit, MI 48231.
Ford Division, Ford Marketing Corporation, Rotunda Drive and South-field, Dearborn, MI 48121.
GMC Truck & Coach Division, General Motors Corporation, 660 South Blvd. East, Pontiac, MI 48053.
Jeep Division, American Motors Corporation, 14250 Plymouth Rd., Detroit, MI 48232.
International Trucks, 401 N. Michigan Ave., Chicago, IL 60611.
Plymouth Division, Chrysler Motors Corporation, PO Box 1919, Detroit, MI 48231.

Associations and Clubs

The principal 4 x 4 associations and some of the bigger clubs are:
Off-Road Competitors Association, 12224 Royal Rd., El Cajon, CA 92021. This association is for drivers who compete in recognized events.
Score International, 2701 E. Anaheim, Wilmington, CA 90744. Membership is open to all 4 x 4 enthusiasts for $15 a year, which includes quarterly publication, racing bulletins, T-shirt, membership card, decal, etc. Score sponsors various West Coast events including the Score Parker 400, the Score Baja 500, the Score Baja 1,000 and the Score Riverside Race (closed course).
Midwest 4-Wheel Drive Association, Rte. 1, Canton, SD 57013. This is an association of off-road clubs and does not extend membership to individual drivers.
Badgerland 4 x 4 Club, contact Tom Wallner, Tire Heaven, 1334 N. Van Buren, Milwaukee, WI 53202. (414) 273-7912.
Minnesota Go-4 Wheelers, 1516 Albany St., St. Paul, MN 55118.
Flatlanders Club, PO Box 2176, Love's Park, IL 61111.

Author Paul DuPre, sporting a joyous grin with one of his ORVs as a backdrop, leaps for joy.

Well-groomed trails throughout the Snow Belt assure the author and thousands of other snowmobile enthusiasts of many enjoyable winter weekends.

The author, relaxing in one of the numerous vehicles which he has driven for fun and profit.

Noted off-road racing champion Tom Wallner (right), and co-driver Paul DuPre, are protected against facial scratches from brush and low tree branches by wire "windshield". Vehicle is a specially rigged Bronco which has won many events.